DATE DUE

The Myth of
Sex Addiction

The Myth of
Sex Addiction

David J. Ley

ROWMAN & LITTLEFIELD PUBLISHERS, INC.
Lanham • Boulder • New York • Toronto • Plymouth, UK

Published by Rowman & Littlefield Publishers, Inc.
A wholly owned subsidary of The Rowman & Littlefield Publishing Group, Inc.
4501 Forbes Boulevard, Suite 200, Lanham, Maryland 20706
http://www.rowmanlittlefield.com

Estover Road, Plymouth PL6 7PY, United Kingdom

British Library Cataloguing in Publication Information Available

Library of Congress Cataloging-in-Publication Data
Ley, David J., 1973–
    The myth of sex addiction / David J. Ley.
        p. cm.
    Includes bibliographical references and index.
    ISBN 978-1-4422-1304-3 (cloth : alk. paper) —
    ISBN 978-1-4422-1306-7 (electronic)
    1. Sex. 2. Sex addiction. 3. Women—Sexual behavior. 4. Men—Sexual behavior.
I. Title.
HQ21.L49 2011
306.77—dc23   2011043765

∞™ The paper used in this publication meets the minimum requirements of American National Standard for Information Sciences—Permanence of Paper for Printed Library Materials, ANSI/NISO Z39.48-1992.

Printed in the United States of America

Dedication

$\mathcal{T}$his work is dedicated, first and foremost, to the many clients who have allowed me to join them in their journeys through life, as they struggle to make healthy decisions in their relationships and sexual behaviors. Along the way, I have met numerous men and women who shared the pain and shame they have experienced from being labeled sex addicts. Hopefully this book can help others like them.

Secondly, this work couldn't have happened without the many men in my life, family, friends, and colleagues, who exemplify the ability to lead healthy, responsible lives, with respect for themselves and others.

Finally, this work is dedicated to my family and loved ones, who have always stood behind me with love, trust, support, and belief.

Contents

Acknowledgments

I greatly acknowledge the support of my employer for supporting my clinical and professional development. A great many kind and supportive colleagues assisted me in understanding the controversy inherent in sex addiction, and identifying the ways in which this label is a problem for our society and the fields of mental health and sexuality. This work couldn't have happened without their assistance. Any errors or misstatements are solely my own.

In no particular order, my sincere gratitude and appreciation goes out to

Phil McGraw, PhD
Marty Klein, PhD
Jason Winters, PhD
Tory Clarke, PhD
Allen Frances, MD
Charles Moser, PhD, MD
David Ortmann, LCSW
Alfredo Aragon, PhD
Tony Dipasquale
Roy Baumeister, PhD
Curtis Bergstrand, PhD
Sari Van Anders, PhD
Angela Kilman

Self Serve Sexuality Resource Center
Steven Ratcliff
Steven Braveman, MA, LMFT
Brenda Wolfe, PhD
Richard Sprott, PhD
Matt Tandy, LPCC
Danielle Cossett, LISW
Janet Hardy
Christopher Ryan, PhD
William Henkin, PhD
Jeff Rudski, PhD
Rory Reid, PhD
Charles Samenow, MD

Introduction

Power is the ultimate aphrodisiac.

—Henry Kissinger[1]

In 1998, the United States was aghast and fascinated by the sexual scandal that embroiled the nation's highest executive, and a young nubile intern in a blue dress. Rumors of infidelity had dogged Bill Clinton for years, dating back to his days as governor of Arkansas. But suddenly his alleged trysts were on the lips of everyone in the country, and the news industry was covering every sordid aspect of the case.

The scandal unfolded, drawing in Congress and nearly the entire government. People started asking why Clinton would do this, and whether his choices represented an underlying moral failing, or an illness. If so, what did they mean for the fate of our country, of for the future of his marriage?

Dolly Kyle Browning, one of Clinton's oldest female friends, confronted the president, suggesting that he was addicted to sex.[2] Former president Gerald Ford labeled Clinton a sexual addict as well, accusing him of having a wandering eye and chasing every skirt he saw, unable and unwilling to control his sexual urges.[3] Recalling that Ford's wife was a famous addict herself, who started a clinic for the treatment of alcohol addiction, one might presume that President Ford would have a keen eye for detecting the insidious and destructive elements of addiction.

Therapists and psychiatrists were quoted by the media, explaining that Clinton's behaviors were clear evidence of the effects of addiction. One psychiatrist opined that it made sense that Clinton could be a sexual addict; after all, hadn't his stepfather had an alcohol problem, and his brother a problem

1

with cocaine?[4] Hillary Clinton once asserted that her husband's philandering emerged from his history of abuse and neglect as a child.[5]

To date, Clinton has never acknowledged or publicly discussed the question of whether he is, or was, addicted to sex. In 2004, in an interview with CBS, he said, "I did something for the worst possible reason. Just because I could."[6] But the scandal catapulted the concepts of sexual addiction into the public consciousness and had everyone discussing the idea that sex was like a drug and that sexual desire could overwhelm even the minds of our best and brightest leaders. But can it? Is sex really like a drug? Can a person become so dependent upon sexual arousal that they make decisions that are out of their control? Is this truly an illness?

In the intervening decades, scandals and allegations of sexual addiction continue to spill from the media, in a never-ending orgy of voyeuristic exploitation. Writing this book, I had no shortage of material to draw upon, and every day, my e-mail was filled with new news alerts about the latest sexual scandal and statements that sex addiction was the cause. But the Clinton scandal set the stage for most scandals that followed and catapulted the concept of sex addiction into a national, media-driven conversation that has overwhelmed the medical and scientific debate about this alleged disorder.

In 2010, I was a guest on several television and radio shows, including *Dr. Phil*. I was there to talk about my first book, *Insatiable Wives*, which told the story of wives who openly had sex with men other than their husband. But people were less interested in talking to me about my book and more interested in hearing my challenges to sex addiction. It turned out that I was one of the few who dared to publicly call this supposed disorder a fraud, and a dangerous one at that. But while the controversy was clear to me, there was little written about it and nothing in the popular press that publicized the fact that there were real scientific questions about the issue of sex addiction.

This book is intended to fill that gap. While I write from a scholarly grounding, this is not a research text. I am writing this book to compete with the huge number of sex addiction books out there, that make wild, unsupported claims from anecdote and personal assumptions, and that convincingly feed the myth that sex addiction is real. I expect to be criticized that I present these arguments in a nonscientific manner, but that's precisely the point. The scientists already know that there are problems in sex addiction. The sex addictionologists themselves are true believers, and little that I say will shake their belief system, grounded as it is in rhetoric and pseudoscience. The great majority of my criticisms are toward the presentation of sex addiction in the media, the popular press, self-help books and groups, and toward the sex addictionologists who make claims that they cannot, or will not, support in a scientific realm. The people who are being swayed by this rhetoric deserve to hear the other side of the story.

I have spent the last year immersed in the literature and research, and the lack of research, frankly, that underlies the concept of sexual addiction. I traced the concept back to the 1980s, when it first emerged into the American field of mental health. I followed the threads of this label even as far back as the writings of physicians in the 1700s. Along the way, I chased related concepts, of the role of sexuality in culture, the differences between male and female sexuality, the neurology of sexuality, and the influence of evolution upon sexual development and behaviors. I explored the question of why, if this isn't truly a medical psychological disorder, then why does society cling to it so tightly? What is it about this concept that is so appealing and intrinsically powerful that it has embedded itself in our national consciousness?

And I asked myself whether it really mattered. Is it really all that important if this is or isn't a disorder? If the label allows people who are in pain and struggling to get help, shouldn't I be satisfied with that? Ultimately, my answer to this question drove the development of this book. I believe that it does matter, for us as a society, for the field of mental health and medicine, and especially for men and our view of masculinity. This diagnosis poses a real risk of stigma and shame to innocent people, simply because their sexual behaviors do not fit what is defined as the social norm (though we truly have little real data about what the norm actually is).

Stefan Bechtel, author of *The Practical Encyclopedia of Sex and Health*, suggests that arguments about whether or not sex addiction is real are equivalent to, well, mental masturbation. "Let's just skip all these dainty intellectual arguments. The fact remains that there are people out there whose sexual appetites have gotten desperately out of control."[7] But criticisms of the concept of sexual addiction are not just intellectual egocentrism. There are real dangers inherent in the sex addiction concept. I believe that for the field of health care, medicine, and mental health to endorse and reify a flawed concept creates a very dangerous slippery slope of moral relativism, where any socially unacceptable behavior is labeled a mental disorder subject to psychiatric treatment.

The concept of sexual addiction is intimately connected to the conflicted sexual morality embedded in our culture at its deepest levels, where sexuality is seen as a dangerous evil temptation that must be constantly constrained and feared. It also reflects the influence of the media and the changing strategies of the 24-7 news and entertainment industry. The concept of sexual addiction is driven by the news and entertainment industry as well as the professional treatment providers, facilities, and industry that serve the needs of self-identified sex addicts.

Lastly, the label of sex addiction affects our efforts to enforce expectations of responsibility, holding ourselves, and especially men, responsible for their choices and actions. If we accept the notion that sexual addiction is a disorder, what is the impact upon our understanding of sexual arousal itself, and upon our view of masculinity and personal responsibility for one's sexual behaviors?

A challenge to those of us who criticize the concept of sex addiction is that we are ignoring the very real suffering of clients who are desperate for help. People around the country are dealing with the effects of their sexual desires and behaviors, as they affect their lives and the lives of those around them. Men and women are struggling with answers to why they or their intimate partners are making unhealthy, destructive sexual decisions, decisions that destroy families, careers, and marriages.

I don't disagree with the idea that there are people who are desperate for help. I just frankly don't think that giving them a label of sex addiction is ultimately going to be helpful to them, to society, or to the field of mental health. I'm troubled by the defensiveness and attacking response to criticism. In fact, over the course of my work on this book, I have received numerous attacks from professionals in the sex addiction field. I have been slandered and accused of poor ethics, being insensitive and uncaring, greedy, and worse, all because I dared to publicly challenge the credibility of this concept. At the same time, I have received strong support from numerous clinicians and researchers who praised my efforts, and told me that the debate was necessary and important. Some even said that they wanted to do what I was doing, but didn't, for fear of the attacking response from their colleagues.

Science progresses through questioning, through dialogue, not by casual acceptance of dogmatic assumptions. Sexologist Marty Klein asserts that America's conflicted moral and religious values about sexuality lead to constant attacks on sexual freedoms, and that those who defend sexual freedom are demonized as pornographers and advocates of child sexual abuse and rape. To defend sexual freedoms puts one at risk of being accused of misogyny, condoning pedophilia, and contributing to the prevalence of rape.[8]

You the reader may be a wife whose husband is viewing pornography till late at night, masturbating alone instead of coming to bed with you. You may be a man who is struggling to resist the temptations of sex outside your marriage, or who is drawn to cheap, anonymous sex. You may be a woman, afraid that you are addicted to love, because of your choices to stay in relationships with unhealthy, abusive men.

You are likely wondering if your problem is that you are addicted to sex, or you may already have been given that label by a professional or by other people in your life. If so, I invite you to come along with me, to learn and understand what it means to say you might be sexually addicted. Learn with me whether this concept really applies in your life or belongs in the field of medicine and mental health. If you decide, as I have, that calling these issues sexual addiction ignores significant scientific problems in the research and understanding of sexuality and leaves out important issues in psychology and personal responsibility, then I invite you to examine with me the things in your life that sexual addiction ignores. Look with me at the ways in which sexuality is a healthy part of your life, and work with me to find ways to enhance your health and well-being.

I've included throughout this book descriptions of real people whose sexual behaviors reflect issues described in the field of sexual addiction. Some of these people have been described in the media or diagnosed as sexual addicts. Some descriptions are amalgams, descriptions of clients who have entered my practice, or those of my colleagues, and I have changed identifying details in order to conceal their identities and protect their confidentiality. In other cases, these descriptions are of people in the public, past and present, whose behaviors illustrate the problems of overpathologization involved in the label of sexual addiction. Inclusion of these vignettes is not intended to suggest that the problems encountered by these individuals are not real and serious, but to underscore the need to understand these people and their sexuality in a larger context, addressing environment and psychology, as well as sexuality.

How Many Definitions Do You Need?

The History of the Sexual Addiction Concept

If I had an hour to solve a problem I'd spend fifty-five minutes thinking about the problem and five minutes thinking about solutions.

—Albert Einstein[1]

In these days of the 24-7 news cycles, with paparazzi photographers and
reporters gleefully trampling through flower beds to get risqué photos of
celebrities in compromising positions, one is hard pressed to find someone
who hasn't heard of the concept of sexual addiction. Sex addiction is an intuitively appealing concept that disintegrates into a morass of conflicting and
ill-defined concepts. The concept seems to make sense, that sex, like drugs or
alcohol, feels good. And because it feels so good, it also makes sense in the
values of our Puritan-descended society that too much of it must inherently
be bad for you.

The advent of the Internet has ushered in an era in which we have
incredible access to sexually oriented materials and can develop sexualized
relationships with other people more easily and anonymously than ever before. As a result of this easy, cheap, and anonymous access, we hear about
men in our churches and communities who lose their jobs and families from
constantly viewing pornography on their computers, and we wonder at the
terrible power that sexual stimulation must hold over our thoughts and feelings, not to mention our behaviors.

Most people recall those early days of puberty, when our hormones raged
through our bodies and we found our genitals responding in new, fascinating ways, ways that were often equal parts of ecstasy, fear, embarrassment,
and shame. A simple fact, supported by a wealth of research, is that people in

Western society treat their sexual urges as secretive. Even though the great majority of people masturbate and begin masturbating in adolescence, few people are willing to openly admit to sexual self-pleasure. As people mature, their willingness to admit to masturbation increases, and many will admit that they have lied about it in the past, for fear of embarrassment, judgment, or rejection.

Most adults today also keep their sexual fantasies secret, rarely sharing them with any other person, even their spouse or lovers. Many people in our culture feel a strong sense of fear and shame around sexuality and believe that sexuality is a force that must be denied, controlled, and suppressed, lest it take over their lives and actions. It is this false, intuitive belief, that our sexuality has a tinge of danger, with which the concept of sexual addiction connects so strongly.

Case Example

Ana Catarian Bezerra is a thirty-six-year-old Brazilian woman who recently won the legal right to masturbate at work while looking at online pornography. Diagnosed with hypersexuality, apparently related to a medical condition and hormonal imbalances, Ana feels the need to masturbate frequently throughout the day, a behavior which has, understandably, interfered with her work as an accountant. But the Brazilian courts considered her needs a medical condition covered under Brazilian law and required her employer to accommodate her medical disability, allowing her the freedom to self-stimulate in her office at work while watching pornography on her work computer.[2]

The concept of sex addiction has a long but troubled history. Though the idea has been around for a long, long time in one form or another, this history reveals the alleged disorder as a cultural and moral concept, not based on science or medicine. Unfortunately, the theories embedded within this framework have been irretrievably muddied and confused by centuries of conflicting and overlapping approaches. Although the current sex addiction concept was really sparked by the writings of Patrick Carnes, PhD, in the 1980s, the underlying premise stretches back much further. The history and origins of the concept reveal clearly the moral and social values that are embedded throughout the theory of sexual addiction.

Addiction literally means to devote oneself to something, to give it a place of preeminence in one's choices. Historically, the concept and term first appeared in Roman law, meaning to surrender to a judgment. The word slowly changed in use, coming to describe a person's sense of devotion to something, an activity or interest.

In the 1600s, Christian clergy first advanced the notion that alcohol addiction reflected a disease. Today, the concept of addiction is intrinsically linked to morality and judgment of socially unfavorable behaviors. In fact, it was only in the twentieth century that the word addiction was first restricted to drugs, specifically heroin.[3]

In modern use, addiction is defined as physiological dependence on a substance, which comes from the chronic use of the substance. Current thinking on addiction has broadened a bit, as research and better understanding has revealed that there are some substances which appear to be addictive but do not generate the levels of physiological dependence that alcohol does. For instance, marijuana does not appear to have any physiological withdrawal symptoms. When people quit marijuana "cold turkey," they complain about difficulties sleeping, relaxing, and socializing, complaints related to the social and psychological role that the drug has taken on in their life. But there does not appear to be any evidence that the body develops a physiological dependency upon the drug the way it does with alcohol or heroin.

It is currently suggested that there are three areas of behavior consistently affected by addiction: managing and responding to motivation-reward, regulating and modulating one's emotions and emotional behaviors, and the ability to inhibit and restrict one's impulses.[4] Thus, a much broader modern definition of addiction now suggests that addiction is a brain disorder, one reflecting the progressive and cumulative changes that occur in an individual's brain over time and with continued use of a drug. In this model, alcohol is addictive as a result of the neurological and cognitive changes that occur in the brain as a person uses alcohol on a progressive daily basis. The brain must adapt to the presence of alcohol in the blood and body fluids.

Traditionally, the medical field has classified a substance as addictive if users of it demonstrate a few specific things:

1. Increased use of the substance is required in order to achieve the same results as when the user first began to use the substance. This is commonly known as *tolerance* and reflects the body and brain's adaptability and ability to more effectively process the substance out of the body, and/or to accommodate to and overcome the effects of the substance.
2. Evidence of physiological dependence upon the substance, such that the body and brain are affected by the absence of the substance. This is manifested in symptoms such as *withdrawals* or delirium tremens (DTs). These symptoms show that the body has adapted to the presence

of the substance within the body so much that when the substance isn't there, the body has trouble readjusting.

3. Continued use of the substance, despite increasingly severe social, biological, and legal consequences.

4. An inordinate amount of time and resources spent on using, obtaining, or recovering from the substance. In other words, this substance begins to "take over" the individual's life.

As our conception of the ideas of dependence and addiction has broadened, there is ever-broadening pressure to include more things within the umbrella of addictions in order to change the way such behaviors are perceived. In 2011, the American Society of Addiction Medicine released a new, controversial definition of addiction, calling it a "chronic brain disorder and not simply a behavioral problem involving too much alcohol, drugs, gambling or sex."[5] The intent of the ASAM's new definition was to increase the understanding of addicts' problems as a result of disease rather than poor choices. Similar attempts to identify behavioral issues as brain disorders have been criticized as well-meaning, but unsupported by research, where biological markers of disorders still remain elusive.[6] In other words, while issues in the brain may contribute to problems such as addiction, to assert that their origin is demonstrably rooted in the biology of the brain is an overstatement. Early psychiatric texts stated that drug addictions were usually symptomatic of a disordered and deficient personality.[7] But now, rather than characterizing heroin addicts as junkies and druggies, the mental health treatment field sees them as people afflicted with the effects of an illness that demands empathy and support. When we discuss treatment needs of heroin users and describe their needs as driven by a chronic illness akin to diabetes, it changes the conversation, as well as the social approach to the behavior. As a result, we as a society are more likely to support the provision of treatment rather than punishment.

But the concept and term of addiction has played an inconsistent role in Western mental health. It has often been argued that the word *addiction* has too many implied meanings; it is too vague and nonspecific, too all encompassing, and too simplistic to explain the complex aspects of sophisticated behaviors. Nowhere is this more clear than in the application of the concept of addiction to sexuality, and the general medical view of sexuality overall.

In 1760, Swiss physician Samuel Tissot published a monograph entitled *L'Onanisme*, where he argued that masturbation deprived the body of essential fluids contained in semen and thereby led to numerous illnesses, notably problems of memory, headaches, and other nervous disorders, including even such problems as gout and rheumatism. Tissot's work was accepted as a scientific treatise and influenced the thinking of medicine for the next two centuries.

A few years later, Dr. Benjamin Rush, who was a signer of the Declaration of Independence, labeled numerous antisocial behaviors as diseases and recommended abstinence and bloodletting as appropriate treatments. Indeed, Dr. Rush's contributions are specifically cited by current supporters of the sex addiction concept as part of the rationale for creating a diagnosis. But these citations neglect to mention Dr. Rush's recommended treatment of leeches and bloodletting.[8] Rush also believed that masturbation was the cause of poor eyesight (Rush literally started the "you'll go blind" myth), epilepsy, poor memory, and tuberculosis. Rush argued that women were particularly vulnerable to the ill effects of masturbation, which would leave them feebleminded and susceptible to evil.

Richard von Krafft-Ebing was a nineteenth century German psychiatrist who was one of the first physicians to describe the various fetishes and perversities of human sexuality. Krafft-Ebing gave names to these patterns of behaviors, such as naming sadism after the Marquis de Sade and his predilection for inflicting pain and suffering as a part of sex, or masochism after Leopold von Sacher-Masoch and his love of being beaten, whipped, and humiliated.

Krafft-Ebing first described and labeled the conditions of nymphomania and satyriasis. His descriptions set the stage for years to come. He described satyriasis as a condition in which a man was "forever disposed to the peril of committing rape," by virtue of being in a constant "rutlike" condition, often with a permanent erection.[9] Krafft-Ebing believed that they are a risk to children and to engaging in exhibitionism, public sexual behaviors, and frequent masturbation. Nymphomania was characterized by women who "were a toy in the grip of a morbid imagination which resolves solely around sexual ideas. . . . Even in their sleep they are pursued by lascivious dreams."[10]

Like Rush and Tissot, Krafft-Ebing denounced masturbation as a destructive influence, which degraded humans, particularly men. Masturbation led to sexual and moral degeneration and even created pedophilia in men who masturbated too much. In an interesting irony, when Krafft-Ebing first published his book labeling deviant sexual behaviors as medical diseases, he was attacked by the "German purity leagues" for promulgating a view that such actions warranted sympathetic treatment rather than legal and social sanctions. Krafft-Ebing's opponents argued that these deviant sexual acts threatened the fabric of society and must be punished and condemned, not diagnosed and treated.[11]

Before Tissot, masturbation was largely tolerated, accepted, and ignored. British nannies reportedly masturbated their young charges to help them sleep.[12] But the medical world turned against masturbation, labeling it disease, sin, and sexual excess. The current prevalence of circumcision in the United States is largely due to efforts by the medical community to prevent masturbation by circumcision. Kellogg's Corn Flakes and graham crackers were both invented by physicians attempting to develop bland foods that would prevent overstimulation of the body and reduce desires to masturbate.[13] Psychiatrists blamed masturbation for the development of sexual perversions, including homosexuality. Until 1968, masturbation itself remained a diagnosable disordered condition in the DSM. Sigmund Freud called masturbation "the primary addiction," arguing that all other addictions merely shadowed our human compulsion for sexual self-stimulation.[14]

It is a fascinating contradiction that during this same historical period, American physicians engaged in manual stimulation of females' genitalia in order to produce "hysterical paroxysms" in their patients as a treatment for hysteria.[15] This treatment actually prompted the development and invention of the first vibrators, which were originally steam powered, and whose use, first by doctors, and then alone at home, promised to bring vibrancy and health back to women. While sexuality (and the use of vibrators) has become far more accepted in our society, the beliefs of the antisex crusaders ultimately had a longer-lasting and more overt influence on the proponents of sexual addiction.

———— ❧ ————

Wilhelm Reich was a psychoanalyst in Germany and New York in the mid 1900s. Reich believed that the orgasm was the healthiest tool in the medical pharmacopeia, and he invented what he called the "Orgone Energy Accumulator," though Woody Allen famously nicknamed it the "Orgasmatron." Actors and celebrities from Sean Connery to Norman Mailer and J. D. Salinger were devotees, believing that by going into these wooden cabinets, their sexual energies were vitalized and their physical and mental health magnified. At Reich's request, Albert Einstein studied his orgone box, attempting to explain its mysterious effects. After two weeks of testing, Einstein decreed the thing to have no effect at all. Reich's celebration of the orgasm, and by extension, human sexuality, was embraced by political activists of the 1950s and 1960s, who used his philosophies to justify their own sexual rebellion. At the encouragement of the American Medical Association, who were concerned about the sexual libertarianism that he exemplified, Reich was prosecuted by the federal government for making false claims about the orgone box's ability to prevent cancer. He died in prison after violating federal orders in the sale and manufacture of his orgasm collecting boxes.[16]

———— ❧ ————

Sexologist John Money suggests that physicians who linked masturbation, and sex in general, to physical disorders were actually mistaking the sex for the cause. In other words, Money suggests that the doctors were blaming sex for illnesses, when in fact it was sexually transmitted diseases, in the form of bacteria, that caused debilitating conditions such as syphilis and gonorrhea. After the discovery of the germs behind these diseases, and effective antibiotic treatments for them, the medical antagonism toward sex and masturbation steadily decreased, until things changed suddenly in the past few decades.

In the early 1980s, a prison psychologist named Patrick Carnes published the book *Out of the Shadows*.[17] In it, Carnes described the sexual excess that he had seen in clients and the destructive influences it played in their lives. He applied the concepts and approach of the twelve-step model of Alcoholics Anonymous and describes the patterns of self-destructive, out-of-control sexual behaviors as sexual addiction. His book has sold widely and has been regarded as a groundbreaking piece of work that has influenced the field of addiction and mental health, and American society in general. In the years since, the concept of sexual addiction has spread through common language and popular culture.

Unfortunately, in contrast to medical diagnoses, which require specificity and diagnostic clarity in order to be useful, the specificity and clarity of the sex addiction concept has broadened over the years as popular culture applies it loosely. In medical treatment, diagnostic precision is critical. As a very basic example, while the effects of a virus and a bacterial infection of the sinuses may look similar, diagnostic precision is necessary to guide effective treatment. Antibiotics given to treat a misdiagnosed virus will have no effect other than perhaps to support the spread of antibiotic-resistant germs. Similarly, the gross lack of clarity of diagnoses and definitions of sexual addiction have led to an explosion of a bewildering variety of definitions and lists of sexual behaviors and problems, all lumped under the general and broad concept of sexual addiction.

In his books, Carnes suggests using the "SAFE Formula" to identify whether sexual behavior is addictive or not. If the behavior is Secret, Abusive (harmful), used to avoid painful Feelings, and if it is Empty (outside of a caring, committed relationship), then a sexual behavior is likely to be addictive, compulsive, and dangerous, according to Carnes.[18]

Carnes' categories reflect heterosexual and monogamous social values and judgments rather than medical or scientific data. Take for instance the issue of secrecy. Homosexual behavior is often kept secret due to fears of social stigma, a secrecy that has everything to do with social views and nothing to do with the individual. A homosexual man might live openly in the United States, but in secret if he travels to Africa. Is he suddenly unhealthy when he steps off the plane in Africa and cloaks his sexuality? Even beyond such overtly alternative sexual practices as homosexuality, masturbation itself, the most common form of human sexual behavior on the planet, is itself kept secret by a majority of people, particularly among children and adolescents. Over 100,000 men responded to the "Great Male 2010 Survey" at AskMen. com. Of respondents, 87 percent indicated that they had secret sexual fantasies their partner knew nothing about, and 61 percent admitted to sexual fantasies about their wife's or girlfriend's friends, fantasies they intentionally kept hidden from their wives and girlfriends.[19] Are 87,000 of these men thus addicted to sex because they have these sexual secrets?

According to Carnes, abusive or harmful sex includes behaviors such as bondage and discipline and sadomasochistic behaviors. In *Don't Call It Love*, Carnes describes this type of sexual behavior in the following way:

> The giving or receiving of pain, also known as sadomasochism or S&M, is a type of sexually addictive behavior in which pain is associated with sexual pleasure. There is a blatant imbalance of power between the giver and the receiver, although both partners may be consenting. . . . Victims may perceive their feelings towards their torturer as loving, but there is no genuine trust or intimacy when a relationship is based on hurting one another.[20]

In contrast to Carnes' blanket pathologizing of this sexual practice, research shows that sadomasochistic behaviors as a part of sex are extremely common and do not indicate the presence of mental illness. Indeed, the sadomasochistic relationship is described as one that requires intense communication and reciprocation, with intense levels of trust and intimacy. Multiple Scandinavian countries have recently removed the categories of sadism and masochism from their listings of mental disorders, in recognition of the large numbers of people who engage in such behaviors with no negative impacts on their lives. Similar considerations are under way in the American mental health field.

Why is it not okay for people to use sex to manage or avoid painful feelings? Carnes and others assert that this is an unhealthy pattern, with little evidence, and in contrast to a wealth of evidence suggesting that sexuality can be an effective and healthy way in which people may exert some control over their emotions. Numerous clinical strategies encourage people to use sex as a means of relaxation and calming, and many people use sex within their relationships in order to overcome feelings of grief, sadness, and loss, and to connect with each other.

Finally, Carnes' view of "empty" sex, and his emphasis upon caring, committed relationships, is laudable but biased, and it ignores the high prevalence of "one-night stands" among significant populations. The rates of casual sex, and what research actually says about it, are reviewed in chapter 12. The primacy of committed, emotionally and physically intimate, and monogamous sex is a cultural and temporal artifact of our society, with a great many exceptions to this view throughout the world and across the ages. Using this criterion, and such a subjective word as "empty," reveals the depths of moral and social judgment embedded in this concept. Examination of the variety of other definitions and sex addiction concepts reveals a similar mishmash of socially driven and subjective criteria that lead to a confusing mix of overlapping diagnostic strategies.

There is a consensus among proponents of sexual addiction that there is a consistent and identifiable problem presented by clients with regard to high levels of problematic sexual behaviors. Unfortunately, that is where the consensus ends. Over the past century of attention to these issues, there is a staggering array of overlapping terms and concepts, all with different definitions and criteria. In 1998, researchers Gold and Heffner published a review article regarding sexual addiction, sexual compulsivity, and hypersexuality. They titled their article "Sexual Addiction: Many Conceptions, Minimal Data," arguing that the concept of sexual addiction was poorly researched, inconsistently defined, and driven more by conjecture and catastrophic assertions rather than empirical research or data. "It is difficult to know to what degree agreement across authors reflects a convergence of clinical observations, and to what extent it represents uncritical acceptance of the assertions about sexual addiction originally presented by Carnes."[21] Little has changed since 1998. Indeed, the situation may have worsened, with the public attention given to these issues as a result of the Bill Clinton and Tiger Woods scandals.

There are an incredible number of overlapping concepts and terms that are used interchangeably in the literature around sexual addiction. The list of terms includes *hypersexuality, nymphomania, satyriasis, Don Juanism, erotomania, hypereroticism, hyperlibido, hyperaesthenia, sexual compulsivity, perversion, dysregulated sexuality, hyperphilia, pseudohypersexuality, sexual addiction, sexual disorder not otherwise specified, perversion,* and *atypical impulse control disorder.*

The satyr was a half goat, half man of legend who served the god Bacchus, also known as Dionysus, the god of wine, debauchery, and revelry. In the original Greek legends, they were strong, hairy men with long ears, but they only acquired their half-goat aspects in later Roman retelling of the legends. In art, satyrs are often portrayed with erections, as a symbol of male sexual virility. In some tellings, the satyr was portrayed as a creature who ejaculated at the slightest touch by a female and was thus left chronically dissatisfied, chasing after a fuller sexual adventure. One of the original alternate titles of the magazine *Playboy* was "Satyr," turned down because the word was too unknown for public recognition.

Satyrs chased after nymphs, female spirits of nature who embodied freedom, loving to dance, sing, and make love. Nymphs were characterized as independent sexual creatures, loving and living outside of social restrictions on female sexuality. Nymphs could be seduced, but they were more often portrayed as seductive themselves, enticing with their boldness and amorous natures.

The array of concepts and overlapping definitions presents a confusing collection of theories and approaches, making it incredibly challenging to sort out whom to believe in these matters. Indeed, "Among AASECT (American Association of Sexuality Educators, Counselors and Therapists), sex addiction is currently the number one issue of debate. New therapists to the Association don't know who to believe because the debate is so strong," describes current sex therapy certification chair for AASECT, Stephen Braveman.[22]

Patrick Carnes initially defined sex addicts in *Out of the Shadows* as "people who cannot stop their behavior which is crippling them and those around them."[23] But Carnes, like the entire field of sex addiction, has continued to evolve the ways in which he defines sex addiction, in ever-broadening ways that capture more and more problem behaviors under the concept of addiction. He later went on to describe addiction more broadly as "a pathological relationship with a mood-altering experience or thing that causes damage to the individual or others."[24]

Carnes' definitions, both the two offered above and the earlier SAFE definition, reveal three main themes that emerge in other definitional strategies, namely focusing upon the specific behaviors and labeling them as pathological themselves; focusing upon the effects of these behaviors and the damage incurred to self and others from these behaviors; and third, focusing upon the internal, invisible motivations and intent of the behaviors and identifying these intents and motivations as inherently unhealthy.

The sex addiction field identifies a number of different types of sexual behaviors as risky and potentially addictive. These behaviors, as we shall see, are also part of the "normal" sexuality of a great many people, and sex addictionologists offer us little ability to determine, for instance, how much prostitution is okay and when it becomes a problem. Summing across the literature, these behaviors include the following:

- Engaging in "fantasy sex"—such as role-playing or dressing up
- Compulsive masturbation

- Anonymous sex with strangers
- Group sex
- Sex in public
- Having multiple sex partners
- An inability to say "no" to sexual advances or requests
- "Cruising" for sex
- Chronic affairs and infidelity
- Use of prostitutes
- Use of pornography
- Engaging in cybersex
- Voyeurism
- Exhibitionism
- Sexual harassment
- Sexual offending
- Compulsive sex within a relationship
- Jumping from one relationship to another
- Seductive role sex (this is based upon the idea that there are people who get hooked on the role of seducer, pursuing conquest after conquest)
- Paying for sex
- Trading sex
- Intrusive sex, where arousal comes from violating a person's boundaries
- Pain-exchange sex, involving sadomasochistic or bondage-discipline behaviors
- Exploitative sex, where sex requires the exploitation of vulnerabilities in others

When the definitions address the effects of these behaviors, they include the emotional effects of these behaviors upon others, as well as the life consequences (such as loss of relationship or job) as a result of the behaviors or the disclosure/discovery of the behaviors. According to some, sex addiction is a disease that leads people to treat others as sexual objects, as less than human, as mere receptacles and sources of sexual gratification.[25] Others claim that "sexual addiction is best described as a progressive intimacy disorder characterised by compulsive sexual thoughts and acts."[26] Repetitive sexual behaviors and promiscuity might be expressions of psychodynamic conflicts, emerging as anger, dominance, or fear. The Society for the Advancement of Sexual Health, formerly known as the National Council on Sexual Addiction and Compulsivity, has defined sexual addiction as "engaging in persistent patterns of sexual behaviour acted out despite increasing negative consequences to self and others."[27]

Case Example

Sherry is a forty-one-year-old African-American female with a long history of depression and mood disorder. She was first diagnosed with bipolar disorder at age thirty-six. She has been married for nine years and until recently had always felt that her sexuality was under control and that she had no real interest in infidelity. "I once kissed a guy who wasn't my husband, back when I was first diagnosed with bipolar. Back then, I was running around crazy a lot of time, doing things I didn't think about."

Since she was first diagnosed with a mood disorder, Sherry has been on various medications to treat depression and mood disturbance. Periods of severe depression have been frequent, periods where "all I could do was cry, just like all the time." She began taking Cymbalta about a year ago. Her depression lifted, and her libido came back for the first time in years, something "which I thought was a good thing, at least at first." Unfortunately, Sherry's libido continued to increase, and she found herself feeling aroused "all of the time." With her husband at work during the day, Sherry began to go online and "found someone to talk to online. I developed an addiction to this person. I felt like he was my safe place because I couldn't talk to my husband, and he wasn't interested in the same thing I was sexually. I started to turn to the other person more and more, especially after my husband found out and hurt me by something that he did. Then, even though I knew I shouldn't talk to this other person, I couldn't stop and kept sneaking and finding ways to talk to him." Though Sherry did have "cybersex" with her online friend, she came to view their relationship as more than just sex. "We did talk a lot about sexual things, but it was more that he became my support system."

Sherry's husband discovered her online affair and read all the messages Sherry had exchanged. He now wants her to go to marriage counseling with him and has threatened to separate from her, even to divorce her, over her actions. "I really do love my husband. I was so hurt, I think I wanted him to hurt like I did somehow. Today was the first time I've not talked to the other guy, and admittedly it's been hard not to try and contact him. I'm not sure if I've got a sex addiction or not. My therapist said it wouldn't hurt if I went to a sex addicts group because at least I'd have more support, but the stuff I've read is all really religious, and I don't believe in God. I just feel really alone right now and like I'm on the downward part of the bipolar cycle. It's like I can feel it happening and I don't know how to stop it, and honestly there's a huge part of me that thinks I deserve to feel this way."

Other theorists suggest that sex addiction is actually an impulse control disorder, where people have difficulties resisting the urges to engage in sexual behaviors, while still other sex addictionologists argue that sexual addiction is in fact the reverse of impulsivity and is actually a manifestation of compulsive behaviors. Compulsions are typically thought of as behaviors that a person feels they *must* engage in, often to make feelings of anxiety and worry go away. So a person might "check" to make sure that their oven is off before leaving the house, sometimes checking it a hundred or more times to relieve their fear that the oven is on and might burn the house down. However, compulsions are driven by a need to reduce or banish anxiety and do not by definition involve behaviors that are pleasurable and rewarding in and of themselves.

Dr. Archibald Hart, psychologist and author of *Thrilled to Death*, suggests that sexual addiction is the result of the pairing of sexuality with adrenaline, as experienced when one experiences a sexual act or arousal, in an illicit way that has the potential for trouble or getting caught. Looking at a dirty magazine, when a teenager, can lead to this pairing of sex and arousal, of thrill of fear and erotic stimulation. Hart argues that this pairing can lead to "grossly distorted" sexuality, particularly in males, contributing to "sexual perversions such as adding pain to sex (sexual sadism and masochism) and, most seriously, rape (a crime that produces high-octane adrenaline)."[28]

Sexual addiction is sometimes defined more simply as problematic sexual promiscuity or as indiscriminate sexual acting out, driven by needs to fulfill nonsexual emotional and social issues, or as "an obsession or intense preoccupation with such a yearning that leads to negative social and/or occupational consequences."[29] It is also defined as behavior that causes problems and is not stopped despite the problems incurred: "sexual fantasy, sexual urges, or sexual behaviors that continue in spite of clinically significant distress or impairment in social, educational, occupation, or other important areas of functioning."[30]

One historical flavor of sex addiction in men has been called "Don Juanism," after a famous literary womanizer. "Don Juanism results from inhibitions, an inhibition and fear of love. By running from woman to woman, and bed to bed, a man need never experience the development of intimacy, dependency, and vulnerability. Compulsively nonmonogamous sex protects a man from the fear of abandonment, rejection and loss."[31] The author of *The Practical Encyclopedia of Sex and Health*, Stefan Bechtel, defined sexual addiction as being similar to nymphomania, calling it a "compulsion to lure a series of casual sex partners for one-night stands, then reject them, because the thrill of newness and conquest is the only thing that enables them to reach orgasm."[32] Bechtel's use of argument by analogy is very common in the field of sex addiction and is covered more fully later in the book as we question the science behind this alleged disorder.

———— ✧ ————

The legend of Don Juan is an oft-told story concerning a Spanish gentleman and libertine, a lover of women who thrills in the chase and pursuit of women.

In Moliere's play *Don Juan*, performed in the 1660s, Don Juan is a Spanish nobleman who pretends to marry young women in order to seduce them, in addition to seducing married women and fighting their enraged husbands. Don Juan is a Catholic who despairs of his sins but believes that he will have time to repent after his days of excess are done. However, in the end of Moliere's play, Juan is dragged down to hell, unmourned by anyone on earth: "By his death everyone gets satisfaction. Heaven offended, laws violated, girls led astray, families dishonored, relatives outraged, wives ruined, husbands driven to despair, they all are satisfied."[33]

According to some theories of sex addiction, different individuals may engage in the same behavior, such as infidelity or masturbation, but the diagnostic distinction lies in the person's motivations or internal needs and in what the sexual behavior is intended to achieve (consciously or unconsciously). Sex addiction is "simply the addictive process being expressed through sex, the compulsive dependence on some form of sexual behavior as a means of regulating one's feelings and sense of self."[34]

Sexologist John Money suggested that disordered sexual behaviors like sex addiction reflect the "lovemaps" that people form in their childhoods and development. A person's lovemap is their internal idea of what "perfect" sex, love, and relationships might look like and feel like. So people with out-of-control sexual behaviors might have lovemaps that make unrestrained, impulsive, dangerous, and self-destructive sexual behaviors the "perfect" ideal to pursue. "The hyperphilic solution is one in which the lovemap defies defacement, so that the sex organs, in adulthood, are used with exaggerated defiance, frequency and compulsiveness, and/or with great multiplicity of partners, in pairs, or in groups."[35] Money goes on to argue that developing a stable, intimate relationship and having lots of sexual partners are mutually exclusive conditions.

SBraga, O'Donohue, and Bancroft are clinicians who crafted a book called *The Sex Addiction Workbook*, one of the most-used self-help books in the field of sex addiction treatment. Their book is filled with useful, thoughtful intervention strategies for people who feel that their sexual behaviors are out of their control. The authors tap-dance around the validity of the sexual addiction concept, avoiding real questions of validity: "We do not view any sexual behaviors as actual addictions in the way that using heroin is an actual addiction, but we've adopted the terminology because it is the language people use to talk about the loss of sexual self-control."[36]

Language is important. If we don't believe that something *is* an addiction, then let's not call it an addiction. To adopt a term that we disagree with, simply because it is popular or sells books, brings significant baggage. When doctors, therapists, and other educated, trained, and titled experts use words in a professional manner, we give those words credibility. While the public might use concepts in nonspecific ways, applying them as metaphors, in the mouths of doctors, they become diagnoses, labels, sentences, and condemnations.

Historically, words such as *moron, retard,* and *imbecile* were clinical words, with specific, clear, and objective meanings. But as the words crept into common usage, the meanings were distorted, their specificity lost to subjectivity as people called each other morons, with no understanding of the true meaning. As a result, in order to preserve the integrity of the clinical concepts, the mental health field adopted new words, replacing the old ones. Unfortunately, in the case of sex addiction, the pattern seems to be running in the reverse direction. The mental health field is adopting the vague, subjective labels and concepts used in general society, and the media. It is no wonder that the field is struggling to establish consistency in the application of these words.

If we allow the frivolous use of the word *addiction* simply to describe any and all behaviors where people feel some loss of self-control, then where do we stop? Are workaholics suddenly "addicted" to work and now eligible for workers' compensation because they worked on weekends and nights and never had a personal life? Are people who schedule their lives around their favorite television shows addicted to soap operas?

Case Example

Tom is a thirty-three-year-old man, married for the past three years, with a young child. Tom came to therapy after his wife found out that Tom went "cruising" at adult bookstores a few times a month, having anonymous sex with other men during these encounters. Tom kept these behaviors secret from his wife and only admitted them when she once accidentally saw him coming out of one such store.

During an interview with the couple, Tom denied any history of previous such behaviors and denied any substance abuse problems. He blamed himself for going to the adult bookstores and said that he had just "gotten horny and didn't think." At this statement, Tom's wife Christie jumped in and said, "That's addiction, right? He's addicted to this, to going to these creepy places and having sex."

After the birth of their daughter, the physical relationship between Tom and Christie diminished under the burdens of parenting, burdens which had worsened after their daughter was diagnosed with a severe illness which required lots of attention from Christie, and put the family under significant financial strain.

Over the course of treatment of the couple, additional details began to surface, including the fact that Tom had been drinking more than he admitted. He got a

DWI and was ordered to attend Alcoholics Anonymous, in addition to continuing his individual and family counseling. Tom admitted that he had been drinking during all of the sexual encounters he'd had at the adult bookstores. Tom first drank alcohol at the age of twelve, when he had sex with an older male neighbor. It was only during therapy that Tom acknowledged that this neighbor was ten years older than he was and that the sexual encounter had actually been sexual abuse. "I thought I was gay; I thought that was why he chose me. It felt good. He made me come for the first time and taught me how to drink, taught me how to masturbate. He showed me porn, and he used to take me out to do stuff with him, like going four-wheeling and stuff. It really felt great, because he was so cool, and I felt so cool, getting to be like him."

Tom began to attend a group therapy for male survivors of sexual abuse and over time became a peer educator in the group, sometimes leading discussions and mentoring other men. He decided that he wasn't bisexual or gay, as he had feared, and through sobriety and focusing on his relationship with his wife, he managed his fears and depression better. He shared in groups sometimes that he still had urges to go to the bookstores and have sex, or that he sometimes masturbated while thinking about other men. "When I do this, I don't beat myself up now. I just look at what's going on in my life and try to figure out what it is that I'm not dealing with, that the alcohol or the sex is a distraction from."[37]

According to the various proponents of sexual addiction, there are numerous different types of sex addiction. In fact, there are so many different types of sex addicts that it seems hard to avoid ending up in one category or another.

Few of these types are established by research or statistics. They are all for the most part derived from anecdotal experiences, based on the history that each different theorist has had in treating sex addicts. Some have suggested that there are separate types of addicts that are biologically driven, psychologically driven (by either fantasy, psychological needs, or psychological disorders such as depression or bipolar disorder), or driven in response to trauma as well as those who are "intimately anorexic," withholding sex from their spouse but acting out sexually in other ways.[38] When we attempt to consider these subtypes within a diagnostic framework, they generate significant confusion. For instance, if the sexual behaviors of a person are related to their history of either trauma or mood disorder, how can we treat these behaviors without diagnosing and treating them as either posttraumatic stress disorder or a mood disorder such as bipolar disorder? It is a violation of the principle of parsimony to render multiple diagnoses (e.g., PTSD *and* sex addiction) when the problem behaviors in the sex addiction diagnosis are the result of the diagnosis of PTSD.

The proposed DSM5 disorder of hypersexual disorder suggests that there are several subtypes of those with hypersexual disorder, subtypes based upon the primary behavior or preference, including masturbation; pornography; sexual behavior with consulting adults—this subtype includes heterosexual and homosexual promiscuity, infidelity, and soliciting of prostitutes; cybersex; telephone sex; and strip clubs.

The research supporting these subtypes is minimal at best, and they are based almost exclusively on therapist anecdotes.[39] There are a great many unanswered questions concerning their use and application in diagnosis and treatment. For instance, what if someone is using voice over Internet protocols to have telephone sex? Are they a cybersex subtype or a telephone sex subtype? It is said that each new technological advancement will invariably be used in some sexual fashion; the automobile yielded a backseat and generations of clandestine sexual encounters; silicone, an inert synthetic compound used in medical applications, was quickly co-opted for use in breast implants and the manufacture of sexual toys. Will we be adding a new subtype to this diagnostic category in response to each new technological advance?

Throughout this text, I will simply use the term *sexual addiction* to describe the basic concepts that are being considered. Though many well-meaning clinicians attempt to distinguish these various concepts, carving out one term or another, there is so much overlap that they remain indistinguishable. Further, as we shall see, there is little research showing that these terms are distinguishable from an individual who simply enjoys sex and wants to have lots of it.

HOW MUCH SEX IS TOO MUCH?

The real danger in labeling hypersexuality is that we do not know what constitutes excessive sexual behavior, and yet we are applying a label which may have pathological symptoms associated with it.

—Rinehart and McCabe[40]

According to the American Psychiatric Association, in order for sex addiction to meet the definition of a mental disorder, it must be shown that sex addiction, or hypersexual disorder, "represents a psychological or behavioral syndrome that is the manifestation of a dysfunction."[41] A syndrome is a cluster of symptoms that form a consistent pattern. So the syndrome associated with the common cold includes sneezing, sniffling, feeling poorly, congestion, coughing, and so forth, reflecting the effects of the attack of a virus upon the body's cells. There does appear to be a cluster of symptoms associated with sex addiction that might meet the definition of a syndrome, though it is a pretty wide syndrome. But what dysfunction does this syndrome reflect?

To establish diagnostic validity, the behaviors of sexual addiction must be distinguished from "mere" excessive sexual activity or high libido. Dr. Eli Coleman and several others suggest that the additional elements of distress, dysfunction, life impairment, depression, anxiety, and obsessions, added on top of the excessive sexual activity, are what catapult high levels of sexuality into the realm of sex addiction.[42] Measuring these distress and dysfunction components becomes a problem when we try to decide if the sexual behaviors are a problem for the person or just those around them. This issue requires more specific attention and is explored in more detail in chapter 6.

Despite efforts to define sex addiction as including these other components of distress and dysfunction, most of the concepts of sex addiction and hypersexuality end up being driven by the simple concept of "too much sex." So, what is too much sex?

Psychiatrist Dr. Martin Kafka suggested that having seven or more orgasms a week over six months was "too much" and was a defining measure of sexual addiction.[43] Unfortunately, there's no real data to back that assertion up. Sex researcher John Money asserted that any attempt to quantify frequency of sex as too much or too little was ultimately doomed. Frequency of sex is only a problem when it consumes someone's time away from other activities, or when two partners are mismatched in their libido and sexual desires (an issue explored in chapter 6).

Kinsey challenged the core notion that there was truly any such thing as "too much sex." He pointed to the frequency distributions of sexual activity, describing them as evenly distributed, such that "no individual has a sexual frequency which differs in anything but the slightest degree from those next on the curve."[44] In other words, there was not a cluster of men at the far end of the spectrum whose sexual behavior was significantly greater than those of other men. Instead, there was a continuous curve, up and down, with regard to sexual behaviors. On this curve, to assert a judgment of too much or too little was a purely relative, subjective statement.

Research studies have found that setting the criteria at the level proposed by Kafka could lead to diagnosing hypersexuality in as much as 40 percent of males and 21 percent of females.[45] In surveys, between 10 and 23 percent of men endorse daily sex or masturbation as their preferred normal, healthy level of sex.[46] If we are engaged in a process that pathologizes such a huge percentage of all males at some point in their lives, then it is clear we may not be fighting a disease but a gender. While Kafka ultimately dropped efforts to include this criterion for hypersexual disorder, the trend of pathologizing male sexuality is one that we will continue to encounter throughout this work.

> For me, a day without great sex is a wasted day.
> —Bill Maher[47]

Dr. Eli Coleman is a psychologist and past president of the Society for the Scientific Study of Sexuality and the World Association for Sexual Health. Coleman previously argued for the use of the term *compulsive sexual behavior*, reflecting the influence of childhood abuse, trauma, and conflicting negative attitudes toward sexuality. However, he now supports the idea that these sexual behaviors reflect the influences of many various causes and histories. Coleman also suggests that this confusing mix of causes, influences, and patterns can easily lead to overdiagnosis when the concepts of sex addiction and hypersexuality are so poorly defined and understood by the general public, not to mention by the mental health field. "We have no clearly defined and agreed upon criteria for this,"[48] he has said, and he has gone on to further state that "sex addiction is a trendy, overused term."[49] Even sex addiction guru Patrick Carnes has suggested that the concepts are unclear and confusing to the public, and he has written that "the words addiction and compulsion as they are currently used and defined are probably inadequate."[50] Just as occurred in the past, when women were diagnosed as nymphomaniacs because female sexuality was not accepted or understood by society, there is tremendous risk of overdiagnosis, especially when the diagnostic concepts of sex addiction are so unclear and inconsistent.

HOKEYPOKEY

You put your left leg in, you put your left leg out, you put your left leg in, and you shake it all about.

Since the 1952 publication of the *Diagnostic and Statistical Manual of Mental Disorders*, commonly called the DSM, the American Psychiatric Association has done the "hokeypokey" dance with sexual addiction. One edition of the book puts it in, and the next edition takes it out. The original version included nymphomania as a diagnosis, but not satyriasis.[51] Nymphomania was itself subsequently deleted from the second edition of the DSM.[52]

In 1974, the DSM-II was amended, removing homosexuality as a mental disorder. The way in which homosexuality was deleted as a diagnosis is a revealing insight into the workings of the DSM itself, and the APA. From 1970 to 1973, gay activists protested at the annual meetings of the APA, creating significant disruption and uproar. In 1973, the trustees of the APA voted to remove homosexuality as a diagnosis, and in 1974, the general membership of the association voted the same way. But while the research by scientists such as Alfred Kinsey was regarded as influential in this vote, Kinsey's research had been around for decades. Instead, what most likely affected the association's members and their votes was the increased social attention and acceptance of homosexuality, combined with the activism of the gay rights movement. "Instead of being engaged in a sober consideration, psychiatrists were swept up in a political controversy. . . . The result was not a conclusion based on an approximation of the scientific truth as dictated by reason, but was instead an action demanded by the ideological temper of the times."[53]

———∞∞∞———

In 1980, the third edition of the manual included diagnoses of both nymphomania and "Don Juanism," describing them as "distress about a pattern of repeated sexual conquests with a succession of individuals who exist only as things to be used."[54] This new language reflected the shift away from a pathology based upon an excess of sexual desire and toward a moralistic stance that pathologized sex when it occurred without love or intimacy. Since 1980 and DSM-III, there have been continued efforts to add hypersexuality as a diagnosis, efforts that have grown in emphasis as the sex addiction movement has gained momentum and popular recognition.

Language specific to sex addiction was removed from the DSM-IV when the committees tasked with evaluating the data and concept determined that inclusion of a sex addiction diagnosis was unwarranted due to "insufficient data."[55] "Hyposexuality" as a specific sexual disorder reflecting very low levels of sexual desire and arousal was included, but at the time, symptoms of hypersexuality were regarded as symptoms of other disorders rather than a discrete syndrome. The category of "sexual disorder not otherwise specified" in the DSM-IV did include a description of "a pattern of repeated sexual relationships involving a succession of lovers who are experienced by the individual only as things to be used."[56]

The *Diagnostic and Statistical Manual of the American Psychiatric Association* is currently due for its fifth revision. The first DSM had 106 diagnoses when it was first published. The current version, DSM-IV TR, has over four hundred diagnoses. In the current development of the DSM5, sex addiction was not included as a diagnosis in the addictive category due to lack of "empirical evidence," despite there being some usefulness to the concept, according to Kafka.[57] Sex addiction as an addictive disorder was declined by the DSM5 task force, along with problems related to shopping, working, and Internet use, all because of a serious "lack of hard data," according to Charles O'Brien, MD, chair of the APA's DSM Substance-Related Disorders Work Group.[58] However, a different presentation was made to the Sexual Disorders Work Group, a set of diagnostic criteria that focus only on specific problems associated with sexual behaviors, without the implication that the behaviors emerge from an addictive process.

Hypersexual disorder is the term applied to the proposed current sex addiction diagnosis in the DSM-V, ostensibly because it is more scientific and less controversy laden than the term *addiction*. Unfortunately, this term is confusing as well. It has been used in medical literature to describe the specific sexual behaviors associated with symptoms of mania, drug abuse, and some brain damage. So carving it out as a separate disorder creates the real possibility that clients whose sexual behavior is symptomatic of these other disorders could mistakenly be diagnosed as hypersexual.

In the "Rationale" section of the DSM5 workgroup's discussion of hypersexual disorder, it is explained that there is a clinical need for this diagnosis because there is a "demand" from consumers and providers of services to recognize and diagnose the groups of people who are seeking and receiving treatment for "out-of-control" sexual behaviors.[59] So, in other words, like the Kevin Costner film *Field of Dreams*, "because they came, we built it." It's a disturbing argument that because there is a group of people saying they have a problem, and because there is an industry and a group of people treating that problem, we should therefore create a diagnosis around it. As others have pointed out, just because there are many people who believe in alien abduction, we have not proposed creating a specific disorder for this condition.

In June 2011, the British Psychological Society responded publicly to the proposed DSM5 development. Given the worldwide impact of the DSM, the BPS's concerns reflect the real issues that those outside America see in our current diagnostic approach. The society expressed very strong concern that many of the DSM5's diagnoses pathologize normal behaviors, treating them as illnesses, and that they are "clearly based on social norms," reflecting "social expectations" and individual variations, rather than illnesses. The concerns of the BPS did not single out hypersexual disorder for specific comment but did address the fact that attributing diagnostic labels to sexual problems ignores the relational and social context of these behaviors. The society's opinion went on to express concern that the APA would venture into diagnosing sexual behaviors as illness, given the tragic history of pathologizing homosexuality, and stated that "the Society would not be able to support considering sexual differences as symptoms of illness."[60]

The justification associated with the proposed criteria for hypersexual disorder acknowledges that it is controversial, and Kafka argues that "the number of 'cases' of hypersexual disorder reported in peer-reviewed journals greatly exceeds the number of cases of some of the codified paraphilic disorders such as Fetishism or Frotteurism."[61] There is a strong argument against Kafka, that the reason for the high numbers of such cases is due to the very wide net that the vague, subjective diagnoses have cast. In contrast to the extensive literature on drug and alcohol use, abuse, addiction, and dependency, there remains a maddening vagueness in the attempt to medicalize sexual behavior problems. This vagueness and lack of clarity permeates the entire sex addiction field, opening the doors to confusing rhetoric and poor science.

> Being "addicted" can become a self fulfilling prophecy and a great excuse for not meeting responsibilities to self, family, school, and the legal system.
> —Allen Frances, MD[62]

In the DSM5 workgroup's justification for hypersexual disorder, published in 2010, it is stated that "significant gaps in basic knowledge remain. . . . For example, developmental risk factors, family history and aggregation studies, cognitive markers, and a distinct neurobiological substrate for hypersexual disorder are not currently known."[63] It also describes that "antecedent, concurrent and predictive validators" are unknown. This means they are saying that at this time they cannot tell who is going to develop hypersexuality and they cannot identify what things consistently come before hypersexuality. They cannot even be consistent in identifying what things hypersexuality actually includes or how they can legitimately know it when they see it.

If these smart, well-meaning, well-funded folks can't generate clear definitions in three decades, then maybe the problem is not in the terminology but in the process, and the goal. The reason why clear medical terminology cannot be created in over thirty years of effort is because this is not a medical issue but a moral and social one.

> The entire concept of hypersexuality is reflective of a sex-negative environment in which it is too easy to stigmatize those who evoke our ambivalence about high rates of sexual activity.
> —Charles Moser, MD[64]

2

Distinguishing Sex from Drugs

Unlike heroin, sex naturally engages issues of intimacy, power, autonomy, and love. Sexual arousal always has meaning. In fact, sexual excitement of any kind is impossible unless its mental and social context is specifically conducive to it. While the desire for sexual pleasure is natural, the how, where and why are not. Sexual desire actually begins in the mind and travels down. The "problem" of sexual addiction always involves the mind and the social world, never the desire itself.[1]

The concepts of addiction are based upon what occurs when an individual introduces a foreign chemical or substance into his or her body and that substance causes some physiological or psychological effect. Many drugs, such as heroine or morphine, create an effect in the body by mimicking, at an exaggerated level, natural processes and biochemical functions of the body. Morphine is an incredibly effective pain medicine that acts by blocking certain pain receptors in the brain, working through its similarity to natural neurochemicals in the brain.

But there are significant problems that arise when we try to apply our understanding of addiction, based upon drug and alcohol research, to sexuality, where no outside substance or chemical is introduced into the body. Sexuality is a natural process that our bodies, brains, and behaviors were actually designed to pursue and enjoy, whether by natural selection, evolution, or a benevolent God. The neurochemical and biological processes are working the way they are supposed to during sexual activity. When we apply the core concepts of addiction to issues of sexuality, we find significant gaps that make it extremely difficult to justify sexual behaviors as a form of addiction.

Tolerance: In the diagnosis and treatment of alcohol and chemical dependency disorders, *tolerance* is the term that describes the fact that it takes more drinks, or more drugs, to reach the same level of intoxication or high than it took when you first began to consume. So, where you got sloppy drunk on a six-pack years ago when you first began to drink, now you can put away twelve or eighteen beers before you really begin to show any effect. Tolerance reflects actual physical changes in the body, as your body becomes more and more efficient at processing out the poison. The liver becomes enlarged over time, and the enzymes in the body and blood that convert alcohol to sugar increase in number and efficiency. Psychological changes occur as well, as the brain learns to cope with the effects of alcohol upon behavior, coping with things like a tendency to slur or stumble by increased caution and deliberateness in moving and speaking.

In sexual addiction, people suggest the concept of tolerance, or at least an analogue process. The suggestions are that it takes more and more stimulation to reach the same level of sexual arousal one once experienced. So where pictures in the lingerie section of the JC Penny catalogue once sent you off the edge, now it takes seeing a live-sex donkey show in Tijuana to get a really satisfying sexual experience.

There's some anecdotal support in the stories of people who present for treatment for sexual behaviors. Unfortunately, there isn't enough data or research on the sexual practices and behaviors of "normal" people to allow a good comparison. Sex addictionologists argue that this pattern is pathological, and part of the disease process of sexual addiction.

There are strong suggestions that this type of tolerance is actually a normal part of sexual development in humans. In fact, this tolerance effect has been intentionally used in the past; in the 1970s, some medical schools required their students to view various types of pornography, including hetero- and homosexual erotica. The intent was to "desensitize" the future doctors, to make them better able to treat sexual conditions, to increase their "tolerance" for sexual materials, and to enable them to treat people as people, regardless of their sexual behaviors.

Adolescents are easily physically aroused by fleeting sexual imagery, whereas adults typically require greater levels and longer continuance of sexual stimulation to reach equal levels of arousal. As males age, the time that it takes to achieve an erection increases, the time that it takes to achieve ejaculation increases, and the latency period, the time in between erections, increases as well. This is not a pathological symptom but a normal part of aging. A progression and change in sexual interests is a part of normal sexual development across the life span.

Sex addiction includes the premise that sex for the sex addict is ultimately unsatisfying and does not lead to the release of anxiety expected or desired. This is based on the idea that people's tolerance for sex increases to the point that sex activity does not achieve the same release it once did. But no research to date supports the notion that people who have more sex lose the ability to enjoy sex. Orgasms do not stop being pleasurable the more of them you have.

People who have more sex with their partners also masturbate more, consume more sexual materials, and think about sex more. There is a sense that sexuality is a muscle that, when exercised, gets stronger. It's just that this stronger muscle doesn't lead you into making unhealthy decisions, like the sex addiction theory would suggest. Further, more sex is not unhealthy but in fact has many beneficial effects (more on this in chapter 5).

Sex addiction theories suggest that a failure to achieve satisfaction from sex drives sex addicts to more and more severe and extreme forms of sex and promiscuity. This isn't a new idea. Carol Groneman, author of the delightful work *Nymphomania: A History*, describes that an inability to be satisfied sexually, to have an orgasm, was deemed one of the hallmarks of nymphomania. But is being "unsatisfied" actually a bad thing? It may be uncomfortable, and people may dislike being unsatisfied, whether in bed or at the dinner table, but does a lack of satisfaction drive people into frenzied uncontrolled and unhealthy behaviors?

> Love enjoys knowing everything about you; desire needs mystery. . . .
> Love is about having; desire is about wanting.
> —Esther Perel[2]

Freud suggested that a failure to be satisfied, sexually or otherwise, is a positive driving force in humans and that the insatiable nature of sexual desires is what drives the great achievements of art, science, and culture. Some suggest that it was Freud's own curiosity about sex that led to the creation of psychoanalysis and modern psychology.[3] Author Robin Wright, in his book *The Moral Animal*, described that "the frequent absence of happiness is what keeps us pursuing it, and thus makes us productive."[4]

We all dream of winning the lottery and suddenly having our financial and material needs all satisfied. But we are all surprised to learn that this windfall of success rarely results in a lasting happiness or life of ease. Even beyond all the friends and relatives who suddenly approach with their hands out, lottery winners find themselves returning to the same level of happiness that they were at before their ticket came up with the winning numbers. For most people, happiness is a relatively constant state. It may fluctuate with time and life's events, but each person has a personal baseline level of contentment that remains their average, and to which they gradually return, regardless of the slings and arrows of fortune.

Researchers have labeled this the "hedonic treadmill," with the image that with each move we make forward, chasing each new happiness, each new thrill, we find ourselves at the same level of internal satisfaction. This is perhaps the closest thing that exists to the concept of tolerance to sexuality within the sex addiction model, and it might conceivably explain the way that people chase new sexual partners and new sexual experiences, without ever being fully sated. Alas, this is a model that applies equally to all people and is relevant to most things in life, not just to sex, and not just to sex addicts.

Withdrawal: There is no clear support in clinical or research literature for any withdrawal syndrome related to interruption of frequent or compulsive sexual behaviors. When someone stops having sex, they don't face the life-threatening and serious physiological consequences of stopping serious alcohol or heroin use. When a male stops having sex, he might, at most, become nervous, report feeling on edge and preoccupied with thoughts of sex, and be likely to experience wet dreams, as this is one of the body's ways of clearing out old, aged semen. But, none of these "symptoms" qualify as withdrawal. As a result, a withdrawal syndrome was not included in the diagnostic paradigm of hypersexual disorder for the DSM5. Similarly, there was no clear evidence of a "tolerance" to sexuality, and thus this key component of addiction also was not included in the currently proposed diagnosis. The lack of these hallmark criteria calls into great question the validity of including sex addiction as an addictive disorder.

In the 1990s, a task force of the American Psychiatric Association considered whether caffeine addiction should be included as a disorder. There was substantial evidence in favor of inclusion of caffeine addiction as a substance-related disorder. Use of caffeine creates a biological and neurological effect. There is a tolerance effect—when caffeine is first used, it has significant physiological and psychological effects that diminish over time, requiring greater doses to reach the same effect. There is withdrawal, in the form of headaches and the grumpiness that my family notes in me in the morning, as I stumble to the coffeemaker. There are negative effects from use, from the amount of money shelled out for double-stuffed half-whipped no-foam lattes with a twist, and the jitteriness and irritability that can result from overconsumption. But, according to Dr. Allen Frances, one of the chief architects of the DSM-IV, caffeine addiction "was left out of the manual because caffeine dependence is so ubiquitous and (for most people) so harmless. It did not seem worthwhile to have sixty million people wake up each morning to the awareness that they had a mental disorder. For those relatively few whose atrial fibrillation or panic disorder is triggered by caffeine, the diagnosis substance dependence not otherwise specified, caffeine, does the trick. All other coffee drinkers can have their morning cup(s) unburdened by mental disorder."[5]

So there is a precedent that things may "look like" an addiction, but it may be acknowledged that there is little overall value, and indeed great social risk, to labeling them as an addiction. And there is precedent for the medical and behavioral health community to resist this label. Unfortunately, the same has not been true for sexual addiction.

THE GATEWAY DRUG THEORY FOR SEX

When you characterize porn as an addiction it tells you that it is hard to break free, that it is a struggle, that relapse is inevitable—all things that have nothing to do with porn. But when you characterize online porn as junk food, the solution is obvious: don't eat it.

—"The Last Psychiatrist"[6]

In drug treatment, there is the concept of "gateway drugs," that is, that certain drugs, notably marijuana, tobacco, and alcohol, serve as an entry point for drug use. The theory goes that since marijuana is perceived as a relatively low-risk drug, people start using it, but they find themselves on a slippery slope of increasing drug use as their marijuana habit expands to include other more dangerous drugs like cocaine, methamphetamine, LSD, and so forth. The gateway drug hypothesis is a popular one with prevention efforts, encouraging the ideas that it's best just to not start at all. In sexual addiction, the concept is applied liberally to consumption of pornography, and even to participation in various kinds of nontraditional sexual behaviors. "Once you start, you won't be able to stop," goes the theory.

However, the science of the gateway theory is marginal at best. More and more studies are showing that drug use and the risk of drug dependency has far more to do with social, biological, and environmental factors. The drugs people choose to use as they first begin using them has more to do with what is easily and readily available to them, and there is often not a clear progression from "mild" drugs to "hard" drugs.

I live and practice in New Mexico, where there is a decades-long problem with black-tar heroin. In contrast to most other areas of the country, treatment providers in New Mexico see people abusing intravenous heroin at far earlier ages. This has to do with the availability of the drug in our state, the family history of drug use, and the limited treatment and prevention resources available in these communities. These kids are no different from other kids in the country. The difference is in their environment.

What does the gateway drug theory have to do with sex? Quite a lot, actually, as there is a strong belief that many forms of sexual stimulation serve as a negative introduction for young men in particular, sending them inexorably careening down a slippery slope, coated in bedroom lubricants, into a morass of depravity and debauchery.

In 1989, serial killer Ted Bundy was interviewed by James Dobson, a psychologist and founder of the conservative Christian group Focus on the Family. Due to be executed the next day, Bundy told Dobson that his problems began with exposure to pornography at a young age. Bundy explained to Dobson that he used to find detective novels and sexual materials in the trash of neighbors, and that this material was so powerful that it took over Bundy's life and thoughts:

> Once you become addicted to it, and I look at this as a kind of addiction, you look for more potent, more explicit, more graphic kinds of material. Like an addiction, you keep craving something which is harder and gives you a greater sense of excitement, until you reach the point where the pornography only goes so far—that jumping off point where you begin to think maybe actually doing it will give you that which is just beyond reading about it and looking at it.[7]

Bundy went on to describe that every violent man he knew in prison was affected by pornography, and that without pornography, his life, and the lives of those he killed, would have been far different.

This proclamation strikes fear in the hearts of parents everywhere and served as gasoline-soaked fuel for the antipornography movement. My God, what parent would allow their children to view pornography if it might turn them into a serial rapist and killer?

Unfortunately, just as in the case with gateway drugs, there is little evidence to support Bundy's assertions. First, we must wonder what the people in his neighborhood were like. If finding their pornography in the trash turned him into a monster, what did it do to them? Was he living in a neighborhood of serial rapists and killers? (Geez, what were their block parties like?) No, of course he wasn't. There was something about Ted Bundy himself, and his life, that led him to make the horrific choices he did. His neighbors who used pornography did not rape and kill the way he did, and neither did the other neighborhood boys who viewed the same materials that Bundy did.

In 1986, the Meese Commission was charged by the United States government to evaluate and investigate the impact of pornography. James Dobson was a part of the commission and helped produce the report that argued that pornography was indeed harmful and should be controlled, despite the fact that most scientists who presented research to the commission testified that there was no real evidence of harm by pornography. A sociologist hired by the commission reported that "no evidence currently exists that actually links fantasies with specific sexual offenses; the relationship at this point remains an inference," though her research and investigation was not cited in the final report prepared by the commission. Other researchers whose work was cited to support the danger of pornography argued that they themselves believed that the real danger was in the violence, not the sexuality.

The Meese Commission's report, and their failed struggle to separate the morality of sexuality from the science of sexual research, serves as a warning sign for the decades since. The arguments against pornography are moralistic and value-driven arguments. That doesn't mean they're wrong, or even that I necessarily disagree with them. But moral arguments *should* remain in the realm of "shoulds" and "shouldn'ts." When moral arguments attempt to step into the world of scientific and medical predictions, they are inevitably weakened and sow confusion. When moral arguments attempt to drive scientific research to support the morality, they result in junk science, research which is invalid and unreliable.

A prime example of this is in the work of Judith Reisman. Judith Reisman is one of the leading opponents of pornography, who argues that pornography exposure releases "erototoxins" into the body, chemicals that alter and damage the mind, and the sexuality of a pornography viewer. Reisman's research to provide the biological evidence behind her alleged erototoxins has been nonexistent, and there is absolutely no evidence to suggest that viewing pornography releases any unique neurochemicals into the body. Reisman has a degree in communications and a long history of provocative speeches, where she alleges that homosexuals are the greatest danger to society, that Jews are behind the availability of abortions, and that people whose brains are "rotted" by pornography should have no protected First Amendments rights.[8] An interesting contradiction in Reisman's theories lies in her own research activities. She acknowledges that in conducting her research, she has viewed many types and examples of pornography. But her brain and rights to free speech are somehow still intact.

Case Example

Jason is a twenty-four-year-old graduate student studying computers. He was diagnosed with Asperger's disorder when he was twelve. Asperger's disorder is a developmental disorder, similar to autism, where individuals have difficulty with social interactions, dealing with change, and communicating about nonconcrete things like feelings. Jason felt so privately inadequate about his social skills and ability to talk to people that he couldn't approach "normal" women for fear of being shamed and rejected. He found solace in constantly exciting himself in Internet chat rooms where he could completely control the interaction and felt safe from the danger of rejection. A component of Asperger's disorder also involves obsessive behaviors, and in Jason, this was expressed as obsessive collecting and viewing of pornography. Most nights of the week, Jason stays on the computer until three or four in the morning and looks at thousands of pornographic images and videos a night, storing many of them on his hard drive. Three months ago, Jason was arrested for downloading child pornography. Though Jason had never shown any interest in sex with children and had no history of sexual abuse or pedophilia, he became obsessed with collecting amateur pornography, the rarer and harder to obtain the better. He had joined pornography chat rooms and groups where child pornography was traded. When one of the groups was busted by the investigation, Jason's participation was revealed. Though child pornography made up only a tiny fraction of the pornography on his computers, they were seized, and he was arrested. With no history of sexual offenses and a psychological evaluation that indicates Jason has no clear indications of pedophilia, he may be able to receive probation or deferred sentence and may not have to serve time in jail. However, his graduate school has expelled him because he was using school computers and Internet access for some of his activity. His probation requirements prohibit him from using computers and the Internet, leaving him unable to get work in his field.

We believe as a society that people under a certain age, seventeen, eighteen, and twenty-one, are unable to handle the complex and potentially dangerous influences of alcohol and sexuality in movies. Protecting these vulnerable people is the reason we have drinking ages and age restrictions on movies and pornography. The concept of sex addiction, and the need to protect people from its danger, was behind Citizens against Pornography's efforts to remove *Playboy* magazine from 7-Eleven stores.[9] Lawyers today sell consultation services, suggesting that "Internet sex addiction" can very easily put a person in violation of the law or lead to a "visit from the FBI. . . . It's never too early to consult a lawyer."[10]

---∞∞∞---

Female Porn

The romantic novel is one of the closest equivalents for women to the male use of pornography. The romantic novel industry is a $1.4 billion dollar a year industry, churning out hundreds and thousands of novels to a hungry, committed audience. The novels reflect women's desire for context and relationship around sexuality and target women's unconscious desires for strong "alpha" men who fall into love and passion, captivated by a woman's beauty.

And women would like men to be more romantic, more passionate, like the men in romance novels; this is not unlike men who sometimes suggest that their wives be like the women in pornography, at least in bed. A group of female fans of romance fiction were once asked their ideas about sexuality. The women responded that they were not interested in adopting male standards but wanted men to learn to be more like them.[11] But there are no concerted efforts to ban or limit the sales or access to romantic novels. When *Playboy* magazines were removed from shelves, romantic novels remained.

People who view pornography tend to be somewhat desensitized to sexual stimuli; it really does become somewhat blasé to them and stops having as much arousal effect. This sounds similar to the tolerance effect. But the same effect is observed in nudists, who report that at first, being surrounded by nudity is sexually arousing, but eventually the arousal effect goes away, and all you see is people.[12] Sexuality becomes separate from nudity, and nudists learn to distinguish nude situations from sexual situations. In treatment of some sexual disorders, such as premature ejaculation, desensitization is an important and effective form of treatment, helping individuals to minimize a very powerful stimulation and manage their response to it.

In recent Canadian research on the effects of pornography, researchers tried to find a control group of college-age males who had not seen pornography.[13] However, the researchers could not find enough college-age males who had not seen pornography in order to determine what impact seeing pornography had on the sexual and relationship behaviors of those men who had seen pornography. They wanted to find men who hadn't seen pornography so they could evaluate their personalities, their sexual behaviors, and their relationships and compare this information to the same information from men who had seen pornography. This is good research: you have an experimental group and a control group, and you compare the two groups to find out what effect the experimental condition has when the two groups are otherwise as similar as possible.

In this research, they couldn't compare Canadian college men to, say, Amazonian tribesmen who have never seen pornography, because there are just too many differences between the two groups to let you say that any results are because of the pornography, rather than the difference between living in a dorm versus a jungle. The results and implications of this study? Pornography actually has little impact upon males' behaviors, and the great majority of the adult male population has viewed pornography. So, thanks to the casual and easy access of the Internet and sexual materials on the Internet, we are awash in pornography exposure. The men on the bus next to you have seen pornography, and your children's teacher has seen pornography, as has your trash collector and your obstetrician. If Bundy and Dobson were right, we would be awash in sexual violence and crime. Nearly every man in the country, and half of all adolescents, must be seething with unrestrainable sexual urges, filled with desires to rape and objectify almost every person they meet.

But we aren't. In fact, rates of sexual violence in the United States are half today what they were in 1993 (the Internet became widely accessible in the 1990s, especially since 1993, when web browsers were made available). Areas of the country that saw increased access to pornography over the past twenty years also saw decreased numbers of rape. In fact, rape and sexual violence diminishes in areas and countries where there is greater access to prostitution and pornography. Since the advent of the Internet, and easy access to sexual imagery, teen pregnancy rates are dropping nationwide by as much as 33 percent. Teen sexual activity itself is actually dropping, by 7 percent, while teen use of condoms has increased by 16 percent. Abortion rates are half what they were in 1990, and rates of sexually transmitted disease (syphilis and gonorrhea) are half to 75 percent less than they were.[14]

Daniel Ariely is a behavioral economist at Harvard who studies the ways in which people's decisions reveal implicit and unconscious patterns. In one fascinating study, Ariely's researchers asked young male college students to respond to questions on a laptop. Then they had the young men respond to the same questions, on the same laptop (now shrink-wrapped in plastic), as the young men masturbated to pornography on the computer. While the men watched the pornography, the questions would pop up randomly, and results showed that—surprise—the men made poorer, less rational and thoughtful decisions while they were physically and sexually aroused. But you know what? Not a single one of these subjects put down the laptop and went out and committed rape. None of them sued Ariely for causing them to develop an addiction to pornography.[15]

Certainly, many of those who perpetrate rape today have been exposed to pornography and may even use pornography on a regular basis. But many more of the individuals who have seen pornography never commit a sexual crime, just as many, many individuals own a gun but never commit a gun-related crime.

MMF

The most common fantasy reported by men is to have a threesome with two women. So, you might expect that Internet pornography would cater to this ubiquitous male fantasy. But research finds that, in fact, Internet pornography is dominated by images of multiple men and a single woman. Why? The answer is fascinating. When studies were done that compared the sexual response of a male watching pornography depicting a single male and multiple females (MFF), versus a single female and multiple males (MMF), the results were startling. In response to MMF pornography, the viewers' ejaculate contained more sperm, and they ejaculated more forcefully. Men watching MMF also gained a second erection sooner.

Evolutionary scientists suggest that this is one of the clues to the nature of sexuality in our prehistoric past. Women and men were not monogamous. For a man to reproduce with a woman, he had to out-compete other men if they were present. Watching his mate have sex with other men triggered his body to produce greater amounts of sperm to "compete" against the sperm of the other men. And, by having more sex with his mate, he was able to further compete against the sperm of other men, increasing the chances that his sperm would win the race to fertilization. The makers of Internet pornography have found, through the effects of the free market, a secret truth to human sexuality, which we might not have known without the contribution of dirty pictures on the Internet. By having more images and videos with multiple men and single women, porn sites garner greater male attention, greater physiological response from these men as they masturbate to these videos, and greater chance the men will either stick around and masturbate more or will come back later. These images are not addictive, but they do trigger a biological and psychological effect that is subtle, powerful, and little understood, which is of great value to the economic forces driving the Internet pornography industry.

—————————

Another criterion for drug and alcohol addiction is that things in life are given up in favor of the drug. So a person who values sports or a hobby stops playing sports, replacing it with time spent drinking or using drugs. Does this happen with sex addicts? Yes, but does it happen more so than it does with people who are not sex addicts? Who can tell? Men and women differ in this. From an evolutionary perspective, in order for men to acquire the opportunity for sex and reproduction, men had to give up resources and activities in pursuit of sex. In fact, much of the reason why men pursue success and acquire worldly goods and status symbols is connected to their desire for sex and their recognition that these are the ways in which men attract women.

Many addicts and alcoholics tell of "hitting bottom" and engaging in shameful acts, things they are embarrassed about and regret, in order to get high, get another fix, or because they were too drunk to make good decisions.

Anecdotally, sex addictionologists report similar things, telling of sex addicts engaging in prostitution and debasing themselves, engaging in behaviors they would not normally engage in when they are horny and turned on, looking for sex. But again, is this truly different from people who are not labeled sex addicts? In men, in fact, this appears to be a universal truth. Research by Ariely found that when sexually aroused, most men will agree to engage in fetishistic behaviors such as spanking that they would not agree to when not already turned on. And a huge number of men admit that they have done things they are ashamed of, that they regret, in pursuit of sex.[16]

The similarities that are highlighted between drug addiction and sex are less substantial than sexual addictionologists would like us to believe. When we are told that sex addiction is "like" drug and alcohol addiction, and that addiction itself is merely the expression of an unhealthy relationship with something, anything, that takes away from a healthy life, the arguments sound convincing and intuitively valid. But it is not truly useful to compare drugs and sex; it just further confuses the issues, particularly when the comparison to drugs and alcohol ignores the differences between them and sex. Comparing sex to drugs brings in all the moral judgment embedded in social views of drug abuse.

In the late 1980s, American media was inundated with stories highlighting the "crack epidemic" and warning of the terrible burdens that society faced due to the addictive and destructive forces of crack cocaine. We were told that "crack babies" would place huge burdens upon the social welfare systems of our country, one day filling up our prisons, with these amoral, brain-damaged children born addicted to crack cocaine. Thankfully, the fears were not true. They were media hype. Cocaine use by pregnant mothers was treated, by society and the media, as "a moral issue rather than a health problem."[17] The analogy between sex and drug use is similarly driven by morals. Analogy is a method of rhetoric and persuasion, not a scientific one, as we will explore in the next chapter.

> The Internet is the crack cocaine of sex addiction. For many sex addicts, their "bar" is their computer, the gateway to their insanity. A true Internet addict doesn't have a chance without some sort of filter, as addicts are compulsive, sneaky and willing to go to any length to get high.
> —Sex addiction therapist Sean McFarland,
> quoted by website Remote WebGuard[18]

3

Valley Girl Science

Like, it's not cool at all! Like, it's all this stuff that tastes like nothing and it's supposed to be so good for you. Why couldn't they, like,
open a Pizza Hut or something?[1]

In the 1980s (just around the time the sex addiction movement really took
off), the word *like* crept into every statement. Apparently it also crept into
the arguments supporting sex addiction. As you read about sex addiction, we
are told that sex addiction is a valid and real diagnosis, because it is "like" so
many other conditions, from drug and alcohol addiction to brain disorders,
posttraumatic stress disorder, eating disorders, and more. Carnes himself
established this approach in *Out of the Shadows*, where he described sex addiction as being inherently similar, and even identical, to alcohol and drug
addiction. Carnes also described sexual addiction as being like the "athlete's
foot of the mind."[2]

Sex addiction is frequently likened to eating disorders, with the parallel
being that, like food, sex is not something that can be, or should be, entirely
given up. Helen Singer Kaplan describes the disorders as explicitly analogous,
with similar patterns and origins in dysfunctional regulatory systems.[3] It has
been suggested that hypersexuality is similar to the lack of control shown in
obesity, binge eating, or bulimia, and that hypoactive sexual desire disorder
is similar to anorexia, reflecting a pathological level of control over sexuality
as anorexia might reflect a control over hunger and eating.[4] Carnes has even
adopted the term *anorexia*, describing "sexual anorexia" as a form of sexual
aversion, whereby people suppress feelings of sexuality, often allegedly due to
a history of sexual abuse.[5]

My colleague Dr. Brenda Wolfe has worked extensively with eating
disorders and even developed a weight management system for the Jenny

41

Craig weight-loss program. When I asked for her thoughts about a parallel between the sex addiction concept and eating disorders, the vehemence of her reply surprised me. She, and many eating disorder specialists, is strongly against any suggestion that eating disorders are "like" an addiction of any kind, including sex addiction. Dr. Wolfe argues that applying an addiction concept to eating disorders clouds issues and actually interferes in treatment. "I argue vehemently against eating disorders being conceptualized as addictions. They certainly share some symptomatology and likely involve overlapping neurochemical processes. However, there are critical differences that make the clumping of them into the same group potentially fatal to any hope of eating disorder recovery."[6] Because one cannot "abstain" from eating, it becomes very difficult to identify what is "excessive" in food consumption when one considers the complex questions and differences between eating healthily and eating excessively. When people are starved of food, they fantasize about it endlessly. But in sex it is the reverse—those who are most sexually active also masturbate the most and have the most frequent sexual fantasies. Those who are "starved" of sex, having chronically low levels of sex, actually report lower levels of masturbation, fantasy, and decreasing levels of desire.

To suggest that an eating disorder is like an addiction supports the beliefs of powerlessness and lack of control in eating disorders. In fact, many people suffering from eating disorders have a tremendous degree of control over themselves, their cravings, and their bodies. They exert control over the food they put in their bodies, and control over their bodies. If we accept that those with sexual behavior problems are as in control of their behaviors as those with eating disorders, we may have to change the sex addiction treatment approach and treat people with sexual behavior problems as people exerting control and power over their sexual choices, rather than seeing them as people who are unable to control their behaviors.

Case Example

In 2007, fifty-two-year-old Felice "Phil" Vanaria pled guilty to official misconduct and bribery after telling a massage worker that if she performed oral sex on him, he would give her a job in county government. At the time, Vanaria worked for Cook County, in a political position, and the massage therapist had applied for a job in the county hospital and was interviewed by Vanaria. He propositioned her in his office and again at her home before she found out that her job application was not on file and his job offers were fictional, at which time she filed charges. He was convicted and sentenced to thirty months probation and ordered into sex addiction treatment. In February 2010, Vanaria was hired as a political fund-raiser by Cook

County commissioner Joseph Mario Moreno, who said Vanaria "is a nice guy who did something stupid."[7]

———∞∞∞———

Multiple Personality Disorder

Now known as dissociative identity disorder in the hokeypokey dance of the DSM, this disorder shares parallels (and cautionary signs) with sex addiction. Like sex addiction, the supporters of multiple personality disorder believed that it resulted from a history of trauma, and research has shown that it is always diagnosed after the fact, after a person has entered treatment. But prospective studies with traumatized individuals show that multiple personalities do not emerge in individuals who have suffered trauma. Research that followed the lives of children abused and traumatized in concentration camps and ghettos in Germany showed that none of those children developed multiple personalities or repressed their memories of the traumas. Diagnosis of multiple personality is limited to a few clinicians, and it is limited culturally—it only appears in countries where clinicians believe in it and diagnose it.

Like the therapists diagnosing sex addiction, the therapists diagnosing multiple personality disorder were well-meaning, good people with good intentions who were trying to help and care for their clients. They were not deceptive or false in their beliefs in multiple personality and their intent to help their clients. But after entering treatment for recovered memories and multiple personality disorder, clients experienced a dramatic and severe increase in self-harming behaviors and suicide attempts. After starting treatment with these well-meaning therapists, clients diagnosed with multiple personality saw their jobs, marriages, and families dissolve at great rates. Their lives were worsened by these well-intentioned but ineffective and damaging diagnoses. Just because therapists who believe in sex addiction mean well does not mean that their efforts result in benign effects.[8] We must remember that, as Camus said, "good intentions may do as much harm as malevolence if they lack understanding."[9]

———∞∞∞———

The arguments that suggest that sexual addiction is "like" one disorder or another are evidence of "reasoning by analogy." Reasoning by analogy is a common strategy used in courtrooms, not because it is a particularly strong method of argument (it is one of the weakest forms of argument, in fact), but because it is so subjective and so easy to manipulate. When we argue by analogy, we get to choose which characteristics we want to highlight and which we want to ignore. I can assert that a banana is like an apple. I can point out that they're both fruit, they both have seeds, the flesh of each is white, and both have skins. But, at the same time, I ignore the fact that they're differently shaped, differently flavored, grow in different climates, and while apples grow on a tree, bananas grow on plants. So, is a banana like an apple? You tell me. It's ultimately all relative. So, when you are told that "of course sex addiction is a real disorder; it's just like drug addiction (or eating disorder, gambling addiction, kleptomania, or sleep disorder, etc.)," know that there are as many differences between these disorders as there are similarities. And the similarities are in many cases so vague that we are left with very little true understanding and little ability to discriminate effectively. The point of science and medicine is to help people to discern truth and to differentiate accurately, something that is difficult to do with the vagueness and lack of precision inherent in sex addiction.

Questioning the Science Itself

If we are uncritical we shall always find what we want: we shall look for, and find, confirmations, and we shall look away from, and not see, whatever might be dangerous to our pet theories. In this way it is only too easy to obtain what appears to be overwhelming evidence in favor of a theory which, if approached critically, would have been refuted.

—Karl Popper[10]

Whatever label is used, whether it's sex addiction, hypersexuality, compulsive sexuality, or what have you, most descriptions sound similar. The various overlapping terms pretty consistently describe folks who have lots of sex, have dangerous sex, have difficulty controlling their sexual behaviors, get in trouble for their sexual behaviors, and hurt themselves and their loved ones with their sex behaviors. The differences only emerge when you start asking what this cluster of behaviors is called, how to specifically identify it, and what causes it. These similarities would seem to give credibility, because so many different people are describing the thing similarly, even when they can't agree on the details.

But no, not really. This consensus is not a good thing, nor is it a sign of good science. First, the overwhelming majority of these descriptions date from after the early 1980s, when Patrick Carnes was first published, describing this pattern in his books about sex addiction. This pattern may really reflect the cumulative social influence of Carnes' persuasive arguments. People may just be seeing what they want to see, or expect to see. And all of these descriptions are emerging within very similar cultural settings. We don't see these descriptions and behaviors arising in sex-positive cultures such as Polynesia. This seemingly common definition probably has more to do with the culture and context in which these observations and descriptions are happening than with the behaviors themselves.

Finally, in the world of science, we like to think that it is data, results, and research that lead to conclusions, *not* agreement. Michael Crichton said, "Whenever you hear the consensus of scientists agrees on something or other, reach for your wallet, because you're being had."[11] If we are told that scientists and researchers and theorists are agreeing on something, despite there being no real empirical research to support it, I'm a bit worried, because it is a sign that something other than science is at play.

Thomas Kuhn was an American physicist and philosopher of science who changed our views of science, arguing that despite our beliefs that science moves on the basis of evidence, it in fact moves like all other human endeavors, on the basis of power and personality. He showed that when "paradigm shifts"—that is, major changes in understanding of science and scientific principles—occur, they happen as a result of consensus between scientists, consensus that happens as critics are silenced or die out, not as a result of evidence piling up and finally convincing the critics they were wrong. One might begin to worry, then, that the constant pressure to add sex addiction as a diagnosis reflects less the influence of scientific research and more the influence of "consensus," powerful personalities, and agreement.

Karl Popper was also a philosopher of science, who saw the same problems that Kuhn did and attempted to help science resolve them. He created the structure known today as the "null hypothesis" and the argument that scientific work should be "falsifiable." In other words, scientists should not set out to prove themselves true but should set out to test whether they can prove their hypothesis is false. If a scientist cannot create an experiment that shows their hypothesis is false, then maybe it is true. But if they create an experiment that shows their hypothesis seems to be true, there are many different possibilities and unknown factors that could have led to that accidental verification.

Popper famously challenged the theories of psychoanalysis and Sigmund Freud, asserting that his theories were untestable. Science could not prove or disprove Freudian theories, because anytime that an answer or result didn't gibe with the predictions, then the field of psychoanalysis had many very clever, and equally untestable, alternate explanations waiting in the wings.

Sex addiction is not falsifiable, as currently identified. Because the theory is so vague and all inclusive, any challenges to the theory can be explained by reference to one of the alternate explanations. For instance, if you showed that a so-called sex addict had not been sexually abused, in contrast to the theory that sexual abuse causes sex addiction, one might receive the challenge that the person might have been sexually abused and suppressed the memory. The definition of sex addiction includes both sexual excess as well as "sexual anorexia," defined as "behavior that is compulsively aversive to sexual activity."[12] How can you argue against or disprove a diagnosis that encapsulates both the presence of a symptom and its absence? Historically, and in a similar vein, the diagnosis of nymphomania was once argued to include and be caused by both the inability of a woman to have an orgasm and a woman's multiorgasmic overresponsiveness to sexual stimulation!

When a person is "acting out" sexually, they're diagnosed with sex addiction. When a person who used to act out sexually is no longer acting out, without ever having received treatment, they are not pronounced cured but are instead labeled as being in the midst of a cyclical phase of attempting to control their behaviors.

Most sex addiction theories describe that addicts engage in sex to manage uncontrollable emotions, as a form of self-medication. But when studies offer evidence that there are addicts who in fact display little if any emotional pain, at least one response has been to suggest that the clients are emotionally numb, using sex to "break through" their numbness and feel something, even pain.[13] Similarly, cereal magnate John Kellogg argued that masturbation resulted in either physical underdevelopment or overdevelopment. If a girl's breasts were too small or a boy's penis too large, both were clear signs that the child's physical development had been tainted by the corrupt influence of self-stimulation. When theories are fluid and unfalsifiable, it is then easy to see what we expect.

If sex addiction theories were specific enough to be tested, we would not be defining the condition though simile, explaining the condition is "like" other conditions. This very "likeness" creates such vague and unclear definitions that the concept is literally ungraspable, constantly mutating to yet another defense.

Mental health professionals are typically trained to be conservative and to diagnose with specificity. If there are symptoms that overlap between two or more disorders, we diagnose the disorder that best captures the patient's overall presentation. This is a problem for the concept of sex addiction. Surveys of sex addicts show that up to 40 percent have anxiety disorders, 50 percent have substance abuse disorders, and 70 percent have mood disorders.[14]

Personality disorders refer to very stable patterns of interpersonal behavior in people, patterns that cause people problems in their life. These patterns, in many cases, involve issues with sexuality and sexual behavior. They include antisocial personality disorder (chronic rule breaking and disregard for the rights of others), dependent personality disorder (constantly living within and dependent upon a relationship and jumping to new overinvolved relationships each time a previous relationship ends), and narcissistic personality disorder (believing the world revolves around you and your needs). Sexuality is a diagnostic and important piece of many of these personality disorders, reflecting aspects of the disturbed relationships these people have. Folks with antisocial personality disorder are typically impulsive, thrill-seeking individuals who don't like following rules, a pattern that plays out in their sexual activities. Dependent personality disorder is associated with the use of sex to acquire new relationships or to pacify partners in order to keep them around. People with borderline personality disorders use sex to get attention, maintain control within a relationship, and push boundaries, creating excitement within the relationship. Those diagnosed with histrionic personality disorder, who are attention seeking in the extreme, use sexually provocative or exhibitionistic behaviors to get attention. Narcissists use sex and sex with other people in the same way they use everything and everybody, simply as a way to fulfill their needs and desires.

Anecdotal reports within sex addiction, and some research, suggests that personality disorder is extremely prevalent in sex addiction. Some estimates suggest that personality disorders and mood disorders are present in almost all cases of sex addiction. Multiple studies show that alleged sex addicts almost always have some other major mental illness.[15] So, when such individuals present for sex addiction treatment, their hypersexual behaviors are most likely to be a symptom of those existing disorders. As one sex therapist and clinician described to me, "The sex addiction diagnosis is a *lazy* diagnosis."[16] It ignores more relevant emotional and psychiatric issues to focus exclusively upon a person's sexual behavior.

Because periods of sexual promiscuity are a frequent symptom for clients with bipolar disorder when they are in a manic phase, we would not normally diagnose hypersexuality *and* bipolar disorder, since bipolar disorder would subsume the symptom of periods of hypersexual behavior. According to the theories of sex addiction, the use of sex to manage negative emotions is identified as a core symptom of unhealthy sexuality and sex addiction. But if those negative emotions reflect the influence of depression or posttraumatic stress disorder, it is more important to diagnose and treat the negative emotions. A diagnosis of sex addiction is superfluous at best and a dangerous distraction from the real treatment needed at worst.

Some in the field of sex addiction have argued that the diagnosis is needed in order to bill insurance companies for services.[17] Unfortunately, in making such an argument, these individuals reveal their ignorance of the above research, showing the incredibly high levels of primary diagnoses,

diagnoses such as depression or anxiety, which are already covered by insurance companies and are likely to be more accurate diagnoses than a label of sex addiction. Such an argument may be pragmatic and oriented toward helping an individual client to access necessary services, but it is not an objective argument that can be applied to populations at large in a scientific manner.

SUBJECTIVE ASSESSMENTS

A nymphomaniac is someone who has more sex than you do.

—Alfred Kinsey[18]

The subjective nature of assessment and diagnosis of sexual addiction is absolutely the biggest problem for those who argue that sexual addiction is real. If the field cannot agree on terminology, it is because of the subjective nature of the concept. "I know it when I see it" may be good enough for the Supreme Court, but neither researchers nor health insurance companies much like relying upon such variable factors. The terms associated with the concept of sexual addiction are inherently subjective in nature; secrecy, emptiness, loneliness, despair, and even obsession are all terms and concepts that are neither good nor bad in essence but rely upon the subjective assessment of the clinician to determine whether they are pathological. There is also a wealth of evidence that such experiences and feelings exist in the sexual lives of those who do not feel out of control of their sex behaviors. Researchers Levine and Troiden argued that "the boundary between 'being in control sexually' and 'being out of control sexually' depends entirely on the therapist's value orientation and purposes."[19]

Unfortunately, there is little clear, consistent, and effective sexual training offered to medical and mental health clinicians. A 1968 study found that fewer than half of medical schools and physicians received adequate training in sexuality.[20] A 2010 study of psychologists found that a similar level of inconsistency and limited training persists even today, with few psychologists receiving any training in the nature of "healthy sexuality," or in the range of normal sexual fantasies and behaviors.[21] Without such training, clinicians are apt to diagnose on the basis of their own subjective experiences and by asking themselves, "Would I do what this client is doing?" rather than basing their treatment and diagnosis of sexual issues on research or an established base of knowledge. As the world is changing and there is greater social acceptance of alternative sexualities such as homosexuality, transgender, nonmonogamy, and sadomasochism, clinicians are receiving little if any training in how to deal with these issues in their practice and in how to identify when these issues are part of or separate from a mental illness.[22] Without such grounding, clinicians are subject to the whims of bias and the subtle influences of culture and morality.

Many, perhaps all, of the behaviors that are considered part of the repertoire of sexual addiction are normal and healthy in different contexts. Indeed, Carnes even acknowledges that sexual addicts are pursuing the "intoxication of young love," when these same behaviors and feelings are normal and healthy.[23] So it is difficult for a therapist with little training in the broad range of sexual behaviors to identify when something is normal and when it is not.

Interrater reliability is one of the best ways to reduce subjectivity in the field of mental health assessment and treatment. It describes a process where we test how consistently and objectively a definition is applied across different people and use this research to establish whether the definition is clear and objective enough that different people can implement it similarly in different situations. Unfortunately, there is little if any data examining interrater reliability in the assessment and diagnosis of sex addiction. Some hope that the criteria laid out for hypersexual disorder in DSM5 will be clear enough to offer some objectivity and reliability. Unfortunately, with the number of poorly defined concepts that remain in hypersexual disorder and the inherent subjectivity in sexuality, I suspect that diagnostic objectivity is going to be a long time coming.

> It's hard for us to accept that other people's most intimate desires
> are different from our own—and when confronted with this fact, we often
> dismiss their desires as deviant or dangerous or just plain hurtful.
> —Ogas & Gaddam[24]

> Empirical science is not able to definitively prove that something doesn't
> exist. The burden of proof rests with those who believe that the phenomenon,
> in this case sexual addiction, exists. And the science supporting sexual addiction,
> as a disorder, has not provided the requisite proof. The research is inadequate,
> as control groups are never included, samples are small and heterogeneous,
> variables are poorly defined (e.g., compulsive masturbation, protracted
> promiscuity, etc.), and correlations are interpreted to claim causation.
> —Jason Winters, PhD[25]

The bulk of the research on sex addiction has focused on proving theories rather than using random selection and control groups to test whether similar results or data can occur in non–sexual addict groups. The research in sex addiction consists of self-selected samples of clients who have self-referred into sex addiction treatment. Why does this matter? If you attempted to test the validity of a certain hypothesis—say, that all people like ice cream (a pretty reasonable hypothesis, right?)—and you gathered your subjects by standing in an ice cream parlor and handing out questionnaires, what do you think the results would say? Probably that 99.99 percent of people like ice cream (there's always one obnoxious person who reads the questionnaire wrong and responds in reverse). But is that a true statement? What about all those people in other parts of the world who have never even tried ice cream? And those poor folks who are lactose intolerant—just the sight of that ice cream parlor makes them sick to their stomach. If you are only getting responses from the people who choose to come to that parlor, then your data, your findings and results, cannot be applied to the general population.

So a reasonable alternative would be to randomly sample the population, for instance choosing names from a phone book and calling them up and asking if they like ice cream. Those results might have some generalizability to a larger population. Similar randomized trials have not been done to study the prevalence of high rates of sexual behaviors in the population at large, rather than just those who walk in the doors of a sex addiction clinic. The closest have been some studies in Europe, which didn't strongly support causal links between high levels of sexual behavior and social or emotional problems.[26]

According to Patrick Carnes' writings, 8 percent of men and 3 percent of women are addicted to sex. Unfortunately, Carnes' research was not published in peer-reviewed literature, and the methodology by which he generates these estimates has been questioned, as he bases them solely upon his observation of clients entering his treatment programs. He has also stated that there are as many as 131 million addicts in our society when one considers the behavioral addictions of gambling and sex, as well as chemical and substance addictions.[27] This is literally *half* the population of the United States.

> People who are looking for a diagnosis of sex addiction don't come to me.
> People who have been labeled as pathological because of their lack of
> monogamy, or their interest in kink, come to me. I get therapy refugees who
> are running away from judgment that their sexuality is their problem.
> —David Ortmann, LCSW[28]

For decades now, the field of sex addiction has been criticized on its poor research base, and cautioned repeatedly, both internally and externally, that better research is critical to support its validity. But instead of producing this research, the field of sex addiction has tried yet again to introduce a sex addiction disorder as a part of the DSM5 addictive disorders workgroup. One argument often made is that a clear set of criteria is needed in order for researchers in sex addiction to compare apples to apples and diagnose consistently.

A sign on my mechanic's wall reads, "Lack of preparation on your part does not constitute a crisis on my part." If the field of sex addiction cannot generate valid, useful, and informative basic empirical research sufficient to defend its need to be recognized as a diagnosis, this lack of data does *not* constitute a reason to create a diagnosis. If the issue of sex addiction were a scientific or medical issue, we wouldn't have to argue for thirty years about the need to generate data and research; we would be overwhelmed with data and research findings. Instead, the field serves as an exemplary case study of the problems described by Kuhn and Popper, where poor scientific methods and the influence of society, politics, and morality have driven theory and argument. So who does sex addiction serve? And why? If sex addiction research does not reflect the influence of science, what are the driving factors behind it?

———⬥———

"The area of sexual addiction has reached a point in its conceptual development that is likely to rapidly culminate in stagnation. The literature on this topic consists largely of theory and conjecture based almost entirely on clinical observation rather than on research findings. . . . It seems clear that aggressive and extensive empirical exploration of the phenomena that are alleged to constitute sexual addiction is urgently needed if we are to ultimately design effective interventions for those suffering from its potentially life-threatening consequences."[29]

4

Eric Sevareid's Law

The chief cause of problems is solutions.

—Eric Sevareid[1]

*O*ne of my favorite sayings has always been, "When all you have is a hammer, every problem looks like a nail." A similar philosophy applies to the treatment of sexual problems. The label of "sex addiction" is a big, lucrative hammer, and every sexual problem is just asking to be "nailed." Sexuality is a complex contextual behavior that involves the influences of environment, history, biology, psychology, internal desires, fears and wishes for the future, and on and on. It is deceptively easy to reduce sexuality to biology and focus exclusively upon the chemical and hormonal influences. But we do this at our peril.

The finances that lie behind the concept of sex addiction are a significant concern. Treatment for sex addiction is not cheap. A month's treatment at some residential sex addiction treatment programs can cost over $37,000. Sex addiction is big business. All the celebrity attention to sex addiction has driven many more people into the offices of sex addiction therapists nationwide. Alexandra Katehakis, a sex addiction therapist with a practice in California, says that "celebrities have been the greatest evangelists for treatment. My practice wouldn't exist without them."[2] High-priced cash-based therapeutic programs and providers exist around the country, serving the needs of self-identified sex addicts. But despite these high-dollar services, there is little if any data to show that their services have any impact. The field of sex addiction treatment is very willing to take your money, but not too interested in publishing research that evaluates whether their treatment works.

There are around nine hundred therapists around the country who have completed training to be a certified sex addiction therapist (CSAT),

53

a certification offered through the International Institute for Trauma and Addiction Professionals (IITAP). IITAP is an institute founded by Patrick Carnes, which sells training modules that are largely based on his work. Completing certification involves completion of four training modules, at a cost of around five thousand dollars, along with receiving thirty hours of supervision from a CSAT-certified therapist (costs for supervision vary between supervisors). Once certified, there is a biannual renewal cost of $150. The parent company of IITAP, apparently owned by Patrick Carnes, has annual revenues around $350,000.[3] Crunching the numbers listed on the IITAP website, it appears that around $70,000 comes in each year, from therapists renewing their certifications, and around $100,000 from advertising revenues, as IITAP sells space on their website and training materials to some of the high-dollar treatment centers who offer CSAT-certified services to sex addicts looking for help.

When compared to many other certification institutes or programs, such as those that certify individuals to be providers in specialty, validated, and effective therapeutic treatments, these costs might not be considered out of line. However, despite IITAP having as part of its goals to "research and implement task-centered approach to treatment,"[4] no research has ever been published in peer-reviewed scientific or medical journals that supports the assertion that CSAT-certified treatment providers are effective, or that the training and therapeutic program they complete has any demonstrated therapeutic effectiveness. Many of the leaders of the efforts to establish a scientific base for sex addiction or hypersexuality, including Dr. Martin Kafka, Dr. Eli Coleman, Dr. Rory Reid, Dr. David Delmonico, and Dr. John Bancroft, have not chosen to be certified by IITAP. Likewise, psychiatrist and editor in chief of the *Journal of Sexual Addiction & Compulsivity* Dr. Charles Samenow is not certified. Collectively, this raises real questions as to the scientific establishment of this program. Like so many of the things in sex addiction, the effectiveness of this treatment program seems to be based upon the "because we say it does" model of argument.

And it's not just therapeutic business now. Sex addiction treatment is business in the entertainment industry as well. The Logo Channel has a reality show called *Sex Rx*, focusing on the therapy needs of a group of LGBT clients treated by Christopher Donaghue, a self-proclaimed specialist in sex addiction treatment. The VH1 channel previously had *Sex Rehab*, with celebrity physician Dr. Drew, which delved into the sexual issues of celebrities and focused on sexual addiction. According to the *Sex Rehab* show's website, 6 percent of the American population is afflicted with sex addiction, though no reference is given to shed light on this number. Further, according to the show's description, "nobody is immune" to sex addiction. In an amusing irony, the sponsored advertisement links on the show's website are all for methods to either delay the male orgasm or treat erectile dysfunction. It sends an odd message—"Sex is dangerous and scary, you need to watch out and control it! And by the way, if you can't have sex, here's a link to buy a pill that will fix you up so you can have sex, which is dangerous and scary by the way!"[5]

The excesses inherent in the concept of sex addiction may be a reflection of society's emphasis upon unrestrained consumerism. I'm reminded of Dan Aykroyd on *Saturday Night Live* as the Conehead who must "consume mass quantities!" We are told every day to consume, to buy, to get credit to buy more and more. We are told that happiness comes from buying, and more happiness comes from more buying. On cable news, every weather report seems to now be called "Extreme Weather," as all we want to hear about are those places where the weather is "out of control." Is it any wonder that people are struggling with moderation in their sexual behaviors? And isn't it interesting that the cure for this "mass consumption of sex" is to consume more medications and expensive treatment?

The New Life Ministries of Laguna Beach, California, runs a three-day seminar for men who say their sexual addiction is threatening their lives and marriages. Paying $1,400 for the seminar (not including hotel room), the men who attend what the church calls their "Every Man's Battle" workshops are there to wage a battle against shame and fear, and the problem of pornography.[6] The Every Man's Battle website sells kits, books, compact discs, DVDs, and self-study resources for adolescents, families, wives, and men of all ages. There is even a kit for soldiers, shipped in a camouflage box, and apparently designed to help men resist sexual urges while deployed in the military.[7] In 2009, this organization made nearly $4 million just from selling their educational materials, and almost $2.5 million from the seminars and workshops they conduct. In 2009, they reported nearly $8.5 million in gross revenues according the tax return documents they filed with the IRS, and since 2003, they have averaged around $8 or $9 million a year in revenue. Stephen Arterburn, the Christian counselor who heads the organization and is the central figure in most of the educational materials, was paid $180,000 a year in salary alone by the organization, a figure that almost certainly doesn't include his speaking fees and royalties.[8]

> Together with the ability to ascertain hypersexual disorder, it is hard to imagine how any person who is sexually active (even if just with himself) could avoid being labeled. This designation will be good for the business of sex addictionologists, but will it be good for patients?
> —J. Paul Fedoroff, MD[9]

One of the only truly scientific studies of treatment of sex addiction came in a double-blind, placebo study of the effect of the medication citalopram on sexual behaviors, which found that it reduced the frequency of masturbation and use of pornography, but it didn't reduce sexual behaviors with partners.[10] This study represents only one of the many medications identified in the literature that may be effective at treatment of sexual behaviors, and it reveals what may be a quiet and pervasive influence in the field.

One of the major groups that would benefit from the inclusion of hypersexual disorder in the DSM5 is the pharmaceutical industry. Some medications, notably the selective serotonin reuptake inhibitors currently prescribed to treat depression and anxiety, have libido-suppressing effects. Physicians sometimes use these medications to reduce or inhibit sexual desire in individuals who display hypersexual behaviors. A psychiatrist once described to me this use of the medication Paxil to reduce the compulsive masturbatory behavior of a demented elderly male in a nursing home. But such use of these medications is what is called "off-label" use. This means the medication is being used in a manner that it is not labeled or FDA approved for.

When a medication is certified or approved for use in treatment of a disorder, it generates a lot of revenue for the drug company. Off-label use, or prescribing a medication for use in something that is not approved by the FDA, is allowed but is limited to those clinicians who have knowledge or understanding that the medication can be used in this nonapproved way. Off-label use also puts prescribing physicians at some ethical and legal risk—they are using a medication in a way that is not formally approved. If negative consequences occur, the physician is at serious risk of being accused of malpractice. Pharmaceutical companies are restricted from marketing of medications for off-label use.

In its first year of sales, Viagra earned over a billion dollars in sales for Pfizer, in what is regarded as the largest and most successful launch of a drug in history. In 2009, Viagra, Cialis, and Levitra, all drugs to treat male sexual difficulties, generated over $4 billion in sales. In recent years, pharmaceutical companies continue to fail to acquire FDA approval for medications intended to treat female sexual dysfunction, now characterized as low sexual desire. More than two dozen different medications have been developed to attempt to treat women who complain (or whose husbands complain) of low sexual desire. With 43 percent of women reporting such complaints, the pharmaceutical companies are drooling over the possibility of sales to these women that might meet, or even exceed, the sales of male-targeted drugs. But the US Federal Drug Administration has denied requests for approval of these medications, as the research continues to show few consistent positive effects. Female sexuality does not respond as simply or consistently to the effects of pharmaceuticals as does male sexuality. But, given the huge profits that potentially await, that hasn't stopped these companies from trying.[11]

———oooo———

"Disease mongering" is the effort by pharmaceutical companies (or others with similar financial interests) to enlarge the market for a treatment by convincing people that they are sick and need medical intervention. Typically, the disease is vague, with nonspecific symptoms spanning a broad spectrum of severity—from everyday experiences many people would not even call "symptoms" to profound suffering. The market for treatment gets enlarged in two ways: by narrowing the definition of health so normal experiences get labeled as pathologic, and by expanding the definition of disease to include earlier, milder, and presymptomatic forms (e.g., regarding a risk factor such as high cholesterol as a disease in itself).

———oooo———

Steve Woloshin and Lisa Schwartz are medical researchers who published an article in 2006 accusing pharmaceutical companies of "disease mongering" in relation to the disorder known as "restless legs syndrome." Woloshin and Schwartz lay out a compelling case against the pharmaceutical companies and their use of the media to encourage greater attention to a syndrome of behaviors in a manner that ultimately resulted in financial gain for the drug company, as their medication was prescribed to treat a disorder that had previously been underdiagnosed, if it was even acknowledged as a true medical disorder. The media was complicit in this, encouraging self-diagnosis in patients and labeling the problem as "the most common disorder your doctor has never heard of."[12] Thus the media became part of the disease-mongering process, such that one could not tell the difference between information and infomercial as the media covered this issue.

In Canada, pharmaceutical companies were recently confronted by scientists who challenged the marketing of testosterone replacement drugs. The pharmaceutical makers were marketing testosterone gels, intended for treatment of men with hypogonadism, highlighting effects that make the drug seem desirable to almost all men. Advertisements suggested that the drugs were effective for men who had "lost that loving feeling," had "low energy," and "low sex drive." Scientists argued that these were symptoms of normal aging and that marketing these drugs to healthy men was dangerous and irresponsible.[13]

Can we expect to start seeing advertisements for SSRIs, suggesting that these medications can help people to be monogamous, focus on work, and stop looking at pornography? Time will tell. Already there are growing references in the scientific and medical literature to medications used off label to treat sexual addiction. Antidepressants such as SSRIs, including Prozac and Paxil, are well known to suppress libido and create physiological impotence in males as well as inhibiting orgasm in females. In a brief review of the literature, I found numerous medical and scientific articles describing the impact of no fewer than fifteen different psychiatric medications on behaviors of hypersexuality, compulsive sexuality, and sexual addiction.

In an amusing irony, many of the drugs that might potentially be marketed as treatments for sex addiction are made by the same companies that are also developing and selling drugs to treat erectile dysfunctions. So these companies stand to make a profit on both ends of male sexuality, enhancing it and suppressing it. In other words, they'll get their money, both coming and going.

In the Arizona desert, about an hour from Phoenix, is The Meadows, an elite treatment center where you can go if you are struggling with addiction to drugs, alcohol, or sex and can afford the steep price tag. For a bit over a thousand dollars a day, you get intense treatment designed to address issues that affected you in your childhood, as well as any traumas that continue to impact your adult life. You do so in a facility with an extremely talented gourmet chef, granite bathrooms, and beautiful fountains, art, and sculpture all around the campus. Notably, there are also giant saguaro cacti all around the facility, giant plants that resemble penises and sex toys so much that they are hard to ignore.

The staff there are dedicated and seem to be good people, genuinely interested in helping people make changes in their lives. But this facility generates close to $2 million a month for the for-profit investment firm that owns the facility. Some sexual addicts choose to stay in their facility long term for treatment, sometimes as long as six months. And all of this is paid for by cash—this program doesn't bill insurance for their treatment.

The Meadows Rehab, where actor David Duchovny has reportedly gone for sexual addiction treatment, is the "ground zero" for the movement to treat sex addiction. The Meadows' senior fellows are Pia Mellody, author of *Facing Love Addiction* and *Breaking Free*; Claudia Black, author of *It Will Never Happen to Me* and *Changing Course*; and Patrick Carnes, author of *Out of the Shadows* and *The Betrayal Bond*. These authors have all written best-selling books on addiction, sex addiction, and codependency. As one critic argues in reference to these senior Meadows fellows, "Sex addiction was invented by a self-help group aided by popular books. It is trying now to move over into a medical condition."[14]

5

Sexual Healing

What you need is sexual healing, being in love with one woman,
where sex and love are joined instead of sexual perversity.

—*Rolling Stone* critic David Ritz to Marvin Gaye, 1982[1]

If sex is inherently dangerous, as the theories behind sexual addiction al-
lege, then why does it feel so good? It's kind of a silly question perhaps, but
it raises the question of what sex is for and what it does in our lives, our
bodies, and our species. According to evolutionary theory, sex feels good and
is reinforcing, so that we desire to have it and thus create new generations
of humans to pass on our genes. There is certainly much more to this story;
after all, if sex were merely serving a reproductive function, then the sexual
interactions of humans would be far shorter and much less significant in our
social lives, our art, and our culture. Sex also serves many other significant
functions in the lives of humans, helping people to bond, develop relationships, establish intimacy, relieve stress, gain exercise, convey and share love,
feel less lonely, celebrate life, and sometimes simply have fun, along with a
myriad of other functions, beyond simple reproduction.

An often overlooked but significant role of sexuality in humans is in the
healing factor that it creates in our lives. In contrast to the idea that too much
sex is dangerous and destructive to our lives and bodies, there is a wealth of
evidence that sex is good for you. In many cases, more sex is even better for
you, both psychologically and physically. This concept presents a significant
challenge to the sex addiction theory. It requires that sex addictionologists
distinguish between high levels of healthy sexual behavior and high levels of
sexual behavior that, for some reason, result in negative consequences. Unfortunately, the muddy theories of sex addiction cannot effectively differentiate

a high libido from an alleged sex addict, and to acknowledge that lots of sex might be healthy is anathema. It is easier to say that the sex is the problem rather than trying to identify the individual issues that might lead an individual into sex-related problems.

A recent development in psychology is the exploration of what is called "positive psychology." It is, in essence, an acceptance that psychology has neglected for a very long time a critical piece of human existence and health. We define the field of mental health not by what is healthy, not by what works, or what is effective in strength and resiliency. Instead, we define the field of mental health by the shadows cast by illness. The field has focused upon abnormal psychology, upon aspects of illness. We are left to understand health only by what is left when we exclude illness. Positive psychology attempts to better understand what mental health is, what the characteristics of resiliency, emotional strength, coping, and personal character actually are, and how we can encourage their growth. It encourages us to help build strengths in people rather than to avoid and suppress their weaknesses.

What does the field of sex addiction compare sexually addictive behaviors to? According to researcher Elaine Hatfield, the field of sexuality and sex research has not yet adopted the approaches of positive psychology and continues to focus upon the negative, dangerous, and potentially harmful aspects of sexuality.[2] There is no clear model of positive, healthy sexuality defined in most sex addiction research. In most cases, we can deduce this only from the things they tell addicts to avoid, only from the shadows they try to suppress. What are we left with when we exclude all of the behaviors that sex addiction labels as pathological?

Case Example

Phillip is a forty-three-year-old Caucasian male with a long history of feelings of depression, since his early twenties. When you first meet him, you wouldn't see this man as struggling with depression. He is outgoing and gregarious, a good listener, and often the life of the party. But Phillip has tried to kill himself three times in the past ten years and was hospitalized in an inpatient psychiatric unit after the last attempt. Phillip feels fundamentally disconnected from other people, and even when he is entertaining to others, there is a running fear in his mind that they are dismissive of him and can see through him, see him the way he really is. "I'm basically a big pile of shit. I know it, and sometimes other people figure it out." Phillip has been married for the past fifteen years. "My wife didn't know how depressed I was when we got married. I think she would leave me if she could, but she comes from a very religious family that just doesn't ever get divorced. But she's

miserable, and I make her that way." For a long time, Phillip has used sexuality
as a way to seek temporary relief from his feelings of self-loathing, sadness, and
loneliness. "When I'm having sex, with my wife, with some woman I pick up, or
even alone, just jerking off to porn, for a little while I can turn off those feelings of
being miserable. They recede into the distance. It's like when I was in the hospital
after a car accident. They gave me morphine. The pain was still there, but it didn't
hurt. It let me pull back from it and made it not so dominant or important." When
Phillip had sex, he felt alive, positive, and momentarily connected to other people,
who liked him enough to take off their clothes and get into bed with him. "It's a
rush. It's like they chose me, even though I'm such a shit; they choose me for sex.
And for a little bit, I feel like maybe I'm not so bad, since they chose me. But then,
afterwards, those feelings come crashing back and bury me in self-loathing, guilt
for cheating, and misery that I'm such a worthless person that I have to use sex as
a way to feel better."

The same issues exist in the sex addiction field's definition of healthy sex that
exist in their definitions of unhealthy sex. They mostly boil down to subjective assessments that make broad generalizations, sometimes addressing intent and motivation, sometimes focusing on the relational aspects of sex, and
other times focusing on certain behaviors, or amounts of behaviors. So, for
instance, in some views, healthy sex involves "a yearning for—or a response
to—a projected, eroticized, comfortable, affectionate and bonding primal
experience."[3] So uncomfortable sex is not mentally healthy sex? I guess it's
like swimming, then. You'd better wait after eating; you don't want to get a
cramp and accidentally have unhealthy sex!

How do you know healthy sex when you see it? Some suggest that the
following components are necessary for sex to be healthy: consensual sex,
legal sex, sex that is "one part" of your life as opposed to the central focus
of it, sex that is not secret, sex that doesn't get you in trouble at work or
financially, sex that is pleasurable for "all of the participants," sex that isn't
harmful, and sex that isn't aggressive or threatening.[4]

I do question how many criteria it takes to be healthy—all of them? One
of them? If you violate one rule is it automatically unhealthy sex? If you fulfill
a single one, is it healthy? It's the exceptions that are troubling to me. There
are many aspects of common sexual behaviors that violate this list but that are
not necessarily unhealthy:

- For many hundreds of years, women were encouraged to "grin and bear
  it," "close your eyes and do your duty for your country," with the message that women don't enjoy sex but do it for their husband and for
  procreation. There are many people, especially women, who have sex but

don't enjoy it. If it is their free choice and they are doing it for reasons of supporting their relationship, is this truly unhealthy?

• Like most people, as an adolescent I worked diligently to keep my masturbation secret. Locked doors, lights off. If anyone ever asked if I masturbated, I flat out denied it. Why? Masturbation is generally regarded in our society as socially unacceptable, even though over the past hundred years this has begun to change. As people age, they grow more willing to acknowledge masturbation. So, is this secret masturbation unhealthy by virtue of its secrecy? I think not. In fact, the reverse is true. Imagine, instead, someone who does not treat masturbation as secret or private. Someone like Diogenes, the "dog philosopher," who was one of Alexander the Great's mentors. Diogenes was infamous for masturbating in public, in the town square, to show his intentional rejection of social rules. I argue that the unsecretive sexual act might be more unhealthy than the secret or private one.

• The laws regarding sex vary dramatically from one state to the next. Sex between two seventeen-year-olds is legal in Nevada, but not in California, where the age of consent is eighteen. So sex on one side of the border is legal and becomes a crime when you step across the state line. How can this criterion be used objectively in determining a mental illness? Almost all states have laws prohibiting sex with individuals who cannot legally consent to the act. Typically this means no sex with minors, but it also applies to those who are cognitively impaired by virtue of brain damage or developmental deficiencies, or due to the influence of alcohol or drugs. Is it unhealthy if my wife and I share a bottle of wine on a bearskin rug in front of a fireplace and have passionate sex? You get to be the one to tell my wife that. I'm not going to.

• Nonharmful, nonaggressive sex—when it comes to rape, I agree. That's not healthy sex. But I note that there are many, many practitioners and devotees of BDSM sexuality, and as we've discussed, there is increasing evidence that this sexual behavior does not represent an illness or unhealthy sex, but merely an individual preference. Estimates suggest that as many as 12 percent of people have incorporated things like spanking into their sexual behaviors at least once. There may be quantitative and qualitative differences between a spanking during sex and dangerous things like asphyxiation during sex. But trying to write down a list of the rules that differentiate "healthy but harmful sex" from "unhealthy and harmful sex" is an impossible task. Passionate sex sometimes damages the body, tearing skin, pulling muscles—minor damage, relatively easily repaired by the body over the next day or two. Differentiating such acts from loving, passionate spanking or discipline activities is unlikely to be easy or objectively applied.

When we examine the recommendations of sex addictionologists to identify their perspectives of healthy sex, we find that it includes many of the following criteria:

- Fewer than seven orgasms a week.
- Sex only when in love.
- Sex only in the context of a monogamous relationship.
- Any alternative relationships or sexuality is suspect.
- Sex should serve the purpose of procreation, or supporting/building a relationship.
- Healthy sex doesn't involve pain.
- Healthy sex is mutually pleasurable.
- Healthy sex is happy sex—if you're sad, angry or lonely, it's probably not a good idea to have sex.
- Masturbation may be normal, but it may involve literally "taking your life into your own hands."

Individual components of this list may make some sense, but taken as a whole, these values highlight the degree of subjective, moral, and relational bias that is intrinsic in the implicit concept of healthy sex within the sex addiction model.

Healthy sex is sex that isn't the focus of your life, according to the theory of sex addiction. "A balanced life is one in which there is meaning and room for everything," and "when there is room in your life for all of the good things life has to offer, there isn't room for any excess."[5] They are basically quoting the words and philosophy that greeted one at the entrance to the ancient Greek temple at Delphi, which said "m dén ágan," or, translated, "Nothing in excess." As opposed to modern Western moralities of "do or do not" (to quote Yoda), the Greek philosophy centered more on walking a middle line, keeping pleasures in balance and not allowing them to overwhelm one's life.

Balance is good, and excess is bad, right? To allow one thing to become an overwhelming focus of one's life is bad and unhealthy. Except that sometimes it isn't. Should Martin Luther King Jr. have taken a more balanced approach to life? Wasn't it a bit excessive to focus his life and career upon a single goal, that of racial equality and civil rights? And Mother Theresa, who devoted her entire life to service of the poor—that's just over the top, isn't it? Shouldn't she have had a more balanced life? But the world would be a lesser place if either of these people had. Chef, wine connoisseur, and author Harvey Steiman once wrote, "All things in moderation, including moderation."[6] Excess is not intrinsically unhealthy and is always relative.

HEALTHY SEX

> Today's public discourse about sexuality is almost exclusively about risks and dangers: abuse, addiction, dysfunction, infection, pedophilia, teen pregnancy, and the struggle of sexual minorities for their civil rights. Public discourse about the physiological and psychological health benefits of sexual expression has been almost entirely absent.[7]

Marvin Gaye sang "Sexual Healing," talking about the value and joy in "getting it on." In life, Marvin was reportedly into kink, BDSM, and pornography. According to biographies, the idea for the song came when *Rolling Stone* magazine critic David Ritz saw Marvin's collection of sadomasochistic pornography and told him that he needed "sexual healing." Marvin's success with the song, though, didn't change his behavior. He allegedly loved to invite groups of men and women to have orgies while he watched, often using drugs and consuming pornography in wild, self-destructive acts. But is there such a thing as sexual healing? Is sex itself a good thing, for the body and mind?

Research is building that makes it very clear that regular sexual activity (including masturbation) promotes health. In contrast to the days when we were told it would make us blind, doctors are now saying that regular sex and frequent orgasms will actually make you live longer. A study from the United Kingdom, at the University of Bristol, that tracked 1,000 men showed that men who had more orgasms in a week lived substantially longer than those who had few or no orgasms. Frequency of sex doesn't affect a woman's life span, but her enjoyment of sex does, as women who report a lifelong history of enjoying sex live longer.[8]

Women's menstrual cycles can be regulated by regular sexual activity. When women are having regular sex on at least a weekly basis, their menstrual cycles are far more predictable and manageable. This keeps various hormones in the body, including estrogen, at positive, healthy levels that promote things like healthy bones and cardiac health.[9]

Since the 1950s, research has been clear that those who masturbate have more fulfilling and satisfactory sexual lives. How can you help a partner to sexually satisfy you if you do not know how to satisfy yourself sexually? In 1988, nurse researcher Beverly Whipple showed that sexual self-stimulation increased a woman's ability to tolerate physical pain, and that the effect did not just come from being "distracted" from the pain by the act of doing something.

The sexual stimulation, endorphins released, and the psychological and biological effects of masturbation made women more able to tolerate physical pain.[10] Sex writer Susie Bright famously described her use of a Hitachi Magic Wand vibrator during delivery of her first child: "I believed that stimulating my clit would be a nice counterpoint to the contractions going on inside my belly. I have a great photograph of me in the delivery room, dilated to six centimeters, with a blissful look on my face and my vibrator nestled against my pubic bone. I had no thought of climaxing, but the pleasure of the rhythm on my clit was like sweet icing on top of the deep, thick contractions in my womb."[11] There is clear evidence that orgasms can banish headaches, even migraine headaches. In the 1950s' sitcom, "Not tonight, Dear, I have a headache" was the standard punch line. Today, based on current research, this should go more like, "Come to bed, Dear, I have a headache and need a good orgasm or two!"

Frequent, good sex improves the chances of conception. Women who have orgasms may be more likely to conceive a child.[12] So, even if you're following the dictum that sex should only be about reproduction, in order for it to "take," you may still need to have it frequently in order to practice and improve the outcomes. In fact, according to recent research by British physician Mike Smith, it takes as long as six months, and over one hundred sexual encounters, for the average woman to conceive.[13]

In direct contradiction to the principles of sex addiction therapists, researchers at the University of Sydney actually encouraged male research participants to masturbate and ejaculate every day for a week (that means they had an orgasm every day of the week—so *seven* times a week). The researchers studied the effect of daily ejaculation on the quality of the sperm and found that daily ejaculations improved the quality of the men's sperm. Further, when the researchers took men that had been identified as having damaged, unhealthy sperm and encouraged those men to masturbate and ejaculate daily, the results were similar. Daily ejaculations, every day for a week, actually healed their sperm and made the men more likely to successfully impregnate a female partner, and made it more likely that their children would be healthier and free of male-related chromosomal disorders. And you know what? Not a single one of those subjects became addicted to their daily orgasms, were unable to stop, or sued the researchers for destroying their lives.[14]

Sexual Medicine

In men and women, regular sex:

- Increases the body's production of collagen, a chemical in our skin that keeps it more supple and resilient, reducing wrinkles.

- Improves mood and relationships with their partners the next day.
- Improves female satisfaction with marriage.
- Even solo sex in women improves the health and happiness of their marriage.
- Improves sleep.
- Lowers rates of endometriosis.
- Reduces rates of cardiac problems.
- Reduces rates of breast, testicular, and prostate cancer.
- Reduces the waistline.
- Reduces appetite.
- Improves social performance and effectiveness in public speaking.
- Reduces general stress and improves feelings of life satisfaction.
- Reduces numbers of days off from work for illness.

———— ⌾ ————

Researchers Gordon Gallup and Rebecca Burch at the State University of New York have published research showing that unprotected sex is actually psychologically beneficial for women, reducing rates of depression and improving memory. Apparently, semen contains high levels of various neurochemicals that increase a woman's sex drive, happiness, memory, and energy levels, all apparently in an evolutionary bid to make women more interested in having more sex. And when women start having protected sex and their bodies are no longer absorbing that semen, their rates of depression increase. Gallup and Burch speculate that this effect might even be involved in some of the symptoms of irritability and moodiness associated with menstruation, as many couples cease sex during menstruation, and these symptoms might actually reflect a *real withdrawal syndrome* that the female body is showing, in response to the removal of that neurochemical-laden semen.[15]

Sex makes you smarter. Really. Hormones released during sexual activity stimulate the brain to work more effectively and efficiently. "Sex promotes our ability to concentrate, lengthens our attention span, and stimulates creativity and ideas. . . . In short, sex makes you smarter," says Professor Habermehl, a German sexologist, describing his research on the effects of orgasm on cognitive activity.[16] Granted, we may be dumber as we pursue sex, but once we've had it, that old IQ comes rarin' back!

In the Netherlands, where they clearly have a better health care system than exists in the United States, research was conducted on the effects of hiring prostitutes for mental patients. Those patients who had regular sex with prostitutes needed less psychiatric medication! While an extreme case, this medical intervention is consistent with other practices, where sexual behaviors labeled as unhealthy by sex addictionologists are often used by sexuality therapists to promote healthy sexual relationships. In 2010, a minor scandal erupted in England around the use of taxpayer money to fly a mentally disabled young man to Amsterdam to have sex with a prostitute. The funds came from a British reform program called "Putting People First," which explicitly supported the sexual rights and needs of those with disabilities, paying for trips to strip clubs and sexual education courses, as well as trips to Amsterdam, where prostitution is available legally.[17]

— ∞∞ —

Trading Sex

Esquire magazine writer Kelly Oxford suggests that couples should "trade" sex for favors, encouraging husbands and wives to do things like exchanging sexual acts, like oral sex, for favors like doing the dishes. "The negotiation process quickly becomes its own thrill." By engaging with each other on this level, the couple creates a thrill, a source of fun and excitement in their sexual lives, so long as neither person is asking for something the other won't or can't do. It's a way to explore fantasies together, even when one partner is only interested insomuch as they are interested in either getting something they want or pleasing their partner. Though the field of sex addiction would label this as unhealthy—trading sex for something, and a situation where both partners are not necessarily enjoying themselves—Oxford sees it as a fun way in which sexual heat has roared back into her life, and she feels secure in the sexual attention of her husband. "Sex bartering has been a part of my married life for so long that it's hard to believe there are couples who haven't thought of this yet."[18]

— ∞∞ —

Sex therapists regularly use techniques with patients and couples, techniques which appear completely contradictory to the ideas of sex addiction. One such technique is called "simmering," a sexual therapy technique used to increase or sustain arousal, developing and creating feelings of sexual arousal throughout the day. Clients are encouraged to practice having sexual thoughts throughout the day, exercising their sexual and genital muscles to increase their sexual responsiveness to their partners. In essence, therapists are directing their patients to think about sex all day long, whenever they can, to enhance their feelings of arousal when they get home with their partner. These therapists are *not* being sued for malpractice by clients saying that this technique caused them to turn into a sexual addict and made them unable to stop thinking about sex, unable to work because of the overwhelming drive created by this therapeutic technique.

Though it is labeled by sex addiction therapists as a dangerous sexual behavior that can be addictive, role-playing during sex is a way that millions of couples add spice, fun, and excitement to their lives. In fact, it is a common technique that therapists encourage couples to explore to enhance their sexual relationships, to introduce a sense of drama and fun and mutual play into their lives. There is no research that identifies how much is too much role-playing and no comparisons between the role-playing of normal, healthy couples and that of supposed sex addicts.

Sometimes, refusing to tolerate an uncomfortable situation any longer and refusing to suppress parts of oneself creates the opportunity for people to change their lives around. In Esther Perel's book *Mating in Captivity*, she tells the story of Charles and Rose, a married couple who approached her for treatment related to their history of low sexuality in their marriage for several years. Though the couple were compatible in many ways, sexuality wasn't one of them. Perel quotes Charles as saying, "Sex with Rose is nice, but it's always kind of flat. Sometimes I can deal with the low intensity; other times it's been unbearable." Charles was surprised by his wife's resistance when he approached her and discussed the idea of him pursuing sexual relationships outside the marriage. Given his wife's lack of enthusiasm for sex, Charles had assumed she wouldn't have a problem. But when she did, and the couple began to deal with the real sexual issues in their marriage, they began making love again, as Rose found that "the more he eludes her, the more she wants him."[19] Perel makes the point that as the couple tried to stay within the lines of monogamy, they actually weakened their marriage and relationship. Once they started to confront these assumptions and the truths they had hidden from, their relationship at once became more genuine, more passionate, and more authentic.

FANTASTIC SEX

Was it a dream where you see yourself standing in sort of sun-god robes on a pyramid with a thousand naked women screaming and throwing little pickles at you? . . . Why am I the only one who has that dream?

—*Real Genius*[20]

Susan Peabody suggests that "love addicts" often engage in excessive fantasizing and daydreaming and are preoccupied by thoughts of their lover and being with them.[21] Celebrity psychiatrist and actor Reef Karim (and what an odd statement it makes about our society and mental health to write the words "celebrity psychiatrist and actor") argues that sexual fantasy is a dangerous component of sexual addiction. He asserts that sexual fantasy must be interrupted in order for a sex addict to recover, saying, "Fantasy allows the client to have a complete process in their minds regarding sexual acting out/in that no one else can see. Thus, the client can be in full relapse sitting in here in treatment."[22] Patrick Carnes asserts that sexual fantasy can be healthy, but only for "reasonably healthy couples" who use fantasy to "move toward rather than away from the partner."[23] Carnes at least acknowledges that fantasy is not intrinsically dangerous and destructive. But he suggests that fantasy may only be safe or healthy if you're doing it with a partner, and then only if you and your partner are "reasonably healthy" (whatever that is) and are using it to improve your relationship. This is sure to be surprising news to the huge numbers of people who report having secret fantasies about other people during sex with their spouse or partner.

Many people worry about their sexual fantasies. In fact, sexual fantasies are one of the things people often keep most secret in their lives, rarely even sharing them with their spouses or closest friends, for fear of their sexual fantasies being judged unhealthy, perverted, or strange. Freud suggested that sexual fantasies are the window into a person's personality deficits—for instance, a person with a deep-seated sense of low self-esteem might be extremely aroused by fantasies of being watched while being sexual. But what do sexual fantasies *really* mean? Do disturbed people have disturbed fantasies and healthy people have healthy fantasies? Can we tell the difference between healthy and unhealthy fantasies?

In the 1970s, author Nancy Friday ripped the lid off the secret world of sexual fantasies, publishing the works *My Secret Garden, Forbidden Flowers*, and *Men in Love*. Friday's books were a revelation, as she published the fantasies of normal men and women. Many of these people fantasized about things most would call unhealthy: rape, violence, bestiality, incest, and even pedophilia. But despite these fantasies, Friday's work showed that these were normal men and women, leading normal, healthy, and productive lives. While even Friday admitted that she found herself often disturbed by some of the fantasies people shared with her, she ultimately found that fantasies served functional purposes in people's lives. She wrote about the way in which sexual fantasies help men deal with feelings of anger and rage and loss, as they live in a world where in order to be with women, they must give up some of their fantasies of what it is to be a man. In the dance of male-female relationships, and a man's desire to be with women, "fantasies are invented. At least for a sexual moment, magic is called in, reality altered, the perceived nature of women changed; the conflict is healed. Fantasies are the triumph of love over rage."[24]

A majority of people acknowledge that they have sexually fantasized about other people while they were in a relationship. In 2001, researchers at the University of Vermont conducted research into the prevalence of fantasies about somebody other than one's primary partner. They found that about 80 percent of married women sexually fantasize about men other than their husband, while 98 percent of men fantasize about women other than their wife. Environment and context has much more effect on female fantasies than it does on men's. In women, things like how long they've been married and whether they are actually having extramarital affairs increased the chances that women would fantasize about someone other than their husband. These factors don't predict fantasy in men—in men, simply being male predicts that they will fantasize about people other than their wives or partners—length of relationship, happy or not, cheating or not, doesn't have any predictive value. In other words, it's hard to go higher than 98 percent.[25] Sexual fantasies, even fantasies that we keep secret, and that our partners might not like, are in fact normative. The overwhelming majority of men and women have them. How can we possibly limit, manage, or restrict sexual fantasies for people at anything other than an individual, case-by-case basis?

Gender Differences in Sexual Fantasy

Sexual fantasy differs between men and women, in qualitative and quantitative ways:

- Women tend to fantasize sexually about known individuals—past boyfriends, coworkers, friends, or their tennis coach.
- Men fantasize about people they don't know, or faceless people.
- Women's sexual fantasies tend to include aspects of intimacy and relationship.
- Men's fantasies as often include mere body parts and mechanical imagery, with no thoughts about relationship.
- Women's fantasies include components of romance, building a scene in which the woman can be carried away on tides of passion.
- Men's fantasies jump straight to the sex.

The Rape Fantasy

One of the hardest presentations I've ever given was at a conference on treating sexual assault. My presentation set the stage, inviting people to consider the broad range of sexual behaviors that fall under the concept of normal. In the content, I explored the issue of the female rape fantasy, how it presents in therapy, and its relation to the effects of assault. As I presented, I recall looking cautiously toward several women in the audience who I knew were there as advocates for rape victims.

Sexual fantasy about rape is exceedingly common among women, with as many as 25 to 65 percent of women endorsing some form of this fantasy, at least once in their lives, in one form or another. One study of female college students found that 65 percent of them acknowledged a fantasy of being forced in sex, though only 32 percent said yes when the word *rape* was actually used in the research questionnaire.[26]

Some women who have experienced the tragedy of sexual assault go on to be tormented by tremendous psychological turmoil over sexual fantasies of rape and forceful sex. They feel angry and upset with themselves, confused that they and their bodies are responding with sexual arousal to a fantasy similar to an event that was so traumatic and devastating. Many women (and not a few men) I've spoken to over the years have disclosed to me their personal fantasies of being forced to have sex, usually with embarrassment, shame, and fear. They struggle over what this fantasy means about them as a person, as a woman or a man, and as a victim. Women have told me that they struggle with being a feminist and yet still getting aroused at the idea of being taken by a man against their will.

There is a general assumption, among people, advocates, and therapists, that for a victim of sexual assault to fantasize about being violated, there must be something wrong. I disagree. The prevalence of the fantasy of rape among women and men who have never experienced such events suggests that the rape fantasy probably occurs independent of a traumatic event.

What does the rape fantasy mean? Lots of things. And perhaps in that it means nothing. Our society romanticizes rape and violence in complex and confusing ways, in movies and novels. I don't believe that women in general, or sexual assault victims specifically, are retraumatizing themselves by revisiting these experiences and fantasies. For many, I believe that, like any fantasy or daydream, it is a way for a person to mentally assert control over a situation in which they were powerless. The great majority of sexual assaults go unreported, and in many ways, the majority of victims move forward successfully in their lives. People do better when they move forward after a trauma, maintaining a sense of personal autonomy and power, developing a narrative that they, not the event and situation, nor the perpetrator, are in charge of their lives and actions.

Sometimes, we as clinicians have to pull back and give up our disease-model thinking. We should not automatically characterize this fantasy as a symptom of an illness, resulting from a history of rape or sexual assault.

Instead, we may need to consider the possibility that this fantasy represents a normal, even a healthy, attempt by a person to regain some control over their sexuality, and the way in which their traumatic history affects them.

After my presentation, one of the women I had been cautiously watching came up to me. She presented that day, on her own experience as a victim of rape. She hugged me and thanked me for my presentation. She shared that she also had experienced such fantasies and had struggled with them and her own reaction to them. She left, saying that my talk had helped her and had given her permission to free her mind, her body, and her sexuality, and to stop tearing herself up over her fantasies. It was nice that I was able to give her one less thing to worry about.

———ɚଚଛୖ———

There may truly be no connection between fantasy and reality when it comes to sex. In fact, there are many people who report that when they have attempted to fulfill a fantasy, they end up disappointed by the mundane reality of real-world sex with real-world people. In the real world, one cannot manipulate reality to create large, ever-responsive penises and cannot provide an endless wardrobe of costumes. In the real world, one must deal with the pesky realities of other peoples' needs and feelings, must deal with the issues of our bodies and their biological and physical capacities. To quote a researcher of sex fantasies, "Sometimes, a mindfuck is better than the other kind."[27]

Wendy Maltz and Suzie Boss, authors of *Private Thoughts: Exploring the Power of Women's Sexual Fantasies*,[28] see sexual fantasies as a healthy and valuable tool. In contrast to the theory that sex should never be used for management or shifting of emotions, Maltz and Boss explicitly recommend that sexual fantasies can be used to manage anxiety, to enhance feelings of self-esteem and attractiveness, and to relieve stress and tension. They argue that sexual fantasies are one very effective way for women to overcome fears of performance issues during sex and to enhance their sexual arousal during sexual encounters. Even when kept secret, such fantasies indirectly improve the sexual experience of the fantasizer's partner. Maltz and Boss suggest a radical thing: women can use sexual fantasies to overcome the impact of a history of sexual abuse. They describe a woman who fantasized during sex about being a dominatrix, "biting and pulling the hair" of a stranger (not the man she was having sex with). In this way, she was able to express internally the rage that she felt over her traumatic history, but still was able to enjoy sex with her current partner.[29]

Columnist Dan Savage once ran an article describing the sad story of a husband, writing to ask for help with his concerns about his wife's sexual fantasy and role-play. During sex, his wife asked him to pretend to be her father and to pretend to molest her. The husband was concerned this might be based on a true event in his wife's past and worried about whether he should or shouldn't participate. With a wealth of experience viewing the sexual fantasies and behaviors people often don't even share with their psychologists, Savage suggested that the husband had a right to ask his wife about the origins of her frightening fantasy. But he also pointed out that this fantasy might be a way in which the wife was reestablishing control over her sexuality and recovering from a history of trauma.[30] I appreciate Dan's response, because frankly, most therapists I know would have run screaming for the hills at this story. In fact, I asked a few therapists I know, giving them the scenario. Their standard response was that the wife, and the couple, needed therapy. They roundly declared that the husband shouldn't fulfill the wife's fantasy and that the fantasy itself was almost certainly evidence that she had been abused and had never dealt with it. None of them acknowledged that this fantasy might be part of the woman's healing process.

British psychotherapist Brett Kahr is the author of *Who's Been Sleeping in Your Head*, and he conducted a large multinational study of sexual fantasies. He suggests that sexual fantasies serve many useful functions, based upon his interviews with 3,000 people. He describes fantasies as ways to relieve boredom; cheer people up; achieve momentary, controllable escapes from the real world and its depressing realities; offer the opportunities to explore novel sex with unattainable people and in unattainable ways without leaving one's bedroom; and increase sexual response to one's partner. He goes on to suggest further that fantasies can be ways to effectively self-medicate one's feelings and problems, sooth oneself, distract from pain and stress, express anger and loss safely and covertly, and even overcome loss and changes in relationships.[31]

Like Nancy Friday's work, Brett Kahr shows the surprising range of disturbing, frightening, and challenging fantasies that exist in the heads of people that are living healthy, successful lives. One of the most surprising was the tale of an older Jewish woman whose parents had died in the Holocaust. And yet this grandmotherly woman revealed that her most powerful orgasms came from fantasies of her being sexually examined and abused by Nazis while strapped nude to a surgical table.[32] But this woman was psychologically healthy, and this fantasy was not an indicator of disturbance.

Kahr even argues that the fantasies he saw in the most disturbed people tended to be fantasies that were extremely simplistic and two dimensional. He saw no relationship in his research on over 23,000 sexual fantasies between disturbing, complex sexual fantasies and any level of mental disturbance. The ability to fantasize, to daydream, and to explore internal worlds of imagination is a valuable, even critical component of the human mind. It reflects our ability to manipulate thoughts, ideas, perceptions, and reality, all within the private confines of our own minds. Kahr suggests that without fantasies, our minds would be sterile, "bleak" places. He views sexual fantasies as inherent "extensions of our capacity for creativity, the very imaginal creativity" that is present in the worlds of artists, painters, and composers.[33]

Sometimes our sexual fantasies and thoughts disturb and frighten us, and if we share them with others, they may frighten them as well. But there is truly no real evidence that these fantasies can become burning desires that must be satiated, that they take over a person's mind in such a way that, eventually, fulfilling the fantasy becomes the most important thing in a person's life. Otherwise—from reading the research by Kahr, Nancy Friday, Seymour Fisher, and others, works that reveal the large level of socially unacceptable and often frightening and disturbing fantasies that live inside the heads of normal people around us—there should be extraordinary amounts of incest, bestiality, group sex, homosexuality, and other behaviors going on every day, among almost everyone in society. Fear of rejection and stigma leads people to keep these fantasies secret from everyone, often even their wives, husbands, and therapists. Friday has described that she has received numerous letters from people, all saying that they believed they were the only ones with such fantasies and that her works have led them to accept that they are not as sick or disturbed as they secretly feared.[34]

Kahr asserted, "I must conclude that the minds of American and British citizens contain much diversity and complexity, and therefore, speaking about a 'normal' fantasy may well be meaningless."[35] He offers examples of the frightening, disturbing fantasies he has heard from doctors, therapists, priests, and nurses, but he describes that these fantasies were never enacted and probably never would be. Sexual fantasies can be contained within one's mind and do not drive a person to enact them.

I believe that the fear of these fantasies, implicit in the concept of sex addiction, reflects a fear of our inability to fully control even our own minds and thoughts. How can it be that we can have thoughts pop into our minds, that we can have fantasies that trigger enormous sexual arousal, at the same time that they trigger shudders of revulsion? It is a scary thought that we live inside our own minds and cannot even control them. Reaction to this fear drives the belief that we must suppress and avoid these fantasies. But perhaps our private sexual fantasies, kept secret, serve a role of maintaining a sense of control over the uncontrollable aspects of our lives and minds. "Perhaps we all do need to have some arena of absolute privacy or secrecy in order to feel more fully in control of our mind."[36] The secrecy and privacy of sexual fantasies may reflect a healthy process, and a way in which people maintain healthy relationships, while using fantasy to explore different, sometimes unacceptable, desires and thoughts.

Case Example

Ronald is a forty-seven-year-old businessman who has been extremely successful in his career, but he has a very long history of chronic infidelity that has affected his marriage and work. He has a master's degree in business administration and has been the CEO of several companies in several different areas of high-tech industry and manufacturing. He is currently married, for the second time, to a woman fifteen years younger than him, with whom he has two children. He has three children from his first marriage. Ron married his current wife, Phyllis, after his affair with her ended his first marriage.

Ron sought couples and marriage treatment from an outpatient psychotherapist after Phyllis discovered that he has had multiple affairs during their marriage and threatened him with divorce. Ron is very committed to avoiding divorce, due to the financial impact it would have upon him and his lifestyle, and because he would lose contact with his children. "After my first divorce, I mostly lost contact with my kids. They're all strangers now. I hardly see or talk to them, and I don't want that to happen again."

Ron actually attended his first session of therapy with a letter from another counselor, which stated that Ron had been diagnosed as a sexual addict. During the first session with his wife, Ron said, "I'm not saying that it's not my fault, but Phyllis needs to understand that me having sex with other women is not really something I can control."

Over the course of marital therapy, Ron was able to begin to acknowledge how much his parents' marriage had affected his own marriage and sexual behaviors. Ron's father was a very assertive, dominant man, who sometimes verbally or physically threatened his wife. One of Ron's earliest memories was comforting his mother after she had been hit by his father. "My mom and dad stayed married and shouldn't have. They were in this awful cycle where he would be violent, and my mom would stop having sex with him, and then my dad would get more and more upset and angry and finally explode." All his life, Ron had feared that he could become like his father and be aggressive toward women. Exploring his various affairs, it became clear that Ron had sex with women whom he wanted to make happy, and with women at work that he felt somewhat responsible for. Every "happy" sexual encounter made Ron feel like he was different from his father, able to keep women happy, treat them right, and have sex, all without violence or aggression.

Patrick Carnes has said, "What people are doing sexually often is a window into their deepest wounding, or their deepest desire, or who they are as a person, and so our culture needs to see the opportunity in that, and that sex is not the enemy. The enemy is us, and it's what we do with our sexuality." But Carnes' idea, while intuitively feeling valid, is not supported by research.

We simply don't know enough about sexual fantasies, and their connections to personality, behavior, and sexuality, to evaluate whether people's sexual desires and behaviors really have deep-seated connections to who they are and what they have encountered in their lives. Because sexual fantasies are so universally secret and private, we don't know enough about them in a non-clinical population to truly judge whether the fantasies we see in a population of alleged sex addicts are truly representative of their psychic "wounds" or whether they represent "covert relapse." The building evidence suggests that disturbed, conflicted, and even bizarre and frightening sexual fantasies do not reflect deep-seated psychological disturbance. The application of these concepts in the field of sex addiction reflects metaphorical thoughts rather than scientific approaches. Characterizing the struggle around sexuality as a battle against an internal enemy is a concept contradicted by a wealth of evidence, showing that sex is healthy, and even frightening sexual fantasies may be part of a healing process.

In chapter 6, we explore this concept further and challenge one of the core ideas in sex addiction, that using sex to cope with feelings is unhealthy, and the use of neurological language to suggest that your problems with sexuality lie in your brain, hence making sexual addiction a disease.

6

Feeling Sexy

It is only when the affectionate, that is, personal factor of a love relation gives place entirely to the sensual one, that it is possible for two people to have sexual intercourse in the presence of others or for there to be simultaneous sexual acts in a group, as occurs at an orgy. But at that point a regression has taken place to an early stage in sexual relations, at which being in love as yet played no part, and all sexual objects were judged to be of equal sexual value.

—Sigmund Freud[1]

I have a pretty stressful job. On a regular basis, I spend my days hearing about awful things that happen to people, from abuse, trauma, and loss. I hear about feelings of shame and guilt that drive people to isolate and even hurt themselves. Patients that come to me are usually in pain, and have been for a long time. On top of the pain that is shared with me in my office, I've got the stresses of dealing with managed care organizations and governmental bureaucracies, all of which seem determined to find ways to not pay for the services people need in order to heal.

When I'm stressed out after a day of banging my head against these brick walls, there's a special thing I like to do. I dress up in special clothes and get together with friends. I choose one special person each time, usually someone different, though sometimes there are people there that I know, whom I trust. Other people pair off in the large room and engage with their partners, just as I do with mine. We start out slowly, my partner and I, but pretty quickly we're in each other's space, and things get aggressive. Soon, we're both breathing hard and sweating heavily, our bodies sliding against each other. Sometimes, I'm on top of my partner, and other times, my partner is on top of me. It's not uncommon for me to end up with bruises and marks that are a little hard to explain as things get rough. But the stress that I've carried around all day vanishes in this purely physical encounter.

But I'm not describing some kind of anonymous group sexual encounter. Instead, a few nights a week, I go to a gym and do martial arts with friends, practicing a form of grappling called Brazilian jiu jitsu. The exercise and confidence that I gain from it is one of the healthiest things in my life. The health and benefit is holistic as well, affecting my emotions, psychology, and spirit, as well as my body.

What is the difference between exercise of this kind, or running a marathon, lifting weights, dancing, and sex? The endorphins released in the body, the changes to heart rate and muscle tone, and even the calories burned are similar. But according to the criteria of sex addiction, if you are using sex to manage feelings, to deal with stress or boredom, or to manage anger or anxiety, it is unhealthy and dangerous. In the proposed criteria for hypersexual disorder in the DSM5, it is described as "repetitive use of sexuality in response to negative feelings, such as anger, sadness or boredom."[2]

If you run five miles every morning and feel grumpy, lethargic, and irritable on days that you don't get to run, there's nothing wrong with you. In fact, there is a national organization of "streakers"—not folks who run naked, but people who have uninterrupted "streaks" of running at least a mile a day, in some cases for as many as thirty years. The leading streaker, Mark Covert of California, has been running daily since 1968 and says, "I guess some might call it an obsession."[3] But if you start every day with an orgasm and feel frustrated and distracted on those days that you don't get to, is it fair to say there is something wrong with you and something dangerous in your sexuality?

The proposed definition of hypersexual disorder suggests that using sex to avoid boredom is unhealthy. Others assert that sex addicts attempt to "to control pleasure and pain by inducing experiences that (1) alleviate boredom; (2) promote a feeling of well-being; and (3) provide an escape from pain and sorrow."[4]

Why? Have these folks never fantasized about being stuck on a deserted island with someone they have a crush on? The whole point of the fantasy is being so bored there's nothing to do but sex. Is it wrong for sex to be fun, diverting, and entertaining?

My wife and I were once trapped in a Colorado hotel room by a blizzard and five feet of snow. The satellite television was out, and we couldn't get further than the soda machine down the hall. We were bored out of our minds and had tons of sex. We love each other, enjoy each others' bodies, and there was very little else to do. Eventually the snow melted, and we returned to the rest of the world, though both of us were a little sore and tired. Was this unhealthy because we were using sex to avoid boredom?

The field of sex addictionologists sees a certain limited sample of people. They see people come through their doors who typically have some pretty serious emotional and psychological problems going on. One hundred percent of the people who seek sex addiction treatment have some other major mental illness, including alcohol and drug addictions, mood disorders, and personality disorders. When everybody that comes through your door is having problems with their lives and feelings, *and* they're having problems related to their sexual choices and behaviors, it's easy to make the logical error of assuming causality, to believe that the one issue (mental problems) is related to the second issue (sexual behaviors). The problem is that they are not seeing the many people with that same sexual behavior who have no life difficulties—those people don't need their help. When the sex addiction field labels sex to alleviate boredom as unhealthy, it separates the behavior from the person and labels the behavior as intrinsically unhealthy.

Research by Quadlund found that so-called sexual compulsives were indistinguishable from "noncompulsives." Sexual compulsives were not more neurotic, anxious, psychotic, or emotionally disturbed than those who did not identify as sexual compulsives. The sole feature that distinguished the two groups? Those who were noncompulsive reported more feelings of "love and relaxation" related to sexual behaviors. This isn't good news for the sexual addiction field; remember, the healthy folks are not supposed to use sex for "relaxation"; it's supposed to be the addicts who use sex in unhealthy ways to manage anxiety.

In the previous chapter discussing sexual fantasies, we reviewed the research and prevalence of feelings of "being out of control" in female sexual fantasies. Feelings of being out of control sexually might sometimes reflect normal levels of sexual desire, and feelings of sexual arousal that are generally accepted, but conflict with a person's moral and sexual values. So a person raised to believe that masturbation, sex for pleasure as opposed to reproduction, or sex without love are all sins might feel tormented by their inability to control and restrain themselves from desires toward such sexual behaviors, even when these desires and behaviors are relatively normal in the general population.

Dr. Marty Klein, writer, counselor, and sexuality advocate, makes the fascinating and provocative point that "feeling out of control, and *being* out of control, are two different things."[5] When I ride a roller coaster, I often feel like I am on the verge of flying out of the seat. This is a frightening feeling, and even though my brain might know that very few people ever die in roller coaster accidents, my body doesn't know this and feels like it is on the verge of near death. This unconscious feeling is so powerful that in some research, after people ride roller coasters, they are more sexually aroused, but not with their existing partners. After riding a roller coaster, people (both men and women) are more interested in having sex with someone they've never had sex with before. One interpretation of this effect is the suggestion that this is an evolutionary process, whereby we are unconsciously driven to reproduce after a near-death experience, with a new partner, to increase the chances of our genes living on in a new generation.

In our culture, we rarely teach people that feeling out of control is something different from being out of control. Many people drink alcohol as a "social lubricant," drinking it as "liquid courage," to reduce their inhibitions in social settings. They drink it specifically to feel less in control, because they want to have fun, and they feel that their internal controls are somehow in the way.

However, the law is clear, and so is our society. Even when you choose to feel less in control of yourself, you are still responsible for the choices you make. But sex addiction seems to set forth a much different idea, one that suggests that when it comes to sexual feelings, you cannot control them when they get too powerful. Sex addiction theory asserts that with sex, feeling out of control and *being* out of control are the same thing. Douglas Weiss refers to sex addiction as "self-will run riot" and suggests that it is actually impossible for a sex addict to control him- or herself without help from professionals: "If addicts want to do it themselves, failure is around the corner for them and their loved ones."[6] Other writers have even argued that unless a diagnosis of sexual addiction is added to the DSM5, then clients will "continue to experience the problems associated with their addictions."[7] When we fail to teach people that self-control *is* possible, even when you have the excited feeling of being somewhat out of control, either because you took a drink, are riding a roller coaster, or are turned on, we are confusing feelings with commands and demands. We need to help people understand what feelings actually are and the role they play in peoples' lives and decisions.

NOTHING MORE THAN FEELINGS

What are feelings, anyway? What are they for? Why do we have them? Why do good feelings feel good and bad feelings suck? One way that we conceptualize emotions is to think of them in two dimensions: their "valence," or whether the emotion is positive or negative, like an atom is either positive or negative; and the strength of the emotion. Some emotions are positive and strong (like love), and some are strong and negative (like anger), while others may be weak and negative (mild irritation), or weak and positive (nostalgia for instance).

The role of this emotional theory in addictions is the belief that an addictive behavior becomes addictive either by providing a strong positive emotion or by reducing the power of a strong negative emotion, such as anxiety or fear. So, in this theory, alcohol could become addictive both by inducing a sense of euphoria and positive feeling in you after you take a drink, *or* by reducing the strength of a feeling of stress when you drink a beer after a long, hard day at work.

Applying this to sexuality, sexual behavior induces a strong, perhaps the strongest, feeling of positive pleasure in individuals. This strong pleasure is felt in many ways around sexuality, psychologically and physically. For instance, a person experiences pleasure at the thought of being able to have sex, during the buildup and preparations for having sex, both from the anticipation of the physical pleasure to come *and* from the psychological sensations of knowing that you are attractive enough to another person that they are choosing to have sex with you. So shouldn't such a strong, positive feeling be potentially addictive?

Similarly, when you consider the degree to which sexual behavior reduces the strength of negative feelings, sexuality is clearly a powerful factor. Many people use sexuality as a means to reduce or manage negative feelings, whether through masturbation as a means to reduce stress, pursuit of sexual relationships with others as a way to make feelings of loneliness go away, and as a way to manage feelings of grief, loss, and fear.

It is a common belief that many babies are born nine months after tragic, fearsome events, as couples join physically to celebrate their survival of these events. While research supporting this belief is weak, there is an intrinsic, atavistic sense of validity in it, that after encountering death, tragedy, and fear, people join with each other and celebrate life through sexuality in a way that is not unhealthy or disordered, using sexual contact as a way to unify and cope with grief and loss. In 2005, researchers "discovered" that pornography use and loneliness go together, with greater use of pornography when people are feeling alone and sad.[8] This explains why hotel rooms and cable porn go together so well, generating millions of dollars of pornography sales by big hotel chains to lonely businesspeople.

———⊶∞⊷———

Kleptomania

The disorder of kleptomania has interesting parallels to sex addiction. Both involve significant issues of anxiety, where someone steals to make anxiety go away, or allegedly uses sex as a way to relieve stress in their lives. Despite significant social consequences and embarrassment, kleptomaniacs often keep stealing. Kleptomaniacs experience a tremendous sense of relief when they steal, so strong that some kleptomaniacs have even compared it to orgasm.

Kleptomania was first described in the 1800s by early psychiatrists, but it was not finally established as an accepted diagnosis for many years. Like sex addiction, there was considerable debate about whether psychiatry was just falling prey to using diagnosis to absolve criminal responsibility. The diagnosis was preferentially applied to wealthy females and was blamed on neurosis, suppressed sexual urges, feelings of inferiority, poor parenting, "cerebral infirmities," "degenerative brain diseases," and most recently, neurochemical disturbance and dysfunction. In the early 1900s, as increasingly lavish department stores were opened, the stores' "intoxicating atmospherics" were blamed for sparking irresistible temptations. Kleptomania has also been in the "hokeypokey" dance of the DSM, in one edition, and out the next.[9]

Kleptomania is classified as an impulse control disorder, not an addiction. A critical component of kleptomania is motivation. Kleptomania is diagnosed when people have no rational desire for stealing but do so anyway. No matter how much a person steals, it's not diagnosed as kleptomania if they are stealing things they want and can't have, or can't afford. It's not diagnosed for the father who steals bread for his starving children. What if the same criteria were applied to sex addiction? Would we lose the ability to diagnose sex addiction in those folks who have lots of reasons for their sexual behavior, but society (or the spouse) doesn't like the reasons?

―∞∞∞―

Despite the common use of sex by people struggling to manage negative emotions, this is defined as inherently pathological and unhealthy in the field of sexual addiction. In the proposed criteria for hypersexual disorder, this is a primary symptom: "repetitive use of sexuality in response to negative feelings, such as anger, sadness or boredom."[10]

There is an idealization of sexuality implicit in the assumptions of those treating and diagnosing sexual addiction, a reflection of the relational view of sex, which mandates that sex is only healthy when it is for procreation or the enhancement of a relationship. Sex is special, this social perspective says. Sex should be intimate. Sex should be spiritual and physical. Charlotte Kasl, PhD, author of *Women, Sex, and Addiction*, says "sex is life affirming only when one is truly present within oneself. Other forms of sex separate us from ourselves."[11] Likewise, Patrick Carnes says, "Sex is about meaning, and spirituality is about meaning. To involve one means to involve the other."[12]

This is a nice, sweet, and wonderful message. It's the same message we give to children: "Sex is special, a special gift that two people can share, when they love each other." But there is another message that children are not mature enough to understand. Sometimes sex isn't wonderful. Sometimes, even between two people who love each other, sex might not be special. It might just be about one partner trying to help the other relax after a long day. How often do couples have sex when one partner is not that "into it" but is having sex out of love for their partner?

The belief that the only good sex is when it is a transcendental, loving, selfless act of union is not new. Russell Trall was a physician and instructor in the 1800s and was actually an instructor of the young physician John Kellogg. Trall was far more sex positive than the cereal magnate Kellogg ever was. Trall argued that unless a sex act was pleasurable to both parties, was generous and harmonious, and involved love as opposed to lust, any children that might result would be flawed. The child of a lustful mating would show the weaknesses they inherited from their parents' corrupt union.[13] So while sex to make babies may be healthy, only good sex makes good babies, went the argument.

There is a moral assumption in the relational view that sex should happen within a meaningful relationship and that sex without such a meaningful relationship is not spiritual and not healthy. But this assumption comes from social values, not from science. Many other societies don't share this view of sex, an issue explored in the next chapter. And the practice of sex outside of committed relationships is explored in chapter 12, but the short answer is that for many, casual sex is not harmful and may even be healthy and emotionally helpful.

Sex addiction theories argue that simply having lots of sex is not a sex addiction, that the diagnosis requires additional features, such as high levels of negative feelings, distress, and life problems related to a person's excessive sexual activity. This is a common feature in the diagnostic strategies employed within the DSM, referred to as the "distress/dysfunction criterion." Essentially, one can only render a diagnosis if there is evidence that the symptoms of the disorder are interfering in the person's life in some way. Sex addictionologists use this factor to argue against those who suggest that they are pathologizing normal behaviors, saying that if the behaviors are normative, the person won't be upset about them or feel that they are out of their control.

However, this doesn't necessarily hold true, and the best example is around masturbation. With such a strong social stigma and secrecy around masturbation, most adolescents who masturbate keep their behaviors secret, worry about getting caught, and often worry that they are masturbating too much. I've seen youth in conservative families who worry that masturbating once a week is "too much" and feel that they cannot control or resist the urge to touch themselves. These youth are extremely ashamed and fearful that their behavior is sinful and abnormal. They would certainly meet the criteria proposed around feelings of distress and lack of control. In some cases, they may actually meet the life impairment criteria as well, when their masturbation has resulted in consequences and punishment in the home. Most of us would scoff at the idea that masturbating once a week is an addiction, but in the concept of sex addiction, this distress/dysfunction element is very loosely and subjectively applied, particularly when the distress and dysfunction is solely driven by the social context in which the individual lives, such as the nature of their marriage.

In fact, some research has suggested that people who seek sex addiction treatment may have extremely high levels of distress, even beyond people who present for problems with gambling and other types of emotional problems. It may well be that the distress reported by such individuals reflects not their sexual issues, but endogenous characteristics related to personality disorders and mood disorders.[14]

The picture of feelings in the sexual addiction model is not clear, and there is disparity in the research. Some research finds that men who self-identify as sex addicts are depressed, other research finds them to be anxious, and some research finds that there is no connection between their feelings and their sexual behaviors. To categorically state that the use of sex to manage feelings is an unhealthy pattern is not well supported, any more than the other moral and socially driven assumptions about sex that are embedded in the concepts of sexual addiction.

Research shows that the use of sexual release to resolve tension is far more common among men than among women, where as many as 80 percent of men will use sex to release stress and tension, while only 25 percent of women use sex in such a manner, choosing things like exercise and television watching to relieve stress instead.[15] This gender difference represents a significant tendency of this tenet of the sex addiction theory to overdiagnose males and is a hint toward what is really going on in the theory of sex addiction, which is explored in the final chapters of this book.

Case Example

Rehabbing Celebrities

For several years, Phil Varone was the drummer for the rock band Skid Row. He has parlayed that success into a new kind of success, using another talent, of which he is very proud. In a new pornographic DVD, released by Vivid Entertainment, Varone has sex with five different women. In interviews, Varone shares that he has

*had sex with over 3,000 women and prefers sex with women "new" to him, such
as the five women who costar in his pornographic feature: "I still feel a charge each
time with each new girl."*

Varone appeared on the Celebrity Rehab *reality show, with celebrity physician and host Dr. Drew, where he was branded a sex addict. Varone disputes the
label of sex addict, asserting, "I never considered myself a sex addict because sex
never screwed up the rest of my life or my ability to function at a high level."*[16]

OBJECTIFICATION

Inherent in most theories of sexual addiction, and particularly evident in
arguments against pornography, is the concept of "objectification." The diagnosis of Don Juanism, which described individuals who treated others as
"things to be used for sex," is based on the belief that objectifying others is a
sign of mental disturbance, or is at least unhealthy. Supposedly by viewing our
sexual partners as objects, we stop them from being human in our minds, and
this puts us at risk for degrading our sexual partners, treating them as nothing
more than meat machines, put there for our sexual gratification.

This does sound troubling. I certainly don't want people viewing me as
merely an object. I have personal experience with this. Born with an obvious physical disability, I have had a lifetime of stares. Many public situations
are uncomfortable for me, as my mind starts to race, thinking about people
looking at me and seeing my disability, and perhaps only my disability. But
despite this personal experience, I acknowledge that objectification is not
necessarily a bad thing.

The military purposefully uses objectification to protect our soldiers and
enhance their fighting abilities. During a war, we dehumanize our opponents,
calling them "Krauts," "Japs," "gooks," "towelheads," and worse. This helps
soldiers to avoid thinking during battle about the humanity, the families, and
the lives of their opponents; they merely fight, and sometimes kill. Surgeons
often objectify their patients, dehumanizing them as a way to manage their
own reluctance to cut into the flesh of another person. Such objectification
helps the surgeon focus on the job at hand.[17] What advice do we give a person
with stage fright or fear of public speaking? "Imagine the audience is naked!"
We don't chastise these people for objectifying their audience, as doing so
allows these people to overcome a difficult and challenging obstacle.

Freud wrote that objectification and even degradation was an integral
part of the sexual act and experience, as one must view one's sexual partner
in some degree of objectification in order to become sexually aroused. Objectification and degradation can be a normal, if not particularly pleasant, part

of sexuality. Sex is not always "nice." Sexual fantasy and behavior reflects the complexity of humans, within the complexity of their social, historical, and physical environments. To attempt to force people to only have "nice" acceptable sexual behaviors and fantasies robs humans of a rich, wide, and varied sexuality. Nancy Friday said, "I do not necessarily expect sex to be pretty; that is to demean it, attenuate its primitive force."[18]

Writer and sexuality counselor Esther Perel also suggests that sometimes objectification is necessary for good sex. "But sexual excitement requires the capacity not to worry, and the pursuit of pleasure requires a degree of selfishness. Some people can't allow themselves this selfishness, because they're too absorbed with the well-being of the beloved."[19] In order to pursue pleasure and sexual gratification in the sexual act, we must at some point become consumed with the imminence and reality of our own orgasm and for a moment be intensely selfish. But when you're trying too hard and are too focused upon your lover's needs, it can be difficult to relax enough to surrender to our own orgasm.

Objectification is a human process that we use in our interactions with others. It is neither good nor bad in itself; it just is. Does it play a role in the actions of individuals who have difficulties controlling their sexual behaviors? Perhaps, but I have yet to see that these individuals have greater difficulties with objectification than do other people, who do not have sexual difficulties. Are there people out there who objectify others to an extreme but are not sexual addicts? Sure—telemarketers and car salesmen come to mind, as do fashion photographers. I may not like what these people do and how they treat others within these roles, but I'm clear that they are not addicted to their behaviors. Objectification of others serves a purpose in their lives.

Case Example

Maria is a forty-five-year-old Hispanic female whose husband brought her to treatment, concerned that she was a sexual addict. They married as teenagers. Over the course of their marriage and relationship, Maria has had twenty-one different affairs, most with her husband's knowledge and consent. For a five-year period while her husband was in school, Maria worked as a prostitute in a "lotion salon." "We used to stand in a line for the men, and it was like being a puppy at the pound; you had to be the 'cutest puppy' in order to get picked." Maria's husband actually enjoys her having sex with other men, and they incorporate that into the couple's sexual fantasy and lovemaking, though Maria refers to this as the "price" she pays for her own sexual freedom to be with other men. Maria is unable to describe what her own sexual fantasies are and views sex as largely unfulfilling for her. "I become for other men whatever they want me to be."

Six months ago, one of Maria's grandchildren died of cancer while Maria was caring for her. Maria was devastated by the loss and felt it was her fault. A short time later, an adult nephew reentered her life after having been taken away from the family by child protective services when he was little. The nephew lived with Maria's family for a while, and Maria ended up having an affair with him, feeling like it was one of the first things she had ever done for herself, and that it was a way to "never lose him again." Since this relationship began, Maria's husband has become afraid that she is addicted to sex and might leave him as she pursues this relationship for her own needs, rather than to fulfill the sexual desires of her husband.

Maria was sexually abused as a young child by an older sibling. She recalls that the first time it happened was after she had a nightmare and went to her parents for comfort. They refused her, but her sibling offered her support and safety and attention, so long as she "let him do anything he wanted to me." Sex for Maria is thus a way for her to be what others want, in exchange for them meeting her emotional needs.

SEXUAL ABUSE

Sexual addictionologists commonly assert that one of the most common pathways to the creation of sex addiction is through a history of childhood sexual abuse. In my career treating the victims of sexual abuse, I've seen numerous females who go through periods when they treat sex cheaply and as a commodity. "It was taken away from me. It's nothing special. Why shouldn't I use it to get what I want?" they've asked me. Young men sexually abused by male perpetrators often go through a phase of questioning their sexuality, as they ask, "What was it about me that drew him to abuse me? Am I really gay or bi, and is that why he chose me?" Male victims of sexual abuse sometimes report higher levels of anonymous sex, though because so few male victims of sexual abuse report their experiences, we are only seeing a very small percentage, which is likely not to be representative of the issues of all-male sexual abuse victims.

But to assert that this is a common pathway to sexual addiction and "out-of-control" erotic behaviors is a stretch beyond the available data. Sex addictionologists present no research that supports this assertion beyond the usual anecdotal descriptions. Forthcoming research from psychiatrist Dr. Martin Kafka and UCLA psychologist Dr. Rory Reid suggests that a history of sexual abuse is not actually prevalent among self-identified sex addicts, particularly among males.[20] Beyond sex addicts, among the general population, the latest statistics suggest that at least one in four women in our country, and one in ten men, will experience sexual abuse of some kind in their lifetime. Even these staggering numbers are regarded as underestimates. If sex addiction was a common result of sexual abuse, we would be flooded with out-of-control sexual behavior to the degree that every day would look like Mardi Gras. In fact, it is only retrospective studies of sex addicts that support this assertion. Studies that look at nonclinical populations find high levels of sexual abuse victims living normal, healthy lives as they have adapted to and overcome what happened to them.

Research in other fields of psychology suggests that the way sex addictionologists view trauma may actually do more harm than good. Research with posttraumatic stress disorder suggests that victims of sexual abuse who never accepted a "victim" role, who did not succumb to feelings of helplessness, and who placed blame and responsibility on the perpetrator ended up suffering the least effects of their experience. There is some current controversy suggesting that therapists' response to histories of trauma may make symptoms of posttraumatic stress worse and engender feelings in victims that they *should* be more impaired. This is an interesting point to consider in light of the sexual addiction movement's assertion that sex addicts are helpless and powerless in the face of sexuality, and where these individuals are seen as "victims" of a disease.

Libido

The high-libido person wants an emotional connection. . . . The sex addict
just wants a fix. It's not about intimacy. It's about getting the fix.
Sex addicts are disconnected during the act itself.
—Douglas Weiss[21]

Allegedly hypersexual behavior often occurs solely within the context of a relationship. One of the most common situations that brings men and couples into treatment for sexual addiction is when one partner is more interested in sex than the other. Sometimes this represents a mild inconvenience, and other times it creates a constant, grinding, and dismaying conflict that can ultimately destroy a relationship.

When one partner describes that the other partner wants sex too much and is pushy and demanding about it, assessment must occur both within the nature of the couple and the nature of the individuals in the marriage, and within the context of what are healthy and normal levels of sexuality within marriage. This conflict happens far more frequently than you might think. In a 1994 study of sex in America, over 30 percent of women reported a marked lack of interest in sex, as compared to only around 15 percent of men.[22] Women, whose levels of sexual desire are already generally lower than those of men, experience greater decline in sexual desire across their life span than do men.

The latter question is particularly challenging, given the complex and shifting nature of this issue across the life span of a person, and a marriage. So, for instance, three to four times a week may be the average and healthy expectation for a marriage in the first year of the marriage, but in most relationships, by the fourth year of monogamy, sex frequency drops off to an average of once or twice per week. However, there are many other factors that influence this, including the ages of the couple, how long they were together before marriage, whether they have children or not, their career status and workload, their physical health, and so forth. There are so many overlapping factors that influence this that it is a challenge for any therapist to answer the question, "How much sex *should* this couple be having?" Peoples' libidos fluctuate, rise, and fall across their lives, affected by a great host of internal and external factors, from seasons, jobs, and family pressures to biological issues such as illness, menopause, or changes in hormone levels.

When one partner wants sex more or less than the other one, who wins, do you think? Does the one who wants sex badger the other into it, by dint of their need? In fact, consistently, when one partner thinks sex once a month is fine, and the other would like it twenty times a month, the average monthly rates of sex are *always* closer to once a month. Economists describe this as an example of the principle of least interest. In any transaction, the person who desires a thing the least has the most control over its ultimate value. When I am in a flea market haggling over a bargain, I can command the best price by pretending that I'm willing to walk away. I get a more favorable price than if the seller believes that I desperately want the thing, in which case they will hold out for all the money I've got. The same plays out in couples and sexuality. The partner who wants sex the least controls the frequency of it, and also controls how much the other partner will have to invest, in terms of time, attention, or dishwashing, in order to have sex.

So when we see someone who is coming in, concerned about having a higher level of sexual desire than their partner, this may not reflect a form of hypersexuality but merely a mismatch in libido within the couple. Some studies suggest that as much as 12 percent of couples experience the effects of mismatched libidos,[23] but given that the libido levels of sexual desire and sexual response fluctuate across the life of all humans, I do not think it is a stretch at all to suggest that almost every sexually intimate couple will experience a period of mismatched levels of sexual desire and sexual response if they stay together long enough. The question is, what do they do when they encounter this dilemma? The theory of sex addiction has us believe that if one partner goes along to satisfy the desire of the other, it is unhealthy. Aside from passive acceptance, there do not seem to be any other healthy options, at least not within the theory of sex addiction, though I dispute whether such passive acceptance is all that healthy itself.

Mismatched libidos is one of the most common explanations behind male sexual infidelity, use of pornography, masturbation, and even men going to strip clubs. An exotic dancer once told me about her professional strategy to present "not like what the guy has at home. He's here to get away from that, to get the fantasy of a woman who wants sex as much as he does."

For dysregulated sexuality to be established as a disorder, it must first be empirically demonstrated that the construct does not simply capture sexual desire. Further, it may be that behaviors considered sexually compulsive, such as protracted promiscuity, compulsive masturbation, pornography addiction, and telephone sex dependence, are merely a means of satisfying a very strong sexual appetite.
—Jason Winters, PhD[24]

When Canadian researcher Jason Winters tried to test the validity of an instrument intended to assess sexual compulsivity, he found that there was no difference between individuals who were self-described sex addicts and those who simply reported high levels of libido. Men with high libidos who were in more restrictive relationships were most likely to have sought treatment for sex addiction. In other words, the distinguishing factor for people seeking sex addiction treatment was the fact that they were in a relationship where there were mismatched libidos. These findings suggest the strong likelihood that what is being labeled as sex addiction may in fact be indistinguishable from a high libido and the conflicts that occur when an individual with a high libido has difficulty expressing his or her sexual desire.

Winters' research raises strong questions as to the validity of arguments that sex addiction diagnosis involves something more than just excessive sex, requiring symptoms of distress, dysfunction, or emotionally unhealthy sexual behaviors. It also suggests that those studies which indicate that higher levels of sexual compulsion or addiction predict higher rates of anonymous sex, dangerous sex, and unprotected sex are actually just measuring the effects of libido, and that it is sexual drive, not pathology, that can lead to risky sexual behaviors.[25]

High libido is more prevalent in men. Buzwell and Rosenthal studied high school students and classed the students into different categories of sex drive and sexual experience. The top two categories were dominated by males—85 percent of the second-from-the-top category were males, and 97 percent of the most sexual category were males, compared to the least sexual category, where there were three girls to every boy.[26]

Researcher Richard Lippa surveyed over 200,000 listeners of the BBC regarding their sexual activity and their sexual attractions. He found that high-libido women were more likely to be bisexual and to show an increase in numbers of sexual partners. But in men, the higher the libido, the more focused these men became, pursuing sexual encounters with either men or women, depending upon the man's sexual orientation. A high libido homosexual male was often a promiscuous homosexual, and a high libido heterosexual pursued promiscuous encounters with women.[27]

Researchers Rinehart and McCabe have shown that people who have "deviant" sexual practices such as voyeurism, prostitution, and exhibitionism show higher levels of depression and obsessive compulsive symptoms, but that people with high libidos who have lots of "nondeviant" sex show no more mental or emotional problems than do nondeviant people who have low amounts of sex. In other words, simply having lots of sex is not associated with mental or emotional problems, but engaging in sexual practices that are deviant (and/or illegal) increases a person's likelihood of having mental problems. It's important to note that no causality is clear in this data. That means that they can't tell from the research which came first, the emotional symptoms or the illegal sex. They can't even tell if the emotional symptoms are the result of the sex itself, or the people's fear of being discovered and punished for their sexual behaviors. In the end, the researchers argue that their research suggests that the labels of sex addiction and hypersexuality may be being applied to behaviors that society deems illegal or inappropriate and may have nothing to do with actual rates of sexual activity. This is important, given that sex addictionologists want to establish that high rates of even "normal" sex are unhealthy.[28]

Women with high libido (defined as having or desiring more than seven orgasms or sexual encounters in a week) often struggle with social acceptance of their sexuality. They are frequently labeled as sluts or whores and taught that their sexuality is negative and unladylike. Such women often have more male friends than female, as they report that men understand them better and don't stigmatize them for their sexuality. Many of these women also report having been labeled as sex addicts. One woman reported being labeled as a sex addict by a therapist after she disclosed that she goes out on weekends "to get laid." The woman's response was, "I like it, but I'm not addicted to it; I'd probably be miserable, but I could go without it." When the woman disclosed that she masturbated daily, her fate was sealed in her therapist's eyes: "The way he was talking, it was awful for me to be doing this."[29]

John Bancroft, former director of the Kinsey Institute, suggests that there may be a "dual-control" explanation for sexual addiction, though he has expressed concern that there is so much variability in the concept of sex addiction that it is premature to diagnose it or include it in the DSM5. Bancroft suggests that people have a sexual arousal system and a system that works to inhibit sexual arousal and libido.

This is parallel to the concept of the sympathetic and parasympathetic nervous systems: the sympathetic system responds to excitement or danger by increasing our heart rate, breathing, and so forth. The parasympathetic system is what then calms our heart and breathing down once the situation has changed. Bancroft suggests that we have a system that responds with sexual arousal to sexual situations, but we also have a system that works to suppress sexual arousal when we need to, for instance due to changes in the environment (such as your girlfriend's parents coming home unexpectedly). Bancroft argues that there are neurological structures in our brains and bodies that support this theory and suggests that sex addiction might reflect people who have highly responsive sexual arousal systems and deficient sexual inhibition systems.[30]

Research by Bancroft and others exploring this concept suggests that this is more true of men than women. Among depressed women, only around 9 percent experience increased sexual arousal, compared to as much as 23 percent of depressed men. As a woman's sexual drive increases, the effects of depression and mood on her sexuality decreases. No such pattern is evident in men. In fact, there appear to be substantial gender differences that may underlie this pattern.

Some research has found that, in fact, all men are able to inhibit their sexual arousal to some degree. An interesting study suggests that men who masturbate compulsively are actually significantly *more* inhibited than those men who are sexually promiscuous with others. This may support the notion that compulsive masturbators are men who fear relationships with others and are too inhibited to be vulnerable in a physically intimate relationship with another, but at the same time have a high level of sexual desire.[31]

Case Example

Peter is a painfully shy nineteen-year-old college student, away from home for the first time and living in the school dormitory of his Christian college. He is an engineering student, with a high GPA, in the first semester of his second year of college. Peter has never had a girlfriend and was socially isolated in high school. He was homeschooled through elementary and middle school and found the social demands of high school to be extremely demanding and overwhelming. Peter's family is extremely religious in a conservative Christian denomination. However, Peter's parents divorced when he was twelve. Due to the divorce, Peter's mother had to return to work and was unable to homeschool her son any longer.

Peter came to therapy, concerned that he was addicted to sex. He sought out a counselor not affiliated with his school, for fear that what he shared in therapy would be released to his school administration. He presented with a great deal of distress that his sexual feelings, urges, and behaviors were out of his control. In interview, Peter shared, extremely reluctantly, that he masturbated two times a month, in the shower in his dormitory. He felt extremely bad that when masturbating, images of pornography came to mind. Though Peter did not view pornography, like most teenagers, he had accidentally stumbled upon pornographic images on the Internet.

Due to his family's conservative views, Peter was not allowed to participate in sexuality education in his high school and has never had sexual contact with anyone else. He is experiencing a great deal of distress over his masturbation and sexual fantasies. "I try not to do it. Sometimes, I avoid showering for days, just to try to not touch myself. I take cold showers sometimes, trying to make the urges go away. But sometimes I have trouble even falling asleep because I think about going in there, into the shower, and doing it again. I go as long as I can, trying not to do it, but then it's just an accident or something, and I touch myself in the shower; and I'm not thinking about it really, kind of out of it even. And next thing I know, I'm hard and doing it. And I try to stop right then, but I can't. I'm terrified that my roommate is going to find out, or that someone might find me in the shower." Speakers had come to Peter's school and talked to the students about the dangers of sex addiction, pornography, and masturbation, explaining in detail how these things had destroyed peoples' lives and marriages. "I really, really want to wait and save all this for marriage. But I can't even talk to a girl right now, for fear that she'll know that I've been touching myself and think I'm a pervert or sicko."

Peter's therapist developed a treatment plan for him, which involved very gentle exploration of sexual education topics, along with attention to Peter's intense anxiety symptoms and social awkwardness. Over the course of six months, Peter's fear of his sexual feelings gradually subsided, though he still viewed masturbation as a sin and something that he wished he didn't do. By focusing on Peter's anxiety symptoms and helping him to practice social skills, Peter gradually came to feel more comfortable with his peers and even began to occasionally go on dates with some of the female students in his classes.

THE MIND-BODY PROBLEM

Calling sex an addiction has an unmistakable tendency to instigate or escalate fighting with one's sexuality. This I can say for certain: If you go to war with your sexuality, you will lose and end up in more trouble than before you started.

—Jack Morin[32]

The theory of sex addiction, according to some, is based upon core experiences of "powerlessness and unmanageability." "When a person becomes addicted, the personality splits into two distinct parts, each denying the existence of the other."[33] This concept is troubling, reflecting a base assumption that addictive behavior, or unhealthy sexual desire, is somehow "other" than a person, somehow outside them. And it supports the idea that we are powerless over these behaviors.

A core weakness in the field of mental health is the issue of dualism, or the separation of mind and body. Philosopher René Descartes, who said "I think therefore I am," helped along the path of this distinction, with the idea that we as human beings are not really part of our bodies but are somehow separate. Like those little aliens in the first *Men in Black* movie, where the tiny little alien controls the big human body from a driver's seat in the body's head, in this approach we "ride" our body but are not part of it. The same distinction is carried further, with the idea that we as a person are somehow different from what we do. Our behaviors do not govern who we are. I can do something awful but still be a good person inside. Those behaviors do not reflect the true me.

This is a belief at the heart of sexual addiction. Sexual behaviors are portrayed as somehow being so powerful that they override our very being, and as if who we are on the inside is somehow lost and overwhelmed by the power of those sexual acts. I must somehow get those behaviors under control in order to reveal the "real me" that was buried under the slippery landslide of sex.

But is this really true? Science suggests that it isn't, that in fact *we are what we do.* Psychology has become increasingly aware of examples that show us that most of what we do in a day, in fact most of our choices, are not conscious. When you choose a soda at a soda machine, you usually don't debate in your head whether you want a cola or a lemon-lime soda. You just push the button and drink what comes out. Your choice was often made unconsciously, by your years of experience drinking soda, by the soda preferences of important people in your life, by the environment and context you are in as you choose a soda, and by a million other factors that are not conscious.

If you tell a person to describe his or her likes and dislikes and then enter that person in a rigged contest where they "win" a thing they just said they disliked, people will all of a sudden like that thing more. In fact, they will reinvent history and tell you that they really didn't dislike the thing as much as they said, or perhaps you just misunderstood them. Having happily won this prize, their mind must resolve the conflict that they are happy they won, even though they won something they didn't really like. This concept is called *cognitive dissonance,* and it is a powerful unconscious force acting on our mind to resolve conflicts, particularly conflicts between our beliefs and our actions.

It appears that our behavior has a far greater impact upon our mind than our mind does upon our behavior. If you tell me that you are sad and I have you sit and "fake smile" for ten minutes, you will start to feel happier. Your brain essentially gets confused, saying "I'm feeling sad, but I'm smiling. I must be happier than I think I am." The muscles and neurons activated by the motion of smiling trigger the release of "happy" neurochemicals, and soon you find yourself feeling more positive than you were. Cognitive behavioral psychology works on these principles. If you want to change how you feel, change what you do. If you feel depressed, don't act depressed. Go out and do the things you would do if you weren't depressed. Socialize, exercise, and soon your mind catches up with your body. This is very different from the theory of sex addiction, where one's sexual desires are characterized as being something that a person must fight against, must declare battle with. Instead, our sexual desires, our sexual behaviors, are as much, and as little, a part of ourselves as our choice between different jobs and different leisure activities.

Case Example

John is a twenty-three-year-old African-American male who lives in a group home for individuals with dual developmental and mental disabilities. John is brought to treatment by group home staff, who report that John is addicted to sex and makes other people uncomfortable by always talking about sex and masturbating in public. John was once almost arrested in a McDonald's after he told the young woman at the counter that he "wanted to eat her pussy." John has been banned from using the house's computer because he so frequently goes to pornographic sites on it and has gotten viruses on the computer several times, not to mention leaving pornographic images on the computer.

As John's therapist engages with him in treatment, she finds that John has had no education or counseling in sexuality and has had few if any role models who helped this young man to understand how to incorporate his sexuality into healthy and responsible social behaviors. John never knew his father and has never returned to his mother's home since one of her boyfriends sexually abused him and John was placed in foster care. John also feels isolated from peers and unable to get the attention he desires. John thinks it is funny when he offends and upsets women and staff with his sexual behaviors, and he thinks that they think it's funny as well. Over time, John's therapist helps him to understand that these women are sometimes frightened and often offended by his behaviors, and that the public nature of his sexuality creates problems for the staff working with him. By working with John to create appropriate and private boundaries around his sexual behaviors and acknowledging his desires as normal and healthy, John's therapist is able to help him live in his group environment with less conflict. John continues to be a sexual person but has learned to show more sexual manners toward his peers and staff, limiting his masturbation and sexualized comments to more appropriate situations and settings.

THIS IS YOUR BRAIN ON SEX

Sexual behavior *is* a highly charged facet of human experience, however, which affects and is affected by biochemical changes in the body and brain that are associated with emotions. Consequently, sexual behavior also has a history of frightening some people so badly that rather than labor to understand it, they seek to suppress it in themselves as well as in others.

—William Henkin PhD[34]

Years ago, working on a hospital unit for individuals with head injuries, I treated a man who suffered a serious head injury in a car accident. Driving a small convertible, his forehead was driven into the windshield frame. After significant time in the hospital and rehabilitation, he returned to work, where he was quickly in trouble due to a new behavior. He liked to sit at his desk and openly read hard-core pornographic magazines. This was before the days of the Internet, so we can only imagine the trouble he might have caused with a desktop window to pornographic movies.

Why did this happen? Was this fellow suddenly supercharged sexually? No. What changed was his ability to restrain impulses. The prefrontal cortex of the brain, the tip of the brain, roughly above and behind your nose, is the place where we are able to think about things, and "think about thinking about things." When we observe ourselves in our mind, it happens there in the prefrontal cortex. I often equate that part of the brain to a governor box, a regulator that we put on engines to prevent them revving too high. I once rented a truck that had a governor box that absolutely refused to allow me to drive over seventy miles an hour—when I got close to seventy, the accelerator would push back against my foot if I tried to keep accelerating. The prefrontal cortex does the same thing in our brain—it pushes back against our desires and intent and allows us to think about things without doing them. I might think about choking somebody I'm upset with and I can imagine it, but I don't do it. I restrain the impulse, using this part of the brain.

The prefrontal cortex is one of the last parts of the brain to mature—one reason that children's and teens are so impulsive. My patient with the head injury? He went from being a person who might think about reading a porn magazine at work but not do it, recognizing the problems it might cause, to a person who did it, simply because he thought it. The problem was not with sexuality but in the impulse control that he applied to his sexual thoughts and desires.

When we apply a sex addiction label to individuals with some other medical or psychological issue, we lose sight of the other things going on, as the sexual behaviors command our attention, as opposed to the true problems, which often lie in people's patterns of relationships, feelings, and choices.

However, a problem for the arguments involving the brain and sex addiction is that there is not a single "pleasure center" in the brain that is involved in our responses to pleasurable activities, substances, and behaviors. There are several different areas of the brain involved in different aspects of the multilayered sensation of pleasure, including excitement, sexual arousal, and happiness, as well as feelings like poignancy and eagerness. One area of the brain, the mesolimbic system, is involved in high-energy pleasure, associated with feelings of strength, confidence, and accomplishment, whereas the opioid system is associated with pleasant feelings of calmness, serenity, and relaxation.

Different drugs stimulate different areas of the brain, resulting in the different effects of different drugs. Methamphetamine triggers the mesolimbic system, leading to that revved-up high, whereas heroin triggers the opioid system, resulting in that lethargic sense of peaceful euphoria. There is no one section of the brain that is our "sexual hard drive." In different people, at different times, different types of sexual activity stimulate different parts of the brain. Stimulation of these various areas of the brain actually serves to increase the overall functioning of the brain. More pleasurable stimulation, through touch, sensory exploration, accomplishments, and so forth, all cause the brain to develop in childhood and to grow and remain healthy throughout adulthood. In addition to the overall survival of the human species, the sense of pleasure serves to increase the mental and physical health of an individual.

Dr. Daniel Amen, a clinical neuroscientist and psychiatrist suggests in his book *Sex on the Brain* that sexual addiction results from deficient functioning in the prefrontal cortex, an area of the brain that inhibits impulsivity. Damage or decreased functioning there can lead to impulsive and poorly planned or considered acts. Dr. Amen has suggested that sexual addiction can also result from a compulsive type of brain deficit and decreased functioning in an area of the brain called the anterior cyngulate gyrus (ACG), an area that helps you "switch" from thought to thought, topic to topic. Thus, the brain can get "stuck" on a single thought or issue, compulsively repeating, like my old scratched LP records. While I was once talking with Dr. Amen backstage in Hollywood, he suggested to me that sex addiction may also reflect a more global social and medical trend of neurological overstimulation, which occurs in our society of excessive consumption.

The brain is certainly involved in sexual behaviors, as it is involved in any human behavior. But attempts to explain sexual misbehaviors based upon single neurological explanations are overly simplistic, reducing complex behaviors to single explanations, reaching beyond our current understanding of the brain. Further, given the heterogeneity of the population labeled as sex addicts, we must expect that, as Dr. Amen suggests, there will be a plethora of brain patterns involved, and that these patterns will not be simple ones.

Case Example

Michael is a fifty-two-year-old Caucasian male who became an engineer, fulfilling a lifelong dream. He describes himself as "heteroflexible," having first encountered bisexuality in his teens. He is currently in his second marriage. In both marriages, he has been able to successfully negotiate the relationships to accept and allow his bisexuality within the marriage. Both wives allowed him to have sex with other men, either with them, or on some occasions without them. Michael refuses to consider himself bisexual or gay and becomes upset when discussing his sexual behaviors with men, for fear that he will be regarded as a homosexual.

Three years ago, Michael's career ended after he suffered neurological damage in an accident where oxygen was cut off to his brain. After his accident, Michael was told that he would probably never walk again, having suffered around 20 percent loss of function, particularly in the frontal regions of the brain, where our impulse control and higher cognitive functions lie. Michael did walk again, but he suffered significant changes to his personality and behavior. Michael became increasingly aggressive, impulsive, and angry. A man who had always been polite and in control of himself, he began cursing and muttering under his breath, as well as swearing at his wife and threatening her in an angry and aggressive way. The couple fought much more often, and many of their fights were about sex.

Michael began engaging in lots of sexual activity, meeting men online and at gay saunas. "I just loving rubbing a guy's penis at a bathhouse," Michael said. Michael justified his behaviors, which were outside the agreement he had with his wife, saying, "She's not giving it up anymore, so I can do what I need to." But his wife's reluctance and withholding was about her fear of sexually transmitted disease from his promiscuous, impulsive, and often unsafe sexual behaviors. When he wasn't having sex with other men, he often downloaded gay pornography to watch and masturbate to.

The couple saw multiple therapists. By two of these therapists, Michael was diagnosed as a sexual addict but was unwilling to engage in the treatment or to admit that his sexual behaviors were a problem, continuing to blame his actions and choices on his wife. Michael's wife, Cynthia, stomped out of her last session, leaving her husband and the therapist's office to walk in a park and decide whether she could remain married to Michael. "He's not the man I married. I know it's not really his fault, but I don't think I can live like this." Michael's problems clearly lie in his changed neurological functioning, and he was referred back to a neurologist; but Michael refuses to seek additional treatment at this time, despite his wife's leaving him. According to his treating clinician, "To say his problem is sex is silly. His problem is in his brain. Trying to get him to embrace the concept of sexual addiction and change his behavior that way is ludicrous."[35]

Brain Bingo

In the 1970s, experiments were done with electrical stimulation of the brain of a subject called "B-19." This gentleman, a twenty-four-year-old male with a history of temporal lobe epilepsy, depression, and drug abuse, was also identified as a homosexual. One reason for the experimental treatment was to attempt to use electrical stimulation of the pleasure centers of the brain to "alter" the subject's sexual orientation. The research was done at Tulane University by Dr. Robert Heath. Electrodes were placed into fourteen areas of B-19's brain and then tested with electrical stimulation. One electrode, placed in the area of the septal region of the brain, a part of the limbic system associated with emotions, generated a significant response when electrically stimulated (previous research with rats and electrical stimulation of this area produced rats who engaged compulsively in self-stimulation, pressing a lever that sent stimulation to this electrode as many as 2,000 times). When the juice was flowing, B-19 reported feelings of sexual arousal, pleasure, and an intense interest in masturbating. Over the course of treatment, B-19 stimulated this electrode with a portable generator, including while masturbating and watching pornographic films of heterosexual activity. Eventually the researchers even brought in a female prostitute, with whom B-19 had his first pleasurable and satisfying heterosexual encounter, accompanied by electrical stimulation of his brain.

Heath reported later that B-19 went on to return to homosexual behavior later in life, and the experimental treatment that Heath pursued is widely regarded as unethical, ineffective, and clinically troubling. But despite direct stimulation of the brain, and despite exhibiting what can best be described as "compulsive self-stimulation," B-19 voluntarily consented to removal of the electrodes. He did not hold the doctor at gunpoint and force the electrodes to be reinserted; nor did he buy a drill and a battery and try to recreate the effect. B-19 serves as a remarkable challenge to the idea that sexual addiction reflects an organic brain change. With neural stimulation and the opportunity to receive such stimulation, under his own control B-19 behaved as an addict would, self-stimulating obsessively. When the electrodes were removed, B-19 returned to a normal life, one much like the life he led prior to the surgery.[36] His brain did not change irrevocably into the brain of an addict, controlling his needs, desires, and behaviors.

—————∞∞∞—————

Reef Karim is a celebrity psychiatrist and sex addiction specialist who states that he diagnoses sex addiction on the basis of brain functioning. "I get asked by a lot of men, 'Doc, am I a sex addict?' Most of the time I say, 'No, you're just a jerk.' I've had a couple of patients that I've been like, 'Okay, I've looked at your neuropsychological testing. You did not meet criteria for sex addiction.'"[37] There are few in the medical or mental health field who agree with Dr. Karim's confidence. Mental health and brain functioning just aren't clear enough or reliable enough to function the way Karim suggests, in sex addiction or even in other well-researched disorders like depression or bipolar disorder.

Dr. Michael First, one of the contributors to the last two editions of the DSM, says that, "in fact, there was a series of research conferences before work on the *DSM-V* actually started, and one question that was put to every single research group is, are we ready to have lab tests or genes or neuroimaging as a diagnostic test? And every single time that question was raised we always got the same answer, which is while this is interesting, while there's data, it's not good enough to help us make a diagnosis. So we're going to have to wait till, you know, who knows when, but certainly not now."[38] There is not at this time a single mental disorder that can be diagnosed on the basis of "bio-markers" or brain scans and testing. This is true for disorders such as schizophrenia and bipolar disorder, which have been studied in incredible detail for decades, and is thus certainly true for such ill-defined concepts as sex addiction.

Recent studies suggest that dopamine, and certain genes that govern the development of the way our brains respond to dopamine, may be involved in the development of certain addictive behaviors. People with a certain type of gene are at higher risk to report more short-term or one-night-stand relationships, along with higher rates of infidelity, gambling, drug and alcohol use, and other adrenaline-fueled activities like skydiving and race car driving. Neuroscientist David Linden argues that this "blunts" the brain's ability to respond to dopamine, requiring higher levels of stimulation to achieve the same effect.[39]

But the picture of dopamine is not as clear as some suggest. It is only one chemical in our brain, and people have different levels of response to it. Even within the very heavily and carefully studied fields of chemical and alcohol addictions, the role of dopamine is only one factor that remains under close scrutiny.[40] But if we do continue to find that dopamine receptors and genes that drive the brain to function in one way or another are related to an individual's "addictive" behaviors, it still only explains a single piece of the puzzle. What are the environmental and personal factors that lead some individuals to choose sex, or alcohol, or drugs, or gambling in response to their brain's functioning, and what are the things that lead other people with that same type of brain chemistry to be able to overcome those predispositions, and not engage in such addictive or destructive behaviors?

"We suspect that the associations we observed between dopaminergic sensation-seeking and sexual behavior may be independent of other evolved mechanisms that promote pair-bond stability and romantic attachments. That is, the motivation to engage in extra-relationship sexual experiences (infidelity) or promiscuous sexual activities (one-night stands) can remain disconnected from any motivation for attachment and commitment even in the presence of strong existing pair-bonds."[41]

In response to arguments that true addictions require chemical changes, sex addictionologists claim that the neurochemistry involved in sex is parallel to drugs in the body, and that too much sex causes the brain to be rewired, becoming dependent upon the neurochemicals released during sex. Unfortunately, their argument doesn't hold up too well. The brain is in fact constantly changing. "The bottom line is, the brain is wired to adapt. There's no question that rewiring goes on all the time."[42] Any significant activity that a person engages in for a period of time leads the brain to adapt, change, and react. When you first learn to ride a bicycle, you wobble, fall, and struggle to steer and pedal at the same time. Quickly, though, your brain and body adapt. Years might pass before you climb on a bicycle again, but when you do, you are quickly able to confidently ride the bicycle again without having to relearn the skills. Why? Because your brain actually changed in the process of learning, and those neuronal connections and pathways that were created as you first learned to navigate the bicycle are still there. The brain changes that might occur when you frequently practice sexuality are no different than those changes associated with any other behavior, particularly if the behavior is rewarding and pleasurable in some way.

Similar brain-based arguments have been made by those who advocate for other disorders and diagnostic categories. Such arguments are routinely rejected by careful scientists, as they oversimplify complex behaviors and ignore the impact of environment and individual differences, shifting focus toward chemical treatments rather than addressing issues of choice, will, and the human consciousness. A 2009 study of the brains of eight men with diagnosed compulsive sexual behaviors found that these men overwhelmingly had other comorbid disorders and that their behaviors in testing closely resembled the patterns of individuals with impulse control disorders.[43] Analyses of the men's brains found no significant differences between their neurological structures and those of a control group. What brain differences were found suggested that the men with sexual problems showed patterns related to anxiety symptoms rather than impulse control problems. So, even when scientists look at the brains of so-called sexual addicts, the confusion remains as to the underlying mechanisms. But the research was clear on one thing. If there were problems in the brains of these individuals, it was related to problems other than sex.

Currently, attempts to identify neurochemical pathways for sexual or pornography addiction are, at best, "speculative not scientific," according to brain researchers Reid, Carpenter, and Fong at UCLA and Brigham Young University.[44] Further, the use of neurological arguments embedded in morally driven campaigns against the dangers of video games, pornography, and certain kinds of sex should be taken with large doses of salt—these arguments are typically expressed by advocates and nonscientists who exaggerate effects and simplify processes, presenting a cartoon version of neurochemistry to support their premises. Right now, and for the foreseeable future, the brain remains a complex, multidetermined "black box" that we are just barely beginning to understand. The role of the brain in complex behaviors such as sex promises to be a riddle for many long years to come. When we solve the riddle, the answers will not be simple ones, as they will have to account for all factors, including the brain, human behavior, learning history, evolutionary influences, environment, free will, and sexual desire.

Case Example

In Insatiable Wives, *I describe the story of Janice, a woman who suffered severe emotional and physical abuse as a child. It was so severe that the woman literally ran away from home and joined the circus, living with the circus for about a year before finally returning home. As an adult, Janice became a sex worker and was unable to have stable relationships, feeling that men ran away from her when they knew her history, or that she herself was too frightened by the level of intimacy and connection a real relationship demanded. But one day Janice met Michael, and a strong connection developed between them. What made their relationship different was that Michael did not ask Janice to be monogamous or give up her sex work.*

For the first ten years of their marriage, Janice continued to have sex with various men, sometimes for money and sometimes for personal reasons and desires. It wasn't about money but about Janice's feelings of self-worth, independence, and freedom. By allowing this woman the freedom to have sex with whomever she chose, Michael gave her the ability to develop an intimate relationship that involved vulnerability and emotional openness in a way that Janice had never experienced. Eventually Janice decided independently to stop her sex work.

Janice's story is a powerful one, because it would have been so easy to consider her sexual behaviors as symptomatic of her traumatic history, to see them as pathological, to characterize her as a sexual addict whose disturbed childhood had warped her view of sex and love. But Janice's story is in fact a story of triumph. Even though she spent years in therapy, it was sexuality, and embracing a nontraditional model of marriage and fidelity, that allowed this woman to accept love and intimacy into her life. So these symptoms of sex addiction, this promiscuity, sex work, and rejection of the monogamy ideal, were actually adaptive. Her sexuality allowed her to overcome the emotional and psychological impact of her early trauma and to heal.[45]

DISEASE MODEL

I once treated a group of men who said when they died, they might as well carve the words "sex offender" on their tombstones. For these men, who had damaged and hurt others by their sexual behaviors, these sexual behaviors had become the sole identity that they held in the views of society. These men were angry, isolated, and stigmatized. And research shows clearly that when such men are isolated and stigmatized, they are at highest risk to reoffend and hurt more people. Why not? What else do they have to lose at that point? Society has told them that their worst acts are all they will ever be, that there is no hope or chance of rehabilitation. Such labeling is counterproductive to helping people take responsibility for their lives, their futures, and their behaviors.

The sex addiction movement identifies people by their behavior, by a single behavior, suggesting that the identity of "sex addict" is the most important aspect of an individual's life. Sex addiction therapists Ralph and Marcus Earle write that a critical component of sexual addiction treatment is that, "to recover, the sex addict needs to say the words 'I am a sex addict.'"[46] The reductionist aspect to this is troubling. It isolates this single behavior from all other behaviors and induces an overfocus upon sexuality, to the exclusion of other issues. As long as we split an individual's sexual behaviors away from who they are as a person, as long as we feed the idea that someone can treat a problem behavior by only addressing the behavior and ignoring the context, we will not be successful at helping people to live whole, full, healthy lives. They may manage a certain behavior, but there are lots more parts to life, and to health.

Calling certain sexual behaviors an addiction or classifying them as a mental disorder labels them as a disease. The disease model includes several assumptions, which get complicated when we apply them to sexual behaviors. Diseases happen to individuals. I don't wake up one morning and decide to develop a cold and a sniffle. The same is true for mental disorders—people don't wake up and decide to be clinically depressed. But sexual behaviors involve choice.

Psychiatrist Thomas Szasz asks the question, "Is every form of suffering illness?"[47] Szasz has been a vocal critic of the way in which psychiatry has been co-opted, used by society to bludgeon and manipulate men, through the mind and the law. Szasz points at the history of psychiatry's attacks on masturbation as an example of how susceptible psychiatry is to subjectivity and how dangerous it is to lose sight of the weaknesses that the field has, despite psychiatry's attempts to present itself as a science.

Szasz's point is well taken, and his question about suffering is revealing of our efforts to label and categorize our struggles. A good example is in the concept of grief, especially when we grieve over the loss of a loved one. We accept as a society that when someone loses someone close to them, grief, anger, sadness, fear, and other negative emotions are a part of the process that one goes through in learning to cope, and in accepting that they now live in a world without their loved one. Traditionally, the field of mental health has established a threshold, and it is only when these negative emotions persist past six months that we consider them symptoms of mental illness. Current proposals in the DSM5 include removal of this limitation, allowing the diagnosis of clinical depression, even in instances of bereavement, after a period of only two weeks. Thus we may begin to medicate grief, treating it as an illness rather than as a normal, if sad and tragic, part of life.

Are we doing the same with sex addiction? Are we diagnosing something that is a part of the normal, if problematic, range of human life and sexuality? I acknowledge that the sexually irresponsible, selfish, dangerous sexual acts of some people cause immense emotional pain to themselves and their loved ones. But just because something hurts, must it be an illness? Christopher Lane, author of *Shyness: How Normal Behavior Became a Sickness*, suggests that suffering can be edifying, teaching us lessons, but that this concept is anathema to modern psychiatry, which seems to have embraced the concept that their goal is to rid the world of suffering and pain.[48]

I often give the following example to clients. Imagine going through the day without the ability to feel pain. You turn on the stove and accidentally rest your hand on the burner. Normally the sense of pain from the heat would lead you to jerk your hand away even faster than the signal of the pain can travel to your brain. Your body is wired such that the pain causes an almost instantaneous reaction. But without the pain? You don't realize your hand is hurt until you smell the flesh burning.

Pain is a signal—nothing more, and nothing less. It is an incredibly important part of life, just as valuable as happiness and joy. Pain and sadness help us to understand and identify what is important in our lives, to value those things, and to motivate us to protect them. If we classify sadness, pain, and suffering as forms of illness, we are in essence arguing that life would be better without them, that we should rid ourselves of suffering and protect ourselves from sadness. There is the implicit statement that we are not strong enough to withstand sadness and loss, which we must be shielded from, and that medicine and psychotherapy must serve to insulate us from these parts of life.

I reject this belief. Life without sadness, without loss and grief, is only a shadow of life. A life without these aspects is not a blessing but a curse. We cannot appreciate the greatness of joy without an understanding of sadness. Without the pain of suffering, we will make the same mistakes again and again. Benjamin Franklin said it well: "Those things that hurt, instruct."[49] The role of painful emotions with our sexuality is no different, no more pathological, than the role of pleasurable emotions with sex. We just don't value the painful emotions and instead view their role in our lives and sex as negative. This has much to do with our cultural views of sex and relationships, issues explored in the following chapter.

7

Culture and Sexuality

We can spend our lives letting the world tell us who we are. Sane or
insane. Saints or sex addicts.

—*Choke*, by Chuck Palahniuk[1]

Sociologists and anthropologists suggest that there are three main ways to
characterize sexuality and eroticism in a society: the procreative, relational,
and recreational views. The procreative views sex as solely a means for reproduction, where sexual pleasure only has value when it occurs within a committed heterosexual relationship and when it is intended or hoped to result
in conception. The relational view is more flexible, putting less emphasis
upon procreation but expecting sex to occur within intimate, caring, and
committed relationships. Procreation is not necessary, such that homosexual
relationships can hold equal value to childless heterosexual relationships, but
sexual relationships that are casual, uncommitted, or nonmonogamous are
of little value, or even of negative value. Sexuality is seen as a way to express
intimacy, love, and commitment. Sexuality without this relational context is
seen as invalid, debased, and immoral. Finally, a recreational view of sexuality suggests that sexuality is focused upon mutual pleasure, regardless of the
level of relationship or not between the sexual actors. There is no need for
commitment or intimacy in the recreational view.[2]

The sex addiction field relies strongly upon the foundations of the
procreational and relational views of sexuality.[3] According to some critics,
the sexual addiction concept came about following social shifts in these
sexual codes, from the 1950s, when procreational sex was mandated by law,
outlawing any nonprocreative sex such as sodomy and homosexuality, to the
1970s, when a recreational ethic toward sex rose up as part of the "free love"

movement. But the rise of AIDS and social shifts toward more conservative values led to the return of more restrictive sexual values. Sex addiction is a concept heavily influenced by social norms and values, with significantly less influence of medical and research arguments.

These different categories of sexual attitudes can be found in survey data of Americans and have a direct relationship with gender and religion. Women are far more likely to endorse relational and procreational views of sexuality, while men are much more likely to endorse recreational and relational views of sex. Men view sex as more playful, fun, and entertaining than do women and are less likely to believe that sex should be reserved for love and marriage. Those with stronger religious beliefs are more likely to endorse views of sex that are traditional in nature, grounded in the procreational or relational models, with more restrictions and views about the "right and wrong" ways sex should be used.[4]

A significant challenge to the concept of sex addiction is that it represents a culturally bound concept reflecting changing social views of sexuality rather than medicine or scientific research. In this view, it makes sense that the sex addiction concept was spawned in the early 1980s, as the United States was gripped with fear of AIDS and the country moved into a socially conservative period, where sexuality was condemned and censored.

As I wrote some of this chapter, I was sitting in a coffee shop in San Francisco. The flamboyantly dressed bearded man in a wedding dress that walked by me would almost certainly have been diagnosed as mentally ill only a few decades ago, solely on the basis of his garb and rejection of social expectations. But today, his rejection of social expectations is a part of the Gay Pride events going on in San Francisco, and even if it weren't Pride Weekend, he still wouldn't be classified as mentally ill without more data.

The field of mental health in America has embraced the notion of cultural sensitivity and recognizes that just because a person has a conflict with the expectations of their culture, it does not make them mentally ill. If a person who is homosexual is not automatically mentally ill in the United States, then they do not suddenly become disordered when they visit an African nation where homosexuality is forbidden. They may violate a law, but their behavior does not become an illness. Cultural beliefs and attitudes toward sexuality vary tremendously, and many cultures do not have the negative views of promiscuity, infidelity, and nontraditional sex that America does. Some cultures are more open, and some are more judgmental and condemning.

The medical and mental health communities are being used to a degree by society, as science and medicine are co-opted by moral and social values and needs. Our medical diagnoses have become "value judgments cloaked as pseudoscientific diagnosis."[5] By pathologizing sexual excess, society enforces the procreational and relational views of sexuality and tries to set limits on the increasing tide of sexual freedom. Labeling sexual excess as an illness offers a way in which to protect monogamy and the "normalcy" of heterosexual relationships, and it offers society a means to excuse the sexual behaviors of male leaders and celebrities, whose sexual behaviors cause them and society embarrassment. By labeling these men as suffering from the effect of an illness, an addiction, we as a society are able to absolve them of guilt and offer the men a means toward restoring their status after public exposure of sexual excess. Sex addiction labels give society, media, and individuals a way to explain the unexplained, and sometimes inexplicable, behaviors of our idols: movie stars, rock stars, politicians, and athletes.

The Appeal of Calling It an Addiction

As the ex-spouse of a "sex addict," I know when I found out I really, really wanted to believe that it was an addiction he had, partly because I thought it would help make it all just a little bit easier to accept (i.e., he has a problem that he can't control, that isn't within his control). However, in the end, he had been right all along about his reasons for doing it: he did it, and did it as often as he could, simply because he could. Learning to accept that you've married someone who could be so intentionally careless with your marriage, with your health, with his health, has taken a long time to move through and to move past. But I understand completely wanting to believe it's an "addiction" over the even more painful truth that it's not.[6]

Should society be able to put restrictions on personal sexual behaviors? The United Nations has taken a stand on protecting the sexual and reproductive rights of all people in the world, arguing that laws that stigmatize certain sexual behaviors and limit sexual knowledge are violations of basic human rights.[7] But in Great Britain, certain levels of bondage and discipline and sadomasochistic behaviors are illegal, even if all parties explicitly consent to them. Videotapes surfaced in England of homosexual men engaging in severe BDSM behaviors, with things like cutting, piercing, branding, whipping, and genital torture. Even though the people in the videos chose to be there and experienced no distress or impairment because of the behaviors, and even though the behaviors did not result in any lasting damage that required medical treatment, the behaviors were deemed illegal, and multiple men involved were arrested. Appeals to the highest courts in England were unsuccessful, as the judges decided that they must protect society from a "cult of violence," and that deriving pleasure from "the infliction of pain was an evil thing." Appeals to the convictions even cited the United Nations' fundamental human rights, asserting that the actors should be free to do what they wanted with their own bodies, and that sadomasochism was essential to the actors' happiness. Nevertheless, appeals were denied, and the convictions of five men were upheld.[8]

So, assuming that a society does have the ability to broadly label certain consensual behaviors as illegal and dangerous and to attempt to restrict or ban them, should mental health be the vehicle for society to change or restrict such behaviors? I think doing so is dangerous in the extreme. Throughout history, there are many such examples, and all represent shameful episodes. In American history, African Americans, Native Americans, and even women were identified as intellectually and morally deficient, labels which justified the lack of rights these groups were allowed. Indeed, the field of psychological testing and intellectual assessment is one of the leveling factors that shows that intellectual and emotional functioning varies more at individual levels, between two people, regardless of gender or race, than they do between large groupings of people. The field of psychology is meant to support the idea that "people are people," regardless of skin color, gender or other factors. The DSM-IV TR says, "Neither deviant behavior (e.g., political, religious, or sexual) nor conflicts that are primarily between the individual and society are mental disorders unless the deviance or conflict is a symptom of a dysfunction in the individual."[9] The American Psychological Association establishes the following in its ethics code, governing the practice of psychology in the United States:

> Psychologists are aware of and respect cultural, individual, and role differences, including those based on age, gender, gender identity, race, ethnicity, culture, national origin, religion, sexual orientation, disability, language, and socioeconomic status and consider these factors when working with members of such groups. Psychologists try to eliminate the effect on their work of biases based on those factors, and they do not knowingly participate in or condone activities of others based upon such prejudices.[10]

This creates a conflict if we accept the diagnosis of sexual addiction when there are cultures that do not embrace the sexual values of monogamy, fidelity, and intimacy.

Throughout history, numerous cultures and religions have incorporated nonmonogamous, nonheterosexual, and nonintimate sexuality into their rituals. Temple prostitutes served their goddess at the same time they serviced unknown men in ancient Greece. Ancient cultures viewed sex as a gift from nature and the gods, and as a way to come into contact with the universe and the gods through sexual ecstasy. Sexual festivals and public orgies played a significant role in many historic cultures. Different orgiastic festivals were organized, with some involving both men and women and some that were reserved for participants of a single sex. Orgies in ancient cultures served to release sexual tension, worship and honor gods, and celebrate and promote fertility in crops. Temples in India and throughout Asia depict sexual acts, including orgies, masturbation, group sex, homosexual acts, sodomy, and oral sex, all included as a part of the social and cultural view of physical and spiritual life. Indeed, many societies celebrated what we would consider pornography as a part of their culture and religion.

Island residents of Melanesia accepted and supported a practice of male infidelity, where a wife looked on her husband's female lovers with a sense of pride, viewing them as reflective of her husband's high status. Thus, a wife could be proud of her husband's success in having mistresses and concubines. But European and colonial laws against infidelity soon stopped this practice, to the lament of many of the men of the island.[11]

On the Polynesian island of Mangaia, a sexually permissive culture existed for many years. Studied by ethnographer Donald Marshall, descriptions of the culture include rampant sexuality from teenage years on. Boys and girls sometimes had as many as sixty or seventy sexual partners by the time they reached adulthood, and there was a cultural "race" toward sexual prowess and promiscuity. More experienced partners were valued by both sexes, for their greater ability to give and share pleasure. Masturbation was encouraged, though considered a private event. As males traveled the Polynesian islands, they were encouraged to be promiscuous and sexually successful in order to uphold their tribe's reputation and status. Marshall described that young people in the culture would often "lose their interest in food," replaced by their pursuit of sex.

And yet the island culture did not collapse; youth and adults were not lost to sexuality, unable to be retrieved. The young men and women aged, matured, married, and had families. They produced food and crops for the tribe. Marriages were sexually satisfactory, and monogamy was not the norm. No one was diagnosed with sex addiction, whether they used those words or not. In fact, Marshall described that some male and female youth were more sexual than others, and this was an accepted range of interest in sexual exploits.[12]

If, as sexual addiction theorists believed, sex is a corrupting dangerous influence that can overwhelm an individual human's ability for self-control, why was this society successful in a culture of sexual permissiveness? Sexual addiction theorists who argue that the risks of sex addiction lie in the brain, and in intrinsic aspects of human biology, would have predicted that at least some of these tribes' members, especially males, would have lost control of themselves in the easy access to sex and would have raped, killed, destroyed, or self-destructed. Sexual pursuits would have so taken over their lives that they could do nothing else and could not stop. Unrestrained, such loss of control would destroy lives and society. But it didn't happen. Sexual behaviors currently identified as pathological may not be, depending upon the cultural context in which they occur. Sexual addiction is thus a "culture-bound syndrome," reflecting cultural values more than universal human psychology.

Case Example

Osho was the assumed name of Chandra Moja Jain, an Eastern mystic who gained international fame and infamy in the 1970s and 1980s as a spiritual leader. Osho led a massive spiritual and self-development organization, from India and the United States, each year receiving over 30,000 visitors, followers, and supplicants. Osho incorporated a great deal of sexuality and eroticism in his teaching and practices, though he argued that once humans had evolved sufficiently, physical sex would no longer be necessary. Until then, Osho claimed that the social pressures put upon sexual expression actually served to increase a sexual obsession in response to suppression, and that free acceptance of sexuality and sexual expression was necessary for individual and social health. As spiritual and world leader of this movement, Osho wasn't above some individual teachings. He claimed to have had sex with more women than any other man in the world: "I have always loved women—and perhaps more women than anybody else. You can see my beard: it has become grey so quickly because I have lived so intensely that I have compressed almost two hundred years into fifty."[13]

Osho went through decades of controversy, arrests, and legal imbroglios, in multiple countries, and his spiritual teachings are still debated. Was he just a charismatic and narcissistic leader, spouting plagiarized pseudomystical truisms, or did he have something to teach the world? In India, where Osho was rejected and ridiculed as the "sex guru" while alive, Osho has since been called one of the ten most influential people in the country's history.[14]

There is a French saying, "It's not good to speak all truths."[15] The French actually have fewer affairs than Americans, but they handle the affairs differently. Sometimes they just leave well enough alone, allowing husbands and wives to have their affairs, without intruding or challenging even obvious lies. They let sleeping dogs lie, and they aren't wracked by guilt over infidelity and the feelings of core betrayal that plagues unfaithful American couples. "They don't think extramarital sex points to larger moral failings."[16]

In many Latin American countries, male infidelity is expected, and even encouraged; it is seen as an expression of a man's virility and "machismo."

At a university party I attended recently, I met a young woman from Colombia. She told me about her boyfriend of eight years who had openly had affairs with seven different women during their relationship, one time even sending her nude pictures of himself with one of his mistresses. According to Stanford researchers, the Latin American concept of machismo is seen as a source of male pride and includes, among other things, a perception that a man has "an expansive and almost uncontrollable sexual appetite," which he demonstrates through his extramarital affairs. The cultural values and norms of these societies lead to women and wives being unable to challenge or criticize the infidelity of the men in their lives. One story told by the Stanford researchers tells of a Latin woman praying before her wedding for three things: that her husband would be faithful to her, that she would not find out when he was unfaithful, and that she would not care when she did discover his infidelity.[17]

Similar patterns are seen in many Asian cultures, where men routinely demonstrate their virility and masculinity through sexual promiscuity with mistresses and prostitutes. An entire industry of sex work exists in Japan, with "hostess bars," sex massage parlors, "soaplands," and sadomasochistic bars, an industry largely fed by the wallets of married men looking for escape in alcohol and the bodies of other women.

In South Africa, some health workers have described what they call the "Alex syndrome," where men are coming in to complain that as they age, they are having difficulty having sex more than once a day. They need to be able to do so, in order to satisfy the sexual needs of both their wives and their mistresses! Among South African men, daily sex is seen as normative, even expected.[18]

Case Example

South African president Jacob Zuma is of Zulu descent and has been president of that African nation since 2009. Zuma is an open polygamist, with three current wives, one wife who is deceased, and another wife whom he divorced. In 2005, the political leader was charged with rape of a thirty-one-year-old woman, an AIDS activist. Zuma denied the charges, claiming that the sex was consensual. Ultimately he was acquitted of the charges as the court agreed with the apparent consensual nature of the act. In February 2010, the African nation was rocked with scandal when it became known that the president acknowledged a "love child" with a former female lover to whom he was not married. Much of the scandal concerned the fact that during the previous trial on rape, Zuma had acknowledged not having used a condom, and this disclosure of the birth of a child out of wedlock also revealed that the president was not a regular user of condoms. South Africa is a nation beset with incredibly high HIV and AIDS rates, and President Zuma had formerly been praised for his open support of HIV prevention initiatives.

In the press, an African minister of Parliament and political opponent to President Zuma argued that the president's behavior revealed not just hypocrisy, but disordered sexuality: "We believe President Zuma needs sex addiction therapy, as was recommended for Tiger Woods who has a similar problem of sleeping around."[19]

Even within American society, there are changing cultural norms about sexuality, monogamy, and even promiscuity. Through American history, the terms hypersexuality and satyriasis have been largely applied to men from minority populations such as African Americans, to mentally deficient males, and to males of lower socioeconomic statuses. In fact, it was the alleged hypersexuality of black men that was used as one argument for their basic "animalistic" and savage nature and to justify slavery. It's interesting that in contrast to this history, the sex addiction label is now applied almost overwhelmingly to white males of the middle and upper classes. However, whenever a society is condemning the sexual practices of a group of people, it is the behaviors of those who go against the sexual morals of society who are at greatest risk for stigma, bias, and oppression. These groups include sexual minorities such as lesbians, gays, bisexuals, and transgendered individuals, as well as those who reject socially prescribed values of monogamy, chastity, and romantic love.

Case Example

Rodney is a twenty-seven-year-old African-American male who has had a fascination with the idea of interracial sex since he was nineteen years old. He grew up in Philadelphia, in a traditionally black neighborhood. As a youth and young man, he had few relationships with people of other races and first encountered the idea of interracial relationships on the Internet, where he found many groups dedicated to the celebration of white women having sex with African-American men. When he was twenty-one, Rodney used the Internet to arrange a meeting with a white woman in a hotel room. This was the first time Rodney had ever had sex, and he spent the night with the woman. After they had sex several times, she called another man she knew, an African-American male police officer, and had sex with him while Rodney watched. When Rodney returned home the next day, to his home with his mother, she accused him of being addicted to sex and to having no self-respect. These are accusations he has heard frequently in the years since. "When black men have sex with white women, we get accused of being 'walking dildos,' of being puppets serving white women in the bedroom, and betraying our race." Since Rodney first began his pursuit of interracial sex, he has had sex with nearly three hundred women. He tells stories of attending parties where women have group sex with several black men at once, and he recounts one incident where a woman flew him across the country to have sex with her. She picked him up at the airport and drove him to a park, where she had sex with him in a parking lot; then she drove him back to the airport for his flight home. Rodney has had some negative encounters in this lifestyle, including one embarrassing incident when a woman berated him, saying that she had "thought his penis would be larger," disappointed by his reality, which was in contrast to her assumption that all black men have inordinately large penises. However, he feels that the worst experiences he has had have been when his sexuality has been demonized and his libido called sick and pathological. "I like sex, and I love women who love sex. Right now, I'm really happy with my life. I have no interest in changing the way I'm living and loving." He quotes a favorite author, who said, "Once you degrade a person's sexuality, you degrade them as a person." Rodney is currently working on his first book, telling the experience of a black man in this lifestyle.

The twelve-step group Sexaholics Anonymous proclaims that "any form of sex with one's self or with partners other than the spouse is progressively addictive and destructive."[20] But many cultures throughout the world do not deify the concept of romantic or passionate love the way American society does. Even through American history, passionate love has been seen at times as a weakness, as something that creates irrational thought and reflects a psychological weakness. In our society, the ideal of love is characterized as a relationship where people feel romantic, committed, and passionate love for one another. Sex, according to sex addiction theories, should only feed the growth of a relationship between two people and should not occur on the basis of feelings of obligation. The cultural practice of arranged marriages contradicts these notions. In arranged marriages, families or community leaders arrange marriages, deciding a match based on the characteristics, needs, and resources of young men and women. The couple is not in love as they marry, though they often report that they grow to love one another over time. Such marriages have surprisingly low divorce rates, only around 5 to 7 percent, compared to the rate of 50 percent in traditional American marriages.

Research by multiple groups has found that there are large groups of young people in our country who don't believe in monogamy, don't believe in the reality of committed relationships, and don't really plan to marry.[21] These young people tend to have sex earlier in life, and they engage in more casual sex, hooking up, rather than pursuing intense, committed, intimate relationships. Many of them grew up in families of divorced parents and have told me that they experienced so much turmoil in their lives as children, living through their parents' divorces, shuttling back and forth between homes and families, that they don't want to put their own children through it, if they even have children. Others have told me that they know that they are enough like their parents that they don't think they could necessarily do any better, and thus they would just like to avoid the whole mess. They see marriage as a temporary relationship as opposed to the expectation of lifelong monogamous marriage that is the norm enforced by the sex addiction movement. In a comprehensive study of college students and casual sex, researchers found that over 20 percent of respondents who were in a committed, ostensibly monogamous relationship admitted to sexual infidelity in the past year.[22]

Openly nonmonogamous relationships are also a growing trend, particularly among the young, fueled by the wide access to electronic social networking. But according to the field of sex addiction, such relationships are inherently unhealthy, and the treatment goal for a sex addict is to learn to incorporate the value that "healthy sexuality must center on the development of an intimate sexual relationship with one partner."[23]

SWINGERS

Swingers, people who routinely have open, consensual sex with people other than their spouses, almost universally keep their sexual activities secret, except from other swingers, due to fear of stigma and rejection. But despite this stigma, research shows that swingers are not mentally disturbed, addicted to drugs, or hippies embracing the concepts of free love long after the end of the sixties. Instead, they tend to be normal, politically conservative, white, middle-class couples with professional backgrounds who value their marriages as much as nonswingers. Where do they differ from nonswingers? According to researcher Richard Jenks, who was one of the first academicians to really look closely at this sexual subgroup, they tend to be people with a high libido who are liberal in sexual attitudes and low in jealousy. Their libido and low jealousy lead them to be comfortable with the idea of stepping outside monogamy within their marriage, and their liberal attitudes toward sexual roles make it easier for them to reject social mandates on marriage. The majority of swingers (who are still swinging) report that their extracurricular sexual activities have actually improved their marriages, and that monogamy was not critical for the health or well-being of their relationship.

"Our sensual appetite is healthier/stronger than the average person. We have incredible endurance. We experience life at a totally different level than anyone else. Our fantasies come true! It's euphoric and addictive. You get a high from the lifestyle. You get a high from life. I am in the lifestyle because I am intellectually stimulated by its members, and physically stimulated through participation."[24]

Swingers have been around for many decades, pursuing sex with other married couples outside the bounds of monogamy. But proponents of polyamory represent a movement that has only taken off in the past twenty years or so, and who argue for the freedom to have "many loves," rather than just sex. Those in polyamory argue for the development of relationships that involve love and sex and intimacy, with more than one person at a time. The polyamory movement is led by mainly female authors and public speakers, including psychologist Deborah Anapol, PhD, author and educator Mim Chapman, and poet and activist Wendy O'Matik. These polyamorous women argue that their rejection of monogamy does not reflect pathology or illness, and in fact represents their commitment toward ethics, instead of engaging in serial monogamy or infidelity. They are choosing to be in control of their lives, their sexuality, and themselves, through an acceptance of themselves, rather than merely accepting the social expectations placed upon them.

The Ethical Slut

Janet Hardy is a self-described "mass of seeming contradictions: mother and slut, dominatrix and homebody, intellectual and showtune queen. . . . Janet has traveled the world as a speaker and teacher on topics ranging from ethical multipartner relationships to erotic spanking and beyond."[25]

In her book *The Ethical Slut*, Hardy describes her life of conscious choices to pursue bisexuality, nonmonogamy, and sexual fulfillment, in violation of many of society's norms regarding sex in general, but especially female sexuality. Hardy never felt that her sexual behaviors were out of her control, even though she was once labeled a sex addict by a friend. In *The Ethical Slut*, the authors write, "Sex-addict' seems to be the latest incarnation of cultural judgment about sluts: a good friend of Janet's once told her, quite seriously, that the reason Janet was so contented was that she was a sex addict who had managed to find a way to make a lifestyle out of her addiction." This shows the subjectivity and morally driven nature of the sex addiction label; even though Hardy has been successful, healthy, and happy, with no evidence of distress or impairment related to her sexuality, she is still labeled a sex addict, on the grounds of her high libido and poor record of conformity with sociosexual norms. Janet was kind enough to describe to me a bit more about her reaction and thoughts to being labeled a sex addict:

> I think what struck me about the comment at the time was its circularity—I was a sex addict, in the speaker's worldview, because I had built my life around exploring and teaching sex, and I had built my life around teaching and exploring sex because I was a sex addict. There were no cracks around the edges of the paradigm, no way to be a sex professional (in any sense of the word, from a PhD in human sexuality to a crack whore) without falling into the abyss of "addiction." Except, perhaps, to make my living doing and writing about sex, but without enjoying it—that might be the only way out.[26]

This changing expectation of monogamy is not necessarily restricted just to young people either. In a recent survey by the American Association of Retired Persons, only around 22 percent of respondents felt that infidelity was wrong, compared with a rate of 41 percent when this question was assessed in 1999.[27] A study at the University of Iowa suggests that as many as one-third of the relationships in large urban areas like Chicago are not sexually exclusive, and one out of every ten relationships involves both male and female partners having sex with others outside the relationship. Sociologist Anthony Paik describes that couples in the United States have "seen a major shift towards nonromantic sexual partnerships." In Paik's study, more women than men reported that they had been sexually monogamous while their male partner had not been, but equal numbers of men and women reported being involved in mutually nonmonogamous relationships, where both they and their partners were sexually involved with others.[28]

There is an assumption in the sex addiction field that heterosexual monogamy is the healthiest form of sexual relationship. But this is an argument that has never been tested and reveals a substantial ethnocentric bias. Multiple studies conducted over the past few decades show that therapists and the mental health field in general have negative and judgmental views of any marriages that are not centered around an assumption of monogamy. When asked, such therapists predict failure for said relationships and automatically attribute the desire and motivation for nonmonogamy to a history of pathology, typically sexual abuse. People who approach therapists and are involved in swinging, polyamory, or open marriages are often met with incredulity and scorn.

I've seen numerous women and men who have shared that they have not told their doctors or therapists about their alternative sexual relationships due to fear of condemnation, or due to the rejection they've already experienced when they were open about their marriages. Other "kink-aware professionals" report the same thing.[29] What this creates is a sample bias. The clinicians see only those couples who cannot keep their sexual behaviors or lifestyles secret, or who come in for some other unrelated pathology. The clinicians do not see the many folks who do not need or want treatment, and who are leading normal healthy lives, even as they engage in alternative sexual and relational practices. A similar pattern is evident in the history of acceptance of homosexuality and acknowledgment of the many healthy and successful people whose sexuality was invisible to society until they started coming out in support of their community. Until we have greater levels of understanding about the wide ranges of human sexual expression and better training and education of therapists about this range of sexual expression, the mental health field is at risk to continue to apply values and assumptions rather than evidence-based treatment.

Case Example

Jason is a fifty-two-year-old manager of a grocery store, currently in his third marriage. Jason has two grown children from his first marriage. His first marriage ended as a result of his wife's discovery of his many years of infidelity and pornography use. Jason's second marriage was to a woman that he had been having an affair with for about five years. Jason's second wife divorced him after one year of marriage and proclaimed that he was a sex addict. "Things changed once we were married," he said. "While we were having an affair, we had lots of sex, all kinds of sex, and even had a couple of threesomes with other people. We even talked about swinging and going to swing clubs. We had a swinger's ad together, with pictures of both of us, though we never met anybody from the ad. But it was like she did a bait and switch on me. Once we got married, all that stuff changed. She wouldn't even talk about swinging, wouldn't watch porn with me, wouldn't do threesomes anymore. But I had enough of that in my first marriage," Jason shared, shaking his head. "I married young, right out of high school, to my high school sweetheart. I had no sexual experience before, and we had kids early, and I started working. The Internet opened a whole new world to me. I didn't know there were people out there that felt like me, that saw sex as fun, as a game, without all the heavy stuff of love and commitment. My first wife couldn't go there at all. We had sex once a month, with the lights off. My second wife was good to go at first, but all that changed. She really did a number on me and made me really question myself, and why I wanted the kind of sex that I want, with people I don't know, who are just there to have fun, to swing and swap. I got really depressed during our marriage when I realized that if I stayed married to her, that wasn't going to be on the table. I finally had to say that if we weren't going to swing together, I was going to do it by myself. She called me a sex addict, and so did the couples' therapist that we went to, saying that I needed to grow up and accept that grown-up sex is really what I need." Jason laughed, shaking his head. "Maybe I'm immature, but you know what? I ain't getting any younger. And I finally decided that this was so important to me that I had to pursue it." Jason and his second wife divorced, and he began to explore the swinging lifestyle, at first as a single male, then with a woman he met and then married, who was already a swinger. "She's a perfect mate for me. She had kids a long time ago too, and she views sex as fun. She's been swinging for a long time. Her first husband died, but she kept swinging. We go to clubs together and have a great time. If I'm a sex addict, then she is too. But since we're together, it works."

LESBIAN, GAY, BISEXUAL, AND TRANSGENDER (LGBT) ISSUES

Historically, the labels of hypersexual and disordered sexualities were often applied to men who had sex with men. Homosexual and bisexual men do sometimes engage in anonymous sexual behaviors with multiple partners, outside of established relationships. Some evolutionary scientists suggest that these behaviors reveal some of the core male sexual drive toward casual promiscuity, when the confines of social values, reproductive issues, and female sexual values are removed from the equation. Others often see this behavior in far less objective terms.

Dr. Charlotte Kasl suggests that, "while some gay men have long-term committed relationships, it is not uncommon for many of them to have five hundred to a thousand partners, perhaps several in one night at a 'bathhouse,' where sex is routinely purveyed as a soulless, emotionless, genital-only event." Kasl goes on to point out that "lesbian women generally have fewer than eight partners and are far more likely to have long-term committed relationships."[30]

I suspect that Dr. Kasl has never actually gone to a bathhouse, nor has she had much anonymous gay sex. I've known committed gay male couples who regularly go to bathhouses together, where they enjoy having sex with other men before the couple returns home together. I've also treated gay men who developed deep relationships and friendships with men they met at bathhouses. For decades, gay bathhouses have been a central if underground part of the male homosexual culture, serving a role that the homosexual community identifies as valuable and important for their identity. To simply label the activities of a stigmatized community as "soulless" is a value judgment, not a clinical or medical one. If Dr. Kasl wants to advocate against gay sex in bathhouses because she thinks it is immoral, fine. But let's not masquerade this as a medical or therapeutic prescription.

Substantial research has also shown that the Internet has become a main way for people to develop an identity as LGBT, as well as those who are "questioning" or just regard themselves as sexually "different." Gay men are far more likely than most other groups to report use of pornography. A consistent finding is that porn (particularly Internet porn) is used by more LGBT men and women, proportionately, compared to heterosexuals.[31] The reason for this seems to be the role that the Internet plays in allowing safe and private sexual expression, and in providing a safe environment for sexual and gender identity to develop for LGBT and questioning people, particularly those in rural environments who have social pressures limiting their identity development and sexual behaviors.[32] In many gay males, as part of the normal stages of coming out and accepting and expressing their homosexuality, they go through a period of sexual promiscuity.[33] Some have suggested that this is an expression of "normative adolescent hypersexuality" emerging in adulthood as males express feelings and needs later in life, feelings that were delayed or suppressed by the social stigma against homosexuality.[34]

Some research has found that those gay men with higher levels of sexual preoccupation and a greater tendency to intentionally choose not to inhibit their sexual behaviors were more likely to be at risk of contracting HIV and to put their partners at risk.[35] I've seen and treated a number of such men, gay men who engage in anonymous, no-strings-attached sex and seek out situations where they can cut loose in sexual "playgrounds." These individuals identify and acknowledge that they like to just let themselves go and give in to "abandon" in their sexual behaviors. "I don't like to think too much in these situations. I go to the bathhouse to just let go, to have wild sex with anybody. I turn off those filters that we have in the real world, about whether somebody is attractive, or whether I would date them or not. It's just about having raw sex," one man told me. As a result, these men are more likely to contract HIV. Because of their sexual behaviors? No, because of their risky, dangerous, and foolish choices to relinquish self-control in situations that are dangerous, like not wearing a seatbelt while driving in a stock-car race.

Monogamy is not a value or expectation that is universal or even widely practiced in homosexual relationships, even lifelong relationships. A great deal of research with gay male couples has found that gay couples are far more likely than heterosexual couples to have agreements to allow sex with outside partners, either in the form of threesomes and group sex, or in the form of outside relationships by one or both parties. This is far more prevalent in gay male couples and less common in lesbian couples. Monogamy in these couples, and the nature of their relationships, is a fluid and individualized concept, with "a relative meaning that each couple defines for themselves," in some cases with couples describing themselves as monogamous but still having sex in some situations with men outside the relationship. "We're sexual beings; that's who we are. And there are differences between sex and intimacy, making love. It can be two different things." These couples make their arrangements work by setting conditions that focus "on the requirement that there be honesty, respect, or discretion around having sex with outside partners."[36]

Physicist, author, and *Newsweek* science editor Charles Panati writes that, "for our gay friends in relationships of fifteen years or more, monogamy without fidelity is the rule, not the exception," going on to explain that such a relationship allows both long-term stability and, at the same time, the "carnal pleasure of a new affair." Panati argues that by separating sexual fidelity, gay couples are able to experience stronger, more stable relationships than are available to many heterosexual couples.[37]

During the 2011 Gay Pride activities in Los Angeles, sex addiction guru Robert Weiss was interviewed about his views of homosexuality. Weiss admirably tried to phrase things in an accepting, nonjudgmental manner, acknowledging that men, and gay men, have more sex with less demand for relationship, and less guilt, and that this is just a result of "how we're built." He acknowledged that the gay community is more accepting of sex in general, and of nonmonogamous relationships. But he argued that intimacy and attachment were still necessary for truly healthy relationships and well-being, and he suggested that the sex positive openness of the gay community could mask or hide sex addiction and ultimately be harmful.[38] Even when the field of sex addiction tries to be open to other values, it still applies and embeds critical ethnocentric values about the role of sexuality in relationships.

Case Example

Donald, a forty-two-year-old gay male who is white and HIV positive, has struggled with monogamy all his life. He's been in an allegedly monogamous relationship for around five years, but he had sex with men outside the relationship on two different occasions. The second time happened when Donald stopped at an adult bookstore one evening and had sex with an anonymous man in one of the video booths. When Donald walked out of the store, he found his partner waiting. His partner had seen Donald's car and had stopped to wait for him.

"Oh it was horrible. I was so embarrassed, and he was so hurt, and I was so ashamed." But as the couple worked through the effects of this event, Donald took responsibility for his behaviors and the issues that had contributed to his choice to have sex with another man. "I broke the agreement (monogamy), and it had horrible consequences. But even then, I just thought, 'You know what? This isn't going to work for me this way. And that's what I was trying to say. . . . I've come to this

realization that a relationship works because it works, not because it's like we've just seen in a book or a movie. And I think my partner is still hankering after that, but little by little he's realizing that what we have in some way is way better, I hope." The couple examined their relationship and their choices. They decided to make new agreements for their relationship, ones that didn't include a mandate for sexual monogamy but did include the need for honesty, respect, and safety.

In 1979, Donald Symons suggested that examination of the sexual lives of male homosexuals was revealing of what core masculine sexuality was, with the restraining influences of females and society removed. His argument was that gay men behave sexually the way all men want to but cannot, because women won't let them. If women were interested in group sex and orgies and anonymous sex in bathrooms, then heterosexual men would be having those activities just as much as gay men.[39] When we compare homosexual males to lesbians and heterosexual couples, we find that homosexual male couples maintain sexual activity more than heterosexual couples do, and many times more than lesbian couples do. In heterosexual couples and lesbian couples, there is a decline in sexual frequency across the length of a relationship, but this same decline is much less steep in male homosexual relationships, suggesting a significant difference in the level of male desire across a relationship.[40]

MSTW

Little research has examined men who seek out sex with transgendered women (MSTW), women who were born as men. There is a huge Internet following and sexual preference of men who fantasize about and pursue "chicks with dicks," or transgendered males, who have used hormone and breast implant treatments to give themselves the bodies of women while retaining their penis and testicles. This fetish is referred to as "gynandromorphophilia." Transsexual pornography is rated higher in Internet searches than is pornography featuring "celebrities" or "Asians," and it is most frequently sought out by self-identified heterosexual men.[41] Men who pursue transgendered women for sex seem to fall into two groups: those who regard themselves as "straight" and those who report being "bisexual." The key difference is in what the man does or thinks about the transgendered woman's penis. The "straight" men actively try to not think about the fact that the person they're with, receiving oral sex from, or perhaps performing anal sex on has a penis. These men try to cognitively distance themselves from their partners' penis, both physically and mentally.

The bisexual-identified men interact, physically and mentally, with their partners' penis. They say that these transgendered women are their sexual ideal, having breasts and the bodies of a woman, combined with the penis of a man. These bi men sometimes perform oral sex on their transgendered partners, as well as receive it.

Some very interesting research with these men suggests that they are looking for casual sex with women who "act like a man in a woman's body." These men describe these transgendered women as being freer, bawdier, and more explicit than women usually are. In bars that are dedicated to the hooking up of men and transgendered women, these transgendered women are often sexually aggressive, reaching out and fondling men, and working hard to make the men "feel wanted." They compliment the men's bodies and looks and interact explicitly with the men's sexuality in a way that women often do not. In contrast to female prostitutes, these transgendered sex workers are described as more warm, friendly, and accepting, and less caustic. "They make you think you have a big cock, even when you don't," said one man interviewed in a "tranny" bar.[42]

When the AIDS crisis hit the male homosexual community, they pulled together in the best tradition of men throughout history. The homosexual community embraced safe sex, and even today, a sexually active homosexual male is nearly three times more likely to use a condom than his straight counterpart. Gay men started social outreach efforts including counseling programs and peer-support efforts, providing meals on wheels to their sick brethren, and starting hospices and home assistance programs to take care of their own. "Their quiet and necessary heroism has humanized and *masculinized* [italics in original] gay men in the eyes of many of their fellow citizens. They had a job to do, and they did it."[43] The differences in the sexual practices of homosexual men had no impact on their empathy, commitment to one another, or their ability to love themselves and each other.

A recent research study in Canada suggests that the people at greatest risk for depression and suicide are sexual minorities who are leading celibate lives. As they suppress their sexualities to conform to social pressures, they are at great risk for severe depression and anguish. Similarly, high rates of depression, anxiety, and mental struggles in lesbian, bisexual, gay, and transgender groups are not believed to reflect the effects of their sexuality but are understood as resulting from internalization of the conflicts between a person's sexuality and the expectations and demands of their society.

The American Psychological Association has taken a strong stand against the practice of using therapy to attempt to convert homosexuals into heterosexuals. This practice, called sexual orientation change efforts (SOCE), or conversion therapy, is driven by faith-based organizations that identify homosexual behavior as a sin, reflective of spiritual and moral failings. The APA created a task force to review the research and practices of SOCE, which found that the research cited by these organizations lacks sufficient rigor or validity to adequately prove that their efforts are successful at changing sexual orientation, and that their efforts only truly appeared to have an effect with people who had behaved in a bisexual manner, rather than those with primary homosexual attractions and behaviors. Changes that were linked to the SOCE were temporary at best, and there were potentially harmful effects, especially upon children and adolescents with sexual minority identifications. The APA set forth a resolution decrying the efforts of changing the sexual orientation of individuals and condemning the use of psychological research and techniques by those in religious/faith-based groups when they are using psychology to justify or excuse their efforts to condemn and change people's sexual behaviors.[44]

Multiple studies reveal that feelings of depression and rates of suicide in LGBTQ populations are predicted not by the individuals' sexuality but by the interaction between their sexuality and their environment. When such individuals live in communities and families that are not accepting of alternative sexualities, rates of depression and suicide attempts are higher.[45] The personal and emotional struggles of some high-libido individuals who enter sex addiction treatment may also emerge from the conflict between their society, their moral and religious values, and their internal desire for sex. This hypothesis is supported by the low rates of social and emotional conflicts in highly sexual individuals in sex-positive cultures, such as the Polynesian islands. This is in fact confirmed increasingly by research such as that of Jason Winters, which finds that those individuals with high libido and high religious values are more likely to seek sex addiction treatment to resolve their internal feelings of conflict.

Case Example

Since age twenty-three, Don has had difficulty controlling a certain behavior, which affects his sleep and fills most of his days, often doing it for much longer than he intended. When he first started, Don was able to limit this activity to a few hours a day. But over time, the role it plays in his life has grown, and he now finds himself actively absorbed in this activity for as much as eleven or twelve hours a day. In the past, Don was able to take breaks from this activity, on weekends and at night. But technology, such as the Internet and cell phones, have made it much more difficult for Don to separate himself and control his immersion in this behavior. Don is now thirty-five and married, with three children. When they married, Tina wasn't aware of the degree to which this behavior controlled her husband. For a long time, he was able to keep it within limits and to restrain his urges, out of respect for Tina. But as stress in his life increases, Don has less control over it and he fights with his wife about it more frequently. Don shares that he feels guilty about it: "I was at my daughter's First Holy Communion, and I found myself in the bathroom, on the phone. I'd like to make it stop, but I don't see how anymore. I can't imagine a life without it."

Don is not a sex addict, but a workaholic. Since he began working as an accountant, Don has devoted more and more of his life to his work. He stays at the office long hours every day. He uses his cell phone and e-mail to continue working from home. Don has tolerance for work, as his capacity and stamina, his ability to stay productive and focused at work, have all grown with practice and experience. When he takes days off from work, he gets nervous and anxious and often has to check his e-mail just to get a "fix."

Don's decade of work has irrevocably altered his brain. His brain adapted to the demands of his work, and he is now able to process complex situations more quickly. Every task accomplished and success achieved at work sends a thrill of neurochemicals through his brain, washing his mind in a bath of pleasing dopamine, oxytocin, and testosterone, all of which combine to lead him on to seeking that next brain chemical high.

Don's overinvolvement at work is unmistakably resulting in social distress and consequences. Tina is threatening to leave him and would rather be divorced than married to a husband she never sees.

So why isn't "workaholism" an addictive behavior? If it was, it would be far more prevalent than sexual addiction. But in current Western values, productivity and the "work ethic" are highly valued. Nowadays, workaholism is known as the "respectable addiction."

The field of mental health treatment is a powerful tool in society's arsenal of efforts to create conformity and control. Like many others, I am concerned that our society has taken the therapeutic couch and used it to replace the diminishing power of the confessional and the pulpit over our citizens' behaviors. Because the science behind sex addiction is so weak, there is enormous potential for misuse of this diagnosis to label, pathologize, and stigmatize the sexual behaviors of individuals who experience social judgment and censure. Historically, the mental health profession inappropriately applied stigma to the LGBT population, and current research suggests that applying the sex addiction diagnostic model would further stigmatize LGBT individuals, as well as those who come from cultures or subgroups with different attitudes toward sexuality.

Julie, a social worker in a psychiatric hospital, shared with me the following: "When we admit a person who is gay or lesbian or transgender, I always get pressure from other people on the team to label the person as hypersexual. It's not that they have done anything on the unit, but people, even doctors, are afraid that just because the patient is LGBT, they are going to act out sexually in the hospital. I've refused to do it, to label these people as hypersexual, and was really blown away that doctors and nurses were using the hypersexual label as a way to isolate these patients."

> Perhaps we should start to contemplate the meaning of our
> society's "addiction" to addiction terminology.
> —William Henkin, PhD[46]

The number of things that we are potentially at risk of becoming addicted to is a staggering list, which makes one wonder if there is anything out there that is not seen as potentially addictive. I polled friends, colleagues, and the Internet to put together the partial list below of things that are alleged to be addictive. Excluding things like alcohol, drugs, caffeine, and nicotine, here is a list of the things that we are told we can become addicted to:

Aggression
Anime
Applause
Arson
Attention
Body building
Body modification
Bottled water
Carbohydrates
Chat rooms
Chewing gum
Chili sauce
Chocolate
Cinnamon toothpicks
Cleaning
Clutter
Collecting
Coupons
Credit cards
Daydreaming
Diuretics
E-mail
Exercise
Food (of any kind)
Gambling
Gossip
Harry Potter

High-fructose corn
   syrup
Hoarding
Internet
Junk food
Laxatives
Lip balm
Love
Lying
Marathon running
Massively multiplayer
   online role-playing
   games
Masturbation
Messiness (there is a
   twelve-step group
   for "messyholics")
Money
Oil (according to
   former President
   George W. Bush,
   the nation is "ad-
   dicted to oil")
Online auctions
Over-the-counter
   nasal sprays
Plastic surgery

Piercings
Politics
Reading
Reality shows
Relationships
Religion
Risky behaviors
Role-playing games
Self-help/support groups
Self-mutilation
Shoplifting
Shopping
Sleep
Smartphones
Soap operas
Social online media
Stealing
Sugar
Tanning beds
Tattooing
Television
Texting
Twinkies
Video games
Violence
Vulgarity (cussing)
Work

The true meaning of this never-ending list of pseudoaddictions is that society *is* addicted all right, to the concept of addiction itself. Once, addiction meant only a few things. But our tolerance grew, and society needed more and more addictions to feed our cravings. If we try to stop, we go into withdrawal, unable to find any way to distract ourselves from responsibility, unable to avoid the consequences of our choices. We use the concept of addiction more every day, despite our growing knowledge that it is destroying our culture, our legal system, and our ability to hold ourselves responsible. Our brains are changed, affected by the neurochemical rushes we get from seeing people on television whose lives have been destroyed by their addictions. We get that rush from our voyeuristic insight into the suffering of others, from the joy and jealousy of watching the mighty fall, and from the relief that it's not us up there watching our lives and successes crumble.

The sex addictionologists are right in a sense. We do live in an "addictive culture." The addiction lies in our society's desire to label problematic behaviors as addictive and compulsive. Where and when do we stop exactly? Where is the twelve-step group that our society can attend to confess its powerlessness over this addiction to addiction and begin to reassert individual responsibility?

—✥—

"The DSM is converting nearly all life's stresses and bad habits into mental disorders. Almost everything we feel and do is listed somewhere in the DSM as an indicator of some dread disorder. This has the effect of creating and trying to enforce social values on the basis of scientific evidence that most people in the field admit is rather weak and unconvincing."[47]

8

Morality and Law

The picture of compulsive sexual behaviors is far more complicated than (male) brain + (nonmonogamous) sexual stimulation = addiction. Dopamine may indeed play a role in all compulsive behaviors, but the narrative of porn as an external factor that takes over your system is a false (and overwhelmingly Christian) explanation that fails to recognize sexual histories and user conceptions of sexuality.[1]

$\mathcal{T}$here is a long history of laws related to sexual behaviors, prohibiting sexual crimes such as rape and sexual abuse. But there is an even longer history of laws and social restrictions on sexual behaviors that do not represent crimes, as we think of them today, but are behaviors that society judges to be immoral or unacceptable. At the same time that these sexual behaviors were declared illegal, they were often also declared evidence of mental illness. These behaviors included masturbation, sodomy, infidelity, and homosexuality, all acts that have now been decriminalized and "demedicalized" in most parts of the United States.

If we accept the evidence presented in chapter 7 that the concept of sex addiction is one that is imbued with cultural morals and social values, then it leads to the question of which morals and which social values. In Western culture, one must acknowledge the huge influence that two social forces have upon our behaviors and lives, most especially our sexual lives. These two influencing forces include the institutions of religion and law.

RELIGION AND SEX ADDICTION

Douglas Weiss is the president of the American Association for Sex Addiction Therapy, one of the leading proponents of sexual addiction, and a favorite of the media, having appeared on numerous television shows, from *The Oprah Winfrey Show* and *Good Morning America* to *The 700 Club*, and a special movie on the Lifetime Channel. Before earning a PhD in psychology, Weiss earned dual master's degrees in divinity and counseling at Southwestern Baptist Theological Seminary. He is the author of numerous books, including *The Final Freedom: Pioneering Sexual Addiction Recovery.*

According to his writings, Doug Weiss himself once suffered from addiction to porn and sex, some twenty-two years ago. Currently, he runs a treatment center in Colorado, which offers a wide range of treatment options to sex addicts, their spouses, and now even their children, offering therapy programs specifically for the adult and teen children of parents who were sex addicts, in the model of Al-Anon, and under the premise that the unique patterns of parenting in sex addicts can lead to unique and treatable problems in their children. Though Weiss's website at Heart to Heart Counseling Center does not make overt Christian or spiritual references, it is important to remember that Weiss earned his degrees in a seminary and specifically defines some of his books as "Christian 12-Step Workbooks."[2] Though Weiss does not normally refer to the Christian aspects of his work when he is cited by the national media in reference to public scandals, Christian principles are prominent in his therapeutic approaches. He has recommended that sex addicts pursue the "Five Commandments" in their road to recovery from sex addiction, advocating that addicts

1. Pray in the morning.
2. Read recovery literature daily.
3. Call someone in recovery daily.
4. Attend twelve-step meetings.
5. Pray again, and thank God daily for sobriety.[3]

Sex Addiction Down Under

Peter Madden is a pastor and self-professed former sex addict running for political office in Sydney, Australia. With the campaign promise that he will "clean up" the immorality of the city, namely the activities of the LGBT population, including the annual Mardi Gras parade, Madden has been attacked as a hypocrite of the first order. Madden acknowledges his hypocrisy and admits that even after he became a pastor, he was secretly indulging in Internet pornography and covert visits to prostitutes. Madden has claimed that he was sexually abused by an older female during much of his childhood and that this history "put seeds of lust" into his life and heart. Through his religious beliefs, Madden overcame his sexual desires and temptations. But

Madden wants to prevent others from suffering the same torments he faced by ridding the city of the forces of "moral depravity." If elected, Madden promises to go after the red-light district of Sydney, where he himself spent so much time, and to do "spiritual battle against the darkness."[4]

───── ❧ ─────

LIFE Ministries is a Christian group focused specifically upon battling sexual addiction. On their website, they describe themselves this way: "L.I.F.E. Ministries is a Christ-centered sexual addiction recovery ministry that provides the Christian community with structure, support, & resources to battle sexual addiction."[5] They further describe that they are "globalizing God's army to battle sexual addiction." The group lists over 250 support groups worldwide affiliated with their mission.

Interestingly enough, when you compare their mission statements to those of the Spirit of Freedom Ministries, "a ministry in family alcoholism, tobacco and other drugs," there is a less moralistically embattled flavor in the ministry dedicated to treating the addiction of alcoholism. The Spirit of Freedom Ministry's website talks about "bringing families together" and helping those dealing with chemical addictions to find hope, freedom, and a new identity.[6] Similarly, the Cancer Ministry states their mission thus: "Our mission is to empower you through knowledge to make a well-informed decision as to how you deal with this diagnosis."[7] So why are Christian advocacy and intervention organizations "empowering" those with cancer and alcoholism but "battling" against sexual addiction? Perhaps the answer lies in the LIFE Ministry's explanation of sex addiction: "All humans have a need for God. There is a hole in each one of us that only He can fill. The sexual addict may use his or her addiction in place of true spirituality—sex becomes the addict's God. It comforts, celebrates, and is always available or present." Crystal Renaud runs "Dirty Girls Ministries" and the "Victory over Porn" therapy group for women. She says that "God created sex. But the enemy has twisted it."[8] In the sixteenth century, sexuality was declared the primary way through which the devil gained influence over women, turning them into witches. Today, the same argument underlies the opposition to pornography, and many aspects of sexuality. Sex addiction has become a moral battle within our culture, a battle against the sin of sexuality, not a medical or psychological health problem.

───── ❧ ─────

Case Example

Religious Sexual Addiction
In May 2011, thirty-year-old New Zealander Nathaniel Enright was convicted of fifty-one sexual charges, including sexually molesting eight teenage girls and trying

to procure other children as young as twelve. Enright was raised in a religious sect called "The Family International," also known as the "Children of God," where adults were encouraged and allowed to have sex with children once the children reached puberty.

During the trial, Enright's attorneys presented a psychological evaluation which described that he had a "compulsive addiction to sex as the result of his religious upbringing," and at sentencing, presiding Judge Samios stated that Enright was "addicted to sex." According to the judge, this addiction "resulted in Enright taking opportunistic and indiscriminate steps to secure sexual partners."[9]

Pastor Craig Gross started the XXX Church in Las Vegas, Nevada, to lead a spiritual campaign against the influence of sex and pornography, preaching to porn stars, strippers, and sex addicts. Gross and his ministry declare that porn is the "#1 most destructive force in our culture." The XXX Church's website also suggests that homosexuality is something to be "diagnosed," something that is a result of the tolerance effect of pornography use as people "seek something different." According to Gross's site, porn-related homosexuality is something to be conquered in order to free people from "the bondage of sexual sin."[10]

The role of religion in mental health is a complex and politically charged issue. The field of behavioral health, and particularly the treatment of alcohol and drug addictions, is currently acknowledging the very real need for spiritual components in treatment and changing people's lives. However, when the issue of sexuality is involved, the role of religious values becomes far more charged and fraught with problems.

In 2011, British psychotherapist Leslie Pilkington had her clinical license suspended and incurred large financial sanctions for attempting to "convert" a gay man. An undercover gay journalist, Patrick Strudwick, visited Pilkington, and she informed him that his homosexuality was evidence of mental illness, a form of addiction, and something that could be cured through the power of religion. In Strudwick's words, Pilkington then proceeded to try to "pray away the gay," praying with and over Strudwick during counseling sessions and giving him prayers to recite when he experienced homosexual attractions.

When Strudwick's reports of his undercover investigation were released, Britain's licensing board undertook an investigation of Pilkington and found that she "had allowed her personal preconceived views about gay lifestyle and sexual orientation to affect her professional relationship in a way that was prejudicial."[11] Pilkington's use of religious principles in the course of professional service was judged to have interfered in her ability to empathize with her clients and led to her providing dogmatic, unprofessional service that ended up as malpractice.

Christian views of sexuality and sexual expression often result in conflicts with the science and practice of medicine as they relate to sexuality, in areas such as abortion, homosexuality, divorce, and so forth. And thus the significant, enmeshed role of religion in the field of sexual addiction raises troubling questions. The weakness and morally driven subjective nature of the research on sexual addiction offers little defense against moral values overriding empirical data. As a result, the concepts of sex addiction are laden with culturally determined values about sexuality driven by moral and religious dogma, not by scientific data or medical facts. Remember that those individuals most prone to seeking treatment for sex addiction are those who have high levels of sexual libido *and* high levels of religious values, which appears to cause internal conflicts that drive them toward treatment for sex addiction.[12]

Christianity has been increasingly "feminized" over the past century, with greater numbers of women attending church and participating in religious teachings and congregations. The values of modern Christianity are described by some as representing a meeker, milder version of religion that men do not connect with. "Many Christian men feel spiritually inadequate and sense that they lost something somewhere along the way, but they just don't know what it is. They lost their own manhood. In becoming 'Christianized' they thought they had to give up being a man and become more like their mother and wife."[13] David Murrow wrote *Why Men Hate Going to Church*, addressing these very issues, and he agrees that men don't see current Christian values as consistent with their view of masculinity. "Christianity based on risk avoidance will never attract men. If our message is full of don'ts, be careful's, and play it safe's, men will turn their backs."[14] Addressing sexual problems mostly in males with religious values that are not popular with many men raises further significant questions about the effectiveness and appropriateness of using faith-based organizations to address sexual problems, whether these organizations are churches or self-help groups.

The role of religion in the treatment and theories of sex addiction is a significant one, and an issue that must be considered as we evaluate the validity of this concept. In chapter 4, I described the New Life Ministry, an organization that makes around $9 million a year providing training, interventions, and materials to "battle" sex addiction. Religion and religious values are deeply embedded in the concept of sex addiction, and before society accepts this diagnosis as dogma, we must carefully examine the forces and motivations that drive it. In Ontario, a sex addiction therapist runs his practice out of an office within the Christian Victory Church.[15] And in 2011, a sex addiction treatment certification program began operation on the campus of a Christian faith-based university.[16] These are just a few examples, out of many, that highlight the critical role that conservative Christian groups play in the sexual addiction field. This isn't to suggest that spirituality and health care shouldn't mix; in fact, much work is now being done to increase the holistic and spiritual nature of behavioral health. But, given the complex moral messages about sexuality that are imbued in Christian traditions, one must be cautious about the risk of those moral values seeping into a mental health approach, as has occurred in sex addiction.

> "What kind of disease is this for which the
> best available treatment is religion?"[17]

One of the strongest criticisms of the twelve-step movement is its inherent religiosity. Courts have strongly supported the notion that Alcoholics Anonymous (AA) and its brethren reflect an organization that is religious in nature. Multiple federal and state courts have found that AA and Narcotics Anonymous are religion-based organizations, due to their principles and practice. As a result, when judges, parole officers, and courts mandate that an individual participate in addiction-recovery programs, they may not mandate only AA or NA but must offer secular, nonreligious options.[18]

I'm not suggesting that twelve-step groups are ineffective, nor am I challenging their principles. I am in fact an advocate of their impact and usefulness and frequently refer clients to their programs. Within the substance abuse treatment programs I supervise, we see that clients who participate in these programs do better, when combined with our treatment, than those who do treatment alone. But when it comes to sex addiction, the nature of their approach and organization indicates that the problem they are best organized to treat is not a medical issue but a moral one. Just because someone benefits from attending twelve-step groups designed to treat sexual addiction does not mean they ever actually had sex addiction. It just means that some components in that group or program helped them to take responsibility for their choices and lives in a way they were not doing before. In my opinion, that's a good thing. It's just not a diagnosis, nor evidence of a medical disorder or a disease.

Case Example

Cheryl is a forty-seven-year-old woman who sought treatment for sex addiction upon the suggestion of her husband Phil. Cheryl was already attending Alcoholics Anonymous, Narcotics Anonymous, and Nicotine Anonymous. Cheryl had been participating in the groups with the very strong encouragement of her husband, who was a self-identified alcoholic in AA with twenty years of sobriety.

Cheryl had been married three times before her marriage to Phil, and she had extramarital affairs in all three marriages, usually when drinking. As she worked through the twelve-step process, she told Phil about these affairs for the first time. Though she told him she had not been tempted during their marriage or since getting sober, Phil became concerned that her infidelity was a sign of sex addiction. Cheryl attended some Sex Addicts Anonymous meetings but did not find them as helpful as her other twelve-step meetings, and so she sought out a therapist in her area to do work with around her sexuality.

Her therapist told her quite clearly that he was not a strong supporter of the twelve-step approach, especially concerning sexuality. However, Cheryl liked the therapist and felt that he understood her better than she had expected. In the first session, she admitted to her therapist that though Phil did not know it, she had in fact already had an affair during their marriage during a particularly tense part of their relationship. Over the course of the therapy, Cheryl and her therapist were able to trace Cheryl's interests and history in extramarital sex to a deep and long-standing anxiety that she felt about being dependent upon another person. Throughout her life, they found that when Cheryl was feeling frightened that her husband or boyfriend might abandon her or be unreliable, she would often have an affair. These affairs were a way for her to feel less dependent, less vulnerable, and even to have a "backup plan" of an alternate male partner should her primary partner in fact leave. As Cheryl and her therapist began to work on these fears, and on her anxiety issues in general, her fear, and her husband's, that her sexuality was out of control began to diminish. Though Cheryl did not disclose to Phil that she'd had an affair early in their marriage, she did talk to him about the origins of her anxiety and fears during a few couples therapy sessions that she and Phil attended.[19]

If we recognize that addiction is voluntary, then we have to conclude that individuals are quite capable of voluntary self-destructive behavior.
—Gene Heyman, PhD[20]

A foolish, self-destructive activity is not necessarily a disease.
—Jeffrey Schaler, PhD[21]

SEX ADDICTION AND THE LAW

Case Examples

In 2011, Kelly Tustison, from a suburb of Chicago, was charged with predatory criminal sexual assault and aggravated sexual abuse of a victim younger than thirteen for sexual abuse of a female relative dating back to 2008. According to reports, Tustison began abusing this female child when she was around three years old, abuse that came to light as the child entered school and disclosed the abuse history to her teachers. According to prosecutors, Tustison told police that he had been "using a female relative to satisfy his sex addiction."[22]

Steven John Ainsworth has been a scourge of Australia for over three decades, preying upon women. While the great majority of rapes and sexual assaults are committed by assailants known to the victim, stranger crimes, like those of Ainsworth, are particularly terrifying because they create the possibility of risk in any and every situation a woman encounters. Ainsworth has been convicted of four rapes and sentenced to prison for fourteen years. According to reports, "Ainsworth had sought treatment for his sexual addiction and a psychological report indicated he was now a different person from the man who committed the offences."[23]

Since the early 1980s, when sex addiction first began to be diagnosed, it has had an inconsistent welcome in court. Many early cases were roundly rejected by the courts, which did not see the concept of sex addiction as valid or valuable in prosecution, defense, or sentencing. But as evidenced by many of the stories and references scattered throughout this book, the concept of sex addiction is being raised in courts much more frequently and is often finding a welcome ear. Judges are ordering men into sex addiction treatment and sometimes excusing men from court appearances when they are in sex addiction treatment.

In treatment of sex offenders, therapists often must strongly resist offenders' efforts to find places to put blame for their abusive behaviors. Some offenders are adept at finding ways and reasons that they are not responsible for their choices and the impact of their choices on others. The tragedy if we allow this is that their victims often end up carrying some of that blame and are robbed of the healing that can only occur when they are able to hold their abuser responsible.

The behaviors of so-called sex addicts often lead to harm and damage for themselves, as well as for those they love and who love them. These men violate trust, lie, deceive, and steal. They violate boundaries and place their own immediate short-term sexual needs and desires above those of all others. Their victims are equally robbed by the concept of sex addiction. Allowing these men to blame their actions on an internal disease, over which they have no power, deprives their victims of true apology and real accountability. It offers a false answer, a pacifier that does not resolve anything and offers no real explanations. All it provides is a label.

Testifying on Sex Addiction

For mental health evidence to be admissible in court, it must fulfill standards of legal proceedings. These rules were developed to create a way to prevent anyone from standing up in court and testifying as a self-proclaimed expert and confusing the issues with information that is subjective, biased, and not based upon generally accepted science. While these standards were developed in cases that did not involve mental health issues, the principles of scientific admissibility still apply.

The standards require that an expert's testimony be based upon reliable information, which is garnered from scientific knowledge. To qualify as scientific knowledge, the information must be based upon research utilizing the scientific method. How does research meet the expectation of using the scientific method? It must meet the following criteria:

- It must involve the testing of hypotheses.
- It must involve empirical testing of real-world data.
- It must be peer reviewed and published. In other words, the research must stand up to criticism by other scientists.
- The error rate, or description of the chances of an accidental positive finding, must be identified.
- The principles must be accepted within the scientific community. This can't be "your pet theory."
- Findings should come from repeatable and verifiable research. If a result happened accidentally one time out of ten, a scientist should not be testifying that this result is a "fact" or is reliable information.

———— ∞ ————

There are many competing hypotheses about sex addiction as evidenced by the plethora of competing definitions. There's plenty of anecdotal and observational reporting, typically from within sex addiction treatment programs, but little real-world empirical testing of these hypotheses. As a result, it would be challenging for anyone to assert that they are testifying on "sufficient facts and data," as opposed to limited personal and anecdotal experience. There is absolutely no data regarding the "error rate" of sex addiction. How often is it misdiagnosed? How often do we diagnose it when the problem is something else? What is the interrater reliability on it as different clinicians render diagnoses on the same case? We do not know, and when we do not know, we should be extremely cautious about predictions and diagnoses. In fact, tests that assess sexual addiction have already been rejected by courts based on these standards, classifying them as inherently unreliable, with no generally accepted standards.

In 2004, a man who had gotten into trouble with gambling sued the maker of a medication he had been prescribed for Parkinson's disorder, claiming that the medication had caused him to gamble compulsively and to lose around $2 million. The courts held that the scientific claims that the medicine could have caused these gambling problems were unsupported scientifically and inadmissible in court. The ruling is relevant to sex addiction as well as gambling. A lawyer involved in the case suggested that allegations of hypersexuality and sex addiction are likely to face the same challenges: "Where the behavior is something that is very amorphous and hard to define and is something that is found in the general population very widely . . . it's going to be an uphill battle [for the plaintiff] because you are just not going to be able to get the data."[24]

There *are* peer-reviewed publications in the field of sex addiction, but it's noteworthy that the "peers" are other professionals who also believe in sex addiction and make their living treating the victims of this alleged disorder. I think most people in the general public would be surprised by the level of skepticism held by the scientific community and the mental health field. In a survey of over 100,000 men on the AskMen.com website, 53 percent believed that sex addiction was an excuse, a fictional disorder, used to avoid responsibility, while 41 percent suggested it could be a real disorder but was being abused as a way to avoid personal responsibility. Only 6 percent of respondents believed the disorder actually was legitimate. In a similar online poll by the Medscape.com site, where users are mostly physicians and healthcare professionals, 67 percent of about 2,000 respondents indicated that they believe sex addiction is not a valid diagnosis or disorder.[25] A study that looked at the "need" for a sex addiction diagnosis and other behavior addiction diagnoses found that over half the clinicians surveyed had reservations about the impact of pathologizing client behaviors and overlap with other disorders.[26]

In fact, the scientific community is so robustly challenging to the lack of research behind sex addiction that I would be extremely surprised if anyone could legitimately testify that sex addiction is generally accepted in the field; after all, if it were, wouldn't it already be a diagnosis?

> Our aim has been to develop models of intervention that assist abusive
> males to cease their abusive behaviors and to relate respectfully to others.
> The models are based on the assumption that these goals can best be achieved
> if the abuse perpetrator accepts full responsibility for his abusive behaviors. . . .
> He must accept his culpability for his actions and bear the full onus
> for ceasing his abuse and changing his behaviour.
> —Alan Jenkins, PhD[27]

One of the other disorders proposed for addition to the DSM5 is a paraphilia, or fetish, toward rape. Dr. Allen Frances suggests that the motivation for this diagnosis may relate to the complex and legally challenging use of the DSM-IV's diagnosis of "paraphilia not otherwise specified—nonconsent" in forensic and legal settings, where it is often used to justify the civil commitment of violent sexual offenders. Legally these individuals can only be committed if there is a mental disorder. If they are just a raping criminal, they can be sent to jail, serve their time, and be released. But if the prosecutors can show that they are a raping criminal with a mental disorder, then they can send them to jail, have them serve their time, and then lock them up indefinitely after that on the basis that they and their disorder pose a risk to society. But the diagnosis currently used for this argument, paraphilia not otherwise specified, is pending a current significant legal challenge on the basis that it is poorly scientifically supported. In a Wisconsin case, *McGee v. Bartow*, which may go before the Supreme Court, it is argued that this use of a mental disorder is not grounded in defensible science and reflects a violation of civil rights.[28] The British Psychological Society singled out the proposed disorder of rape paraphilia for specific criticism, expressing "grave concerns that such views may offer a spurious and unscientific defence to a rapist in a criminal trial."[29]

Should dangerous people be allowed to walk among us and put people at risk? Absolutely not, whenever possible, and when efforts to do so do not affect the innocent. But our legal system works on the principle that it is better to take the risk of freeing the guilty than risk imprisoning the innocent. Should we use the mental health system as a means to lock people away and protect society? Thomas Szasz argues vociferously that the role of psychiatry in involuntary civil commitments of the dangerously mentally ill is a travesty.

It troubles me greatly that in the sexual addiction movement, sexual crimes such as child sexual abuse and rape are blended with other sexual behaviors that do not involve violation of consent. Many of the books and articles about sexual addiction commingle discussions of compulsive masturbators or porn users with pedophiles and rapists. Authors such as Sbraga, O'Donohue, and Carnes offer many anecdotal stories about clients whose sexual behaviors expanded into nonconsensual and criminal activities as their sexuality allegedly became a runaway train that ultimately carried them off a cliff and into illegal acts. Recently, a Montana counselor who specializes in treating sex offenders offered the following proclamation: "Sexual addiction is not a curable thing. It's a treatable thing, it's a manageable problem. But usually adult sex offenders will continue with treatment in some form or fashion for long into their lives. It's a lifetime thing."[30] Not only does this assert that sex addiction and sex offending are one and the same, but it also buys into the same premise, that sexually addictive behaviors represent a chronic condition that cannot be personally controlled but requires treatment, monitoring, and supervision.

Unfortunately, the research in treatment and assessment of sexual abusers and rapists simply doesn't agree with this premise. First, for most sexual offending, sexuality plays only a small part in the act. Rape is not solely an act of sexuality but one of violence, anger, fear, selfishness, and sexual desire wrapped into a frightening ball of pain. Most perpetrators of child sexual offenses are not acting out of a core sexual drive, such as pedophilia, but are acting out based upon poor socialization, a history of trauma and loss, anger and resentment, and sometimes cognitive and emotional deficits. Sexuality is often merely a tool by which such perpetrators express their feelings, and these men and boys often have many other ways in which they express their rage, from violence and drugs to stealing and destructive behaviors.

In research by Bancroft and Vukadnovic, the authors interviewed twenty-two individuals enrolled in Sex Addicts Anonymous. Of these volunteers, two of them were criminals with sex offenses, in the areas of exhibitionism and child sex abuse. These individuals described to the authors that they were not out of control but that there were sexual behaviors they would pursue if they could "get away with it." In the authors' words, "Both of these men obtained some benefit from regarding themselves as sex addicts, but as they did not report out of control sexual behavior they were not included in further analyses."[31]

According to research conducted with self-identified sex addicts, and with sex offenders in treatment, there is substantial overlap between the two groups. Compulsive masturbation and pornography "dependence" are reported for as many as 70 percent and 50 percent of individuals in treatment for paraphilias and sex offending, respectively.[32] Carnes and other writers have suggested that some sexual addicts progress to sexual offending due to the severity of their addiction. There is simply no research based on verifiable data that suggests this theory is true. It seems like the hammer problem—when all you have is a hammer, every problem looks like a nail. When you believe in sex addiction, every sex-related problem seems to be the result, cause, or consequence of sex addiction. This is known as *confirmation bias*, where once you have committed to a theory or belief, you preferentially see and recognize the information that supports your belief while simultaneously ignoring information that contradicts it.

I'm ethically and clinically troubled by this argument, beyond the questions of its scientific merit, as it puts the blame and responsibility for these sexual crimes on the perpetrator's supposed addiction and a disease process rather than placing responsibility on the individuals themselves. Over decades working with sexual offenders, I can tell you that if there is a way that they can avoid responsibility for their actions, they will. I've spent too many long hours challenging folks who are trying to pass the buck and blame everybody but themselves for the choices they make, to endorse this get-out-of-jail card.

There is a surprising inconsistency in the differing social treatment of sex offenders versus sex addicts. If, as is suggested, most sex offenders are really extreme sex addicts, shouldn't we be treating these two groups similarly? But we do not.

The great majority of popular media stories about pedophiles, for instance, imply or outright state that they are unable to be treated. Life sentences for sex offenders are becoming more common as the practice of civil commitment to sex offender treatment centers spreads and gains legal defensibility. In my years working with sex offenders, I can't tell you the number of times laypeople have told me that sex offenders should just be shot and killed, or castrated, or locked away forever. If there is an explicit link between sex offending and sex addiction, will we apply these same assumptions and biases against those diagnosed as sex addicts? Currently, when someone goes on television and confesses to sex addiction, we seem all too willing to accept that joining a twelve-step group or going to a residential treatment program will treat an individual with sex addiction and absolve them of guilt for their actions. What if we treated them with the same scorn, disbelief, and outright hatred that sex offenders receive? I don't think too many athletes, politicians, or television stars would be claiming the label.

Case Example

In 2011, a social worker in Monterey, California, was charged with possession of child pornography after his wife called the police and told them her husband was suicidal. When the police came, they found child pornography plainly visible in the client's home. In April, the social worker missed a court appearance because he was in a residential treatment program for sexual addiction, according to his defense attorney, who stated that such treatment was critical due to his client's suicidality.[33]

Australian psychologist Alan Jenkins wrote *Invitations to Responsibility*, a book that has greatly influenced my work with men and boys who have used their sexuality to hurt others. Instead of attacking these men and creating environments of shame and fear, he instead uses the delightful approach of offering clients questions that confront their failure to exert self-control by giving them questions they cannot refuse, what he calls "irresistible invitations." So, he might suggest asking these men, "Are you ready to take control of your sexual behaviors, or do you still need to be monitored and controlled by other people?" Or, "Do you think you are now mature enough to own your sexual behaviors and take responsibility for them?" "Are you strong enough to accept the consequences for your actions?" "Could you handle a life in which you were in charge of your sexual behaviors?"

Aren't these delightful questions? Wouldn't it be hard to say no? Wouldn't it be almost impossible to say, "No, I'm addicted to sex; I need external controls; and no, I'm not mature enough to be responsible for my sexual behaviors"? Jenkins' approach is very similar to the extremely successful modality of addiction treatment called motivational interviewing.[34] Motivational interviewing was developed by my former professor, psychologist William Miller, PhD, who saw that many who abuse or are dependent upon substances would benefit from assistance in enhancing their internal motivation and commitment to change. The job of a therapist in motivational interviewing is not to force a person to change but to help that person find the internal desire to make better choices, to feed that desire, helping the person to make more choices in their life based upon that desire. Multiple studies around the world have demonstrated that the strategies employed by Miller and Jenkins work. Instead of telling people they cannot control their behaviors without external control, they tell people that they *can* control themselves, they *can* make healthy choices for themselves and those around them, and they *can* have the life they want.

Some research on PTSD has begun to lead to changes in the way we think about treatment and the experiences that create posttraumatic stress. In one study, researchers interviewed flight attendants who had survived plane crashes. They found that they could divide the attendants into two groups. One group consisted of those attendants who felt panicked and out of control during the crash. They felt that the crash was happening to them and that there was nothing they could do during the event but wait to die. The other group experienced a crash as well, but during the event they focused on doing what they could, using their training to preserve the lives of their passengers and themselves. The key difference between the groups was the feeling of being "out of control," something the first group experienced and the second did not. The first group experienced the long-term negative effects of PTSD at far higher rates than the second. Somehow, even though the physical experiences were the same, the different cognitive experience, of being in charge, in control, of something, anything, was protective.

Studies with soldiers and others exposed to trauma and stress have also shown that when a person in a stressful situation does something, *anything*, that they have been trained to do, believing that it will help them retain control, the experience of the trauma is lessened. In military studies, levels of the chemical cortisol, which is related to stress, were lower in soldiers who used their training to prepare for attack, and higher in soldiers who merely worried and waited. So the message is, if you believe that you are powerless, your body does too, and you and your body enter into a spiraling cycle, where your feelings of powerlessness feed on themselves. In contrast, when you find yourself feeling powerless, if you begin to do something, almost anything, that has a chance of improving the situation, you will feel more in control and suffer fewer long-term effects from the experience. But if people tell themselves (or are told) that they are unable to control their behavior, they will indeed be unable to control it.

This is one of my big problems with the social and therapeutic message that our sexuality is an "out-of-control" and dangerous force in our lives, whether that message comes from religious or from legal values. In coverage of the 2011 sex scandal involving the French politician and International Monetary Fund chief Dominique Strauss-Kahn, the media attempted to understand and explain why this powerful French politician would allegedly attempt to rape a woman. French psychiatrists said "there is a loss of control" and that sex addiction "is characterized by a loss of rational control, as well as significant and measurable changes in the neurochemistry of the brain," where "willful rationality is no longer the orchestra conductor."[35] We know now that telling people that something is uncontrollable creates that belief, in some people at least. And this belief, that one's sexuality is an uncontrollable force, can become a self-fulfilling prophecy.

The danger in the implicit assumptions of sex addiction, that sexual arousal poses a risk that can overwhelm people, lies in the implication that it allows people a way to avoid responsibility for their actions. In fascinating research into the roots of evil, psychologist Roy Baumeister found that perpetrators of violence and evil acts on others do two things cognitively. In their minds, these people tell themselves, "It wasn't so bad," as a way to minimize their internal recognition of the harm they've done to others, telling themselves that their actions truly didn't hurt their victims all that much. Secondly, the perpetrators tell themselves, "I couldn't help it," and that it was out of their control.[36] People who hurt others point to things outside themselves, creating irresistible urges and reasons why they were not responsible for their actions.

Baumeister highlights this pattern in the actions of killers, rapists, and Nazi war criminals, all of whom are quick to minimize the harm they did, at the same time that they find ways to place responsibility for their actions on forces they could not control. Even while these people admit that what they did was wrong, they argue that they are not responsible for their actions. Teaching people that their sexual urges are an uncontrollable impulse, a force that is outside themselves, and not a part of who and what they are, is a belief that fosters and promotes evil and harm to others. It does not increase the likelihood that they will behave differently; it merely increases the chances that when they do hurt others, they will be convinced that it's not their fault.

Archibald Hart, author of *Thrilled to Death*, suggests that when men unwittingly pair sex and adrenaline, they set themselves up for an addictive process in which they step onto a roller-coaster chase of ever-increasing highs from ever-increasingly extreme sexual acts, up to and including criminal acts such as rape.[37] To blame sex crimes and disorders on adrenaline and sex addiction is ludicrous. Such acts are complex, determined by a large variety of historical, environmental, and psychological antecedents. Given that Hart is a self-identified Christian psychologist and author, I'm surprised at how readily he gives away a person's individual responsibility for evil and violation of the rights of others. The crime of rape doesn't happen because someone once masturbated to dirty magazines and was afraid of getting caught. Such a view trivializes the immoral, selfish, angry, and destructive choices of a rapist and prevents us from holding such people accountable for their behaviors.

When we allow morals, religious values, and laws to dictate medicine and science, it leads inevitably to the current morass of diagnostic confusion. The muddiness of blending morals, laws, and science supports the current social quagmire of sex addiction, where the diagnosis sometimes excuses people for their behaviors at the same time that it is used by society to stigmatize and pathologize certain behaviors and groups of people. Attending to this dialogue is especially important as we address the complex issues of gender and masculinity that are embedded in sex addiction.

9

Gender and Libido

Human sexuality, especially male sexuality, is polymorphous, or utterly wild (far more so than animal sexuality). Men have had sex with women and with men; with little girls and young boys; with a single partner and in large groups; with total strangers and immediate family members; and with a variety of domesticated animals. They have achieved orgasm with inanimate objects such as leather, shoes, and other pieces of clothing; through urinating and defecating on each other (interested readers can see a photograph of the former at select art museums exhibiting the works of the photographer Robert Mapplethorpe); by dressing in women's garments; by watching other human beings being tortured; by fondling children of either sex; by listening to a woman's disembodied voice (e.g., "phone sex"); and, of course, by looking at pictures of bodies or parts of bodies. There is little, animate or inanimate, that has not excited some men to orgasm. Of course, not all of these practices have been condoned by societies—parent-child incest and seducing another's man's wife have rarely been countenanced—but many have, and all illustrate what the unchanneled, or in Freudian terms, the "unsublimated," sex drive can lead to.

—Dennis Prager[1]

Machismo is a fertile breeding-ground for the seeds of evil.

—Betty Friedan[2]

If you think about all the crazy stories you've ever heard about weird and bizarre sexual hijinks, chances are good that the majority of the stories involve males. Emergency room doctors removing strange things from bodily orifices? That would be male orifices, in almost every case. A person arrested in England for having sex with, and I'm not making this up, pavement and trash bags? Yes, that was an Englishman named Karl Watkins, not an Englishwoman.[3] And who do you think was arrested in 1992 for shooting themselves in the chest while wearing a bulletproof vest and masturbating? That was, of course, a man.[4] At a rate of nearly twenty to one, men are engaged in or interested in kinky and alternative sexual activities far, far more than women. There are core differences in the ways men and women express sexual desires, which emerge in a manner that parallels the concept of sex addiction.

Case Example

In 2011, Edward Smith of Washington State went public with the fact that he prefers to "date" automobiles and has had sex with over a thousand vehicles, ranging from helicopters to Volkswagen Beetles. Smith last dated a human woman fifteen years ago and was unable to consummate the relationship. Since age fifteen, he has had a primary orientation toward sex with vehicles. "Maybe I'm a little bit off the wall but when I see movies like Herbie and Knight Rider, where cars become loveable, huggable characters it's just wonderful. I'm a romantic. I write poetry about cars, I sing to them and talk to them just like a girlfriend. I know what's in my heart and I have no desire to change. I'm not sick and I don't want to hurt anyone, cars are just my preference." Smith is described as having a fetish called "mechaphilia," and he is not the only one, meeting with other vehicle lovers at rallies and car shows. "As far as women go, they never really interested me much. And I'm not gay," he declares.[5]

The history of the concept of nymphomania is a dark and disheartening tale that should serve as a warning sign to us as we consider sex addiction. Carol Groneman has written the definitive tale of this sad episode of medical malpractice in *The History of Nymphomania*. She tells horrific stories of women hospitalized and subjected to surgery and varied torturous "treatments," all in the name of suppressing their dangerous sexuality. Throughout the ages, Groneman describes, the social view of female sexuality has fluctuated. In the Middle Ages, women were seen as being overly sexual and vulnerable to the influences of the Devil through their sexual feelings. In the nineteenth century, women were seen as less sexual, their feelings more tied to their maternal role, and were portrayed as beings who did not enjoy sex, save for the satisfaction it gave their husbands. Groneman sees nymphomania as a metaphor, one that depicts the ways in which medicine, law, and society viewed female sexuality, embodying "the fantasies and fears, the anxieties and dangers, connected to female sexuality through the ages."[6]

Despite the long history of being pathologized and stigmatized for their sexuality, many women with high libidos in today's society have embraced their sexuality, describing it as "a driving force for personal growth" in their lives.[7] Artists like Madonna have embraced their sexuality, celebrating it as a defining and beautiful part of their personality and image.

Sex addictionologists, because they are using anecdote and their own clinical experience, are subject to their own biases. Gender bias creeps in quite often, with differential approaches and diagnoses applied to women and men. Women who engage in sexually addictive behaviors are typically described as "seeking relationships and security."[8] This is uncomfortably close to standard gender-driven views of males and females, and there is no data to back it up. Even proponents of sex addiction acknowledge that the field has given short shrift to females, and that labeling sex addiction in females as "relationship" or "love" addiction is a myth, based upon social views.[9] "From a feminist perspective, the neo-Victorian assumption that women are 'love addicts' fits the still reigning perception of women's sexuality 'as less powerful, less compelling, and less profound than that of men,'" says author Carol Groneman, quoting sexologist Rebecca Chalker.[10]

Case Example

Susan was forty-one, slender and professional, and she still retained her good looks from her days as an exotic dancer. Her husband encouraged her to enter therapy because of his concern about how much she was drinking. But it only took a session or two to find out that there were more significant issues at play. She'd been married for five years, and for the past three, each business trip she took involved her hopping into bed with at least one man. On the most recent trip, a weeklong excursion to Chicago, she slept with three different male coworkers, as well as a man she met in the hotel bar.

Susan knew that if her husband found out about her infidelities, divorce was likely, and the marriage would almost certainly end. She even acknowledged that her husband, who worked in law enforcement, could get violent or aggressive. So why did she do it? Susan had many reasons for her chronic extramarital sex. The strongest reason she described was that the attention from these men brought her the rush that she had felt as a nude dancer, when men's eyes were on her all night long, their attention riveted by her sexuality and confidence. Susan only came to therapy a few times and ended therapy as the therapist began to help her uncover some of the reasons why she felt such a strong lack of confidence and why her self-esteem was so tied to her body and sensuality.

Modern research with sex addicts includes very little information about women. Self-labeled sex addicts are predominantly males. In research with sex addicts and identified hypersexuals, women consistently make up less than 20 percent of the groups. But according to Kafka, "data on women with Hypersexual Disorder are lacking although protracted promiscuous behavior has been reported by contemporary investigators and noted historically as nymphomania."[11] With the long history of the use of research and psychiatry to support the misogyny and suppression inherent in past treatment of females under the guise of the treatment of nymphomania, I shudder to think that we would allow that shameful history to guide current thinking, and that we could allow history to repeat itself.

In contrast to the ways in which nymphomania was used in response to female sexuality in the past, the concept of sexual addiction is very differently applied to males. Women diagnosed with nymphomania were subjected to suppressive treatments, hysterectomies, electroshock, and hydrotherapies. Men diagnosed with sex addiction are told they have a disease, to attend group therapy, or, at worst, to attend a posh residential treatment center for intensive and daily group therapies. "Treatment of nymphomania resulted from the desire of medical science, in particular, and patriarchy, in general, to control women's behavior."[12] In contrast, males with sex addiction are portrayed as "victims of societal side effects, these individuals nevertheless represent bearers of abnormalities, uncontrollable consumers whose disorders are to blame."[13]

Why are the rates of females diagnosed with sex addiction so much lower than male rates? For one thing, the great majority of the sexual behaviors identified as problems are behaviors typically associated with male sexual performance. I also believe that there is a sensitivity and awareness that pathologizing female sexuality may be evidence of an unacceptable gender bias against female sexuality, comparable to calling women sluts. In today's world, this is a guaranteed way to ask for attack, as evidenced by the "slut-walks" organized in 2011 in response to a police officer's comment to college students that females should not dress like sluts if they don't want to get raped or attacked. Women and activists vociferously organized, and marches were held in multiple cities around the world, where women proudly reclaimed the word slut, and men wore T-shirts stating their love of slutty women.[14] The same has not been true in defense of male sexuality. Nobody stands up in support of masculine eroticism.

"To us, a slut is a person of any gender who has the courage to lead life according to the radical proposition that sex is nice and pleasure is good for you. . . . As proud sluts we believe that sex and sexual love are fundamental forces for good—activities with the potential to strengthen intimate bonds, enhance lives, create spiritual awareness, even change the world."[15]

Case Example

In 2002, Catherine Millet published what has been called the "most explicit book about sex ever written by a woman." In it, she recounts her many sexual encounters in orgies and random trysts. Millet is a well-known French art critic who developed a driving interest in promiscuous sex and group sexuality, pursuing anonymous encounters in the French swinging scene. Millet's tales of her sexual exploits contain little real description of pleasure, and she even comments that in all the many, many such sexual encounters, she never experienced an orgasm. Millet said that she feels that many women have fantasies about the kind of sex she pursued, and that she differs only in that she played the fantasies out. She is frank about her difficult childhood but defends against an assumption that her promiscuity emerged from "neurosis." She admits that some of her motivation came from an attempt to abase herself, but she found higher meanings in this, beyond a form of self-hatred, feeling that her sexuality allowed her to embrace "an extraordinary sense of freedom."[16]

It would be easy to diagnose Catherine Millet as a sex addict. Anonymous sex, chronic infidelity, and emotional detachment during sex were all part of her repertoire. Millet grew up in a household where both her mother and her father were casually and constantly unfaithful. Depression was prevalent in her life and her family: Millet lost her mother to suicide as a result of depression and mental illness. But Millet is a woman clearly in charge of her life, her destiny, and her choices. In contrast to the ideas of destructive, progressive, uncontrollable, and addictive sex permeating through a person's life and wreaking havoc, Millet has been extraordinarily successful. Parts of her life might not be what we would encourage others to mimic, but nothing I've read suggests that she regrets her sexual choices:

"I loved particularly the anonymity, the abandonment of orgies. The sensation that one was glorying in this unbelievable freedom, this transcendence. I look back on it with nothing but pleasure. It was very important to me, to my identity, my ego, but it wasn't an addiction. I was never a nymphomaniac."[17]

You don't have to look far to find evidence that being male is seen as a problem. In the 1920s, when testosterone was identified as the hormone behind male aggression, it was used both to treat those seen as too effeminate and was identified as a scourge and cause of war. In the 1960s, the discovery that some men in prison had two Y chromosomes was held up as evidence that being "too male" led to idiocy, violence, and criminality.

In the past decade, boys as young as four years old have been charged with sexual harassment in schools for acts as innocuous as kissing a female peer. In the days of Tom Sawyer, such behavior might have warranted a spanking in the front of the classroom. Now it commands a media spectacle and a circus of outcry regarding the pervasiveness of male assaults against female sexuality. In 2006, a four-year-old boy was suspended from his preschool after he allegedly rubbed his face against a female teacher's chest during a hug. Also in 2006, a five-year-old boy was accused of sexual harassment for pinching a female peer.[18] Christina Hoff Sommers argues that our society is trying to force boys to be like girls, and she asserts that the typical male is "alienated, lonely, emotionally repressed, isolated, at odds with his masculinity, and prone to violence."[19]

As we've seen in previous chapters, the concept of sex addiction is intrinsically tied to cultural views of sexuality, promiscuity, and infidelity. The categories and behaviors of sex addiction include sexual behaviors that are predominantly engaged in by men, including masturbation, infidelity, use of pornography, cybersex, telephone sex, and going to prostitutes and strip clubs. Though the news is filled with sensationalist stories that women's participation in these various activities is increasing, decades of research indicates that male and female sexuality differs in many ways, ways that are surprisingly targeted in theories of sex addiction. The concept of sex addiction reflects in part a social effort to label and constrain many aspects and expressions of male sexuality as a public health problem, to identify the uniquely male aspects of human sexuality as unhealthy, dangerous, and in need of control.

As adolescents enter puberty and their bodies and minds develop toward sexual maturity, hypersexuality is seen as the norm. Sex addictionologists and researchers from Carnes to Kafka acknowledge that there is a core similarity between the sexuality of teenagers going through puberty and adolescent sexual development on the one hand, and descriptions of adult sex addicts on the other. Kafka describes that "the internal state of motivation associated with such behavior may shift from primarily sexual arousal associated with youthfulness to an admixture of sexual arousal, sexual motivation and a maladaptive behavioral response."[20] In fact, some researchers argue that it is likely there are few young adults who would not meet significant criteria for hypersexual disorder.[21]

Television over the past decades has been filled with portrayals of men as mindless buffoons. In *Married with Children*, Al Bundy is a perpetually clueless and horny man who teaches his son the worst parts of masculinity. "The unspoken premise of much of American pop culture today is that a large group of men would like nothing better than to go back to their junior high school locker room and stay there."[22] And why not? In junior high, as our hormones started to rage, we had no shame or guilt about our sexual drives. We were forgiven being perpetually horny and overly focused on breasts and buttocks. Men long for those days of unabashed horniness and ribald celebration, with no need to self-censor or constrain those thoughts and feelings. Men today are told by society, the media, and the field of sex addiction that the sex drive they had as an adolescent was acceptable but is now a dangerous illness. They must "put aside childish things," including a desire for frequent sex.

Sex addictionologists assert that "7–10 percent of men in the U.S. have sexually compulsive traits," and that "one of the fastest growing categories of men with this problem is well-known, successful people."[23] The issue of sexual addiction is not about sex in general; it is about male sexuality, and the sexual practices of those women whose high libidos lead them to behave more like men. This is an attack on masculine eroticism and an attempt to label core aspects of male sexuality as inherently unhealthy and diseased.

> If the message, the only message, to boys is that their sex and sexuality
> is potentially harmful to girls, how will we ever raise them to be
> full partners in healthy relationships?
> —Sharon Lamb[24]

> He who can sleep with a woman and does not, commits a great sin. My boy,
> if a woman calls you to share her bed and you don't go, your soul will be
> destroyed! That woman will sigh before God on judgment day and that woman's
> sigh, whoever you may be and whatever your fine deeds, will cast you into Hell!
> —Zorba the Greek[25]

There is something baser, closer to the core, in male sexuality. Whether it is less masked and controlled than female sex, or whether male sexuality is simply more primitive and primal, getting beneath the surface of male sexual desires can be a frightening and even disturbing process. Nancy Friday, whose books about female sexual fantasies opened the door on sexual fantasy research, shared in her book *Men in Love* that delving into male sexual fantasies left her appalled and disgusted, often requiring that she literally wash her hands to try to shed some of the moral stench she perceived in male fantasies of sadism, aggression, and dominance.

Since psychologists and researchers first began to measure people's attitudes toward sex, it has been clear that men and women see sex differently. On the Sexual Attitudes Survey, developed in 1985 by Hendrick and Hendrick, men and women differ on over 80 percent of the test's most important questions. Women tend to be more conservative about sex, while men are more liberal and permissive. Men are more apt to see casual sex as acceptable and report that they'd like to have as many partners as possible. Women are more prone to see sexuality as an intense, emotional, and spiritually significant event, while men see sex mostly as just a way to enjoy themselves. Women tend to be more sexually responsible than men, and men tend to connect sex and power far more than women do. And most women are much more sexually conventional than men. In general, women masturbate less, are more likely to see the use of sex toys and pornography as abnormal, and place the most value upon penile-vaginal intercourse. Men are more direct about sex than women are.[26] Those women who go against the norms of female sexual behavior are often labeled as being hypersexual and emotionally traumatized, and are often excluded and judged by other women.[27]

Fetishes, or paraphilias, are predominantly, some even say exclusively, a male disorder. With the exception of the behaviors associated with BDSM, there are few women who get compulsively and dependently attached to things like shoes, exhibitionism, or voyeurism in the way that men do.

Some, such as John Money, have suggested that this is because men respond strongly to erotic visual cues in a way that women do not and that fetishes are derived from these visual cues. Other research, such as that of Meredith Chivers, shows that women do respond to erotic images, perhaps even more than men do. But whereas men's experience of psychological arousal usually coincides with physiological arousal (in other words, when their body is turned on, so is their mind), women often experience physiological arousal at the same time they are reporting feeling "nothing." So while women's bodies react with sexual arousal to images of nude men, nude women, and even of primates having sex, the women don't feel turned on, even though their body does.

Other mechanisms, besides visual arousal, are likely to be involved in gender differences as well. In a British study, some baby goats and sheep were switched after birth and raised by mothers of the other species. So a baby goat was raised by sheep, and vice versa. After three years, the animals were switched back. Females adapted easily, adjusting to being back among their own species. Sexually active with the species with which they were raised, the females were willing to mate with their own species after they were returned. But males had a lot more difficulty. They were "stuck" with the sexual attractions they developed in their rearing by the other species. They were unable or unwilling, even after a period of years, to mate with females of their own species.

So pity the poor males, whose sexuality is more proscribed, more narrow, and less malleable and responsive than that of females. In the following pages,

I will highlight the ways in which these differences between male and female sexuality contribute to the very behaviors that are diagnosed as disordered in the field of sex addiction. Further, we will see the ways in which these very differences are intrinsically connected to evolutionarily driven patterns of male behavior that have affected the world throughout history, though we fear and stigmatize the sexual effects that accompany these same attributes. Finally, we will explore the components of both masculinity and male sexuality that are ignored by the field of sex addiction.

Bestiality

Deviant sexual behavior such as bestiality, or sex with animals, is one of the extreme behaviors that sex addiction therapists like to throw out as examples of the depths of depravity to which sex addiction can take a person. In Carnes' book *Out of the Shadows*, he tells the story of a man disclosing sex with animals in a sex addiction group and being surprised to hear that he was not the only one in the group with such an embarrassing story. But is bestiality really related to sex addiction and to irresistible sexual impulses? Research on bestiality suggests in fact that it is related more simply to the nature of access and motivation. Kinsey's research sixty years ago suggested that 40 to 50 percent of men who were adolescents on farms admitted to sexual contact with animals, and in most cases, these contacts were experimental and reflected adolescent sexual exploration within the environment, and with the resources available. Nowadays, such boys might more easily access pornography through the Internet and have no need to explore sexual contact with animals. Thus the reaction and alleged link between sex addiction and bestiality likely has more to do with the social disgust and stigma toward it, and less to do with any real evidence that sex with animals is part of a slippery slope of sexual behaviors.

Is male sex bestial? Is it more primitive, more animalistic than female sexuality? Perhaps. But as Ryan and Jetha point out in their delightful book *Sex at Dawn*, humans are far and away one of the most sexual creatures on earth. Rampant sexuality is more human than animal, they suggest, and "an excessively horny monkey is acting 'human,' while a man or woman uninterested in sex more than once or twice a year would be, strictly speaking, 'acting like an animal.'"[28]

10

Men and Women

Separated before Birth

The greatest hurdle to sexual harmony is ignorance of the fact that members of the other sex (and other sexual orientations) are fundamentally different from ourselves.

—Ogas & Gaddam[1]

"I want a loving, faithful, caring, caretaking wife, and I wanna make love to everything else in long skirts, with bare feet and ripe, juicy mouths. Little boy-girls with small firm breasts and tight asses. Rubenesque round women with big Mother Earth breasts and green eyes. God! I could go on and on."[2]

In the early days of fetal development, there is little difference between female and male children. A developing fetus actually has the genetic blueprints to develop the physiological structure of both male and female genitalia. But the female system is the human default. Without additional triggering or influence, the fetus will develop into a female, growing ovaries, a uterus, and a vagina, while the precursors of the male system simply wither away. But if the developing fetus begins to produce testosterone (referred to as "T" in scientific literature), triggered by the male chromosomes in the developing child, then the child develops into a male, with penis and testes.

Throughout his life, T will continue to affect the male's development, behavior, and physiology. T has a dramatic and notable effect on behaviors related to the alleged symptoms of sex addiction. T suppresses the developing child's immune system and thus serves as a later signal of a robust immune system: only those males with a very strong immune system (a desirable quality to females looking to have strong, successful children) can survive the suppressive effects of high levels of testosterone.

In both men and women (but mostly in men), high T levels are associated with the following:

- Facial structure, including a more symmetrical face, more pronounced bone structure, and a stronger jaw.
- A deeper voice.
- A longer ring finger, larger penis, and larger testicles.
- Higher levels of masturbation and infidelity.
- Because men with higher levels of the male hormone marry less, and have less successful relationships when they do marry, they actually end up having fewer overall sexual encounters. The choice seems to be less sex with more women, or more sex with a single woman.
- Greater chances of being involved in open, or nonmonogamous, relationships, and less satisfaction with monogamy.[3]
- Higher-risk careers such as day trading or investment banking.[4]
- Aggressiveness, assertiveness in personal and professional relationships, and dominance.
- Increased use of pornography (in men and women).
- Higher T levels decrease communication skills—women with higher estrogen, which suppresses T, are better at saying tongue-twisting rhymes, at reading body language, and at communicating their feelings.
- Lower rates of male T predict higher rates of monogamy and longer-term relationships.

A transgender person, Griffin Hansbury, was born female but transitioned to male after college. Griffin has described that prior to treatment with the hormone T, Griffin would admire a beautiful woman on the street and have an internal desire to meet the woman. But after T treatment began, Griffin found that an attractive woman unleashed a wave of desire that would "flood my mind with aggressive pornographic images, just one after another. . . . I felt like a monster a lot of the time. It made me understand men. It made me understand adolescent boys a lot."[5]

But T is not a simple, black-and-white chemical. We cannot simply blame all male behaviors on it, as levels of T interact with the environment, with society and culture, and with individual male choices. Studies of the finger length of ancient remains from Neanderthals and early humans show that males had very high levels of T. As a result, they were likely to be extremely promiscuous and aggressive. The intervening millennia of evolution have reduced these levels, suggesting that the "civilizing" influences of society have affected male biology and the impact of these hormones on male behaviors.

——⟨∞⟩——

Threesomes and Public Sex

In the 2010 AskMen.com sex survey, over 100,000 respondents indicated that having a threesome was the main fantasy of 34 percent of men, and having sex in public the fantasy of 15 percent. In a similar survey of male readers of the *Men's Health* magazine, 55 percent of men would have a threesome with their wife or girlfriend if they could, and 77 percent would really like their wives or girlfriends to be willing to explore having sex in public.[6]

In England, the problem of public sex, called dogging, has become so prevalent that neighborhoods are enacting vigilante-style interventions, using spotlights to scare off doggers from public areas. The English courts convened a special commission to develop a consultation paper on how to amend the laws regarding public nuisance and "outraging public decency," in order to outlaw the public sexual behaviors that are plaguing the country. While some British responses to the problem of dogging have raised the problem of public health and possible transmission of sexually transmitted disease, the great majority of social response has been based upon the simple perception of the acts as embarrassing, inappropriate, and rude. There has not been a major push to label these people's behaviors as disturbed or mentally ill. Immoral? Yes. Criminal? Yes. Sick, mentally ill, or addicted? No.

——⟨∞⟩——

Male T levels drop when they are in a monogamous (heterosexual) relationship and even more when they become a father. The success or failure of a favored football team or politician affects a man's T levels as well. When Barack Obama beat John McCain, levels of T fell in men who had supported McCain.[7] In states that "went" for winning candidates, other research shows that there were spikes in online pornography use, results suggestive of increased libido and sexual desire, effects of that increase in T in men who supported the winning candidates.[8]

When a man is in a relationship that is not monogamous and the man is either polygamous, in an open relationship, or unfaithful, T remains high, compared to men in relationships with a single female.[9] Men with higher levels of T tend to be less interested in relationship commitment or investment and are more apt to engage in multiple short-term relationships. Levels of T both affect a man's tendency to approach a relationship in a certain manner *and* are affected by the nature of the relationships a man is involved in, in a complex and circular fashion.

In most women, a very different pattern emerges. When women engage in casual sex, their T levels drop, and the women's T levels appear more like the levels of women who are in monogamous relationships, and lower than the levels of single, unattached women who are not romantically involved. In other words, when a woman has sex with a man, her body seems to respond instinctively as though there is now a monogamous relationship. So one reason that men and women differ in their approach to casual sex is the fact that such relationships have very different biological effects on the different genders.[10]

Rates of T in males vary in response to their social status, in response to their level of competitiveness and violence (males in a combat or competitive situation have higher levels of T), and in response to the availability of sexual partners. So as we look at the men who are labeled sexual addicts in the media, men who are tall, deep-voiced, assertive, dominant, and successful leaders, they are expressing both the levels of T that helped them achieve these levels of success, and the levels of T that their bodies produce in response to their environments of stress, competition, and dominance. In multiple animal species, from monkeys to wild horses, males will establish temporary periods of dominance over the troop, tribe, or herd. During such periods, these males' bodies produce extremely high levels of T, as the males pursue mating with the females of the group and combat with the other males to maintain their dominance. But when the males get tired, they retire to the edge of the social group, with diminishing levels of T as well as plummeting physical strength, aggression, and libido.

Exciting, cutting-edge research is going on that examines the role of T in the sexual and mating behaviors of both men and women. New patterns are emerging every year, and scientists are beginning to tie these threads together, explaining why and how our hormones affect the human body and our behavior. T is a double-edged sword for men, affecting their sexuality, their lives, and their health. Those men who have higher rates of T are also at higher risk for future cancer and other medical conditions, in what appears to have been an evolutionary tradeoff, where men with higher T are more likely to mate sooner and more frequently, thus producing more children, but are more likely to die sooner. As actor John Derek in the film *Knock on Any Door* said, "Live fast, die young, and have a good-looking corpse!" (This saying is often misattributed to James Dean, who coincidentally was an extremely promiscuous bisexual man, allegedly drawn to various kinks, including sadomasochism and anonymous gay sex, toward the end of his short life.)[11]

Vigorous Men

In volume 5 of *Studies in the Psychology of Sex*, physician Havelock Ellis referenced a French psychiatrist, Gustave Bouchereau, who once described that "the men most liable to satyriasis are those with vigorous nervous system, developed muscles, abundant hair on body, dark complexion and white teeth."[12] Dark complexion and white teeth aside, likely representing the history of racism in the concept of satyriasis, the rest of these characteristics mirror the effects of high levels of testosterone in men. Bouchereau also believed that nymphomania and satyriasis were not themselves actual disorders, but merely symptoms of other afflictions, whether it be brain lesions, childhood trauma, or "excessive abstinence."[13]

DIFFERENT LEVELS OF DESIRE

According to a 1993 meta-analysis (a research method of examining trends and patterns across many different research studies, combining all of their results) by Oliver and Hyde, the single greatest difference between men and women's sexual behaviors is in masturbation.[14] Men just masturbate more than women do. Even as it becomes more acceptable for women to admit to sexual desire and masturbation, rates of female masturbation still don't approach the near universal rates of male masturbation.

Case Example

Salvador Dali: *The Great Masturbator*
In 1929, Dali painted The Great Masturbator, *a work that he kept in his private collection until after his death. The painting is believed to be an expression of Dali's conflicted feelings about sex, and his use of masturbation as his primary sexual outlet. In adolescence, Dali reportedly discovered that his penis was smaller than those of his peers, and he developed a fear of sex in general, and was afraid that he would never be able to sexually satisfy a woman. Dali was apparently a virgin when he fell in love with his future wife Gala, who was then married to another artist. Throughout their marriage, she had many other male lovers, with Dali's encouragement. It is believed that Dali only ever had sex with Gala, though throughout his later life he allegedly arranged orgies for him to watch while masturbating.[15]*

This single difference is the most likely explanation for gender differences in porn use. Men use porn more, and when they do, they use it to masturbate, in contrast to the relational use of pornography by women (women tend to watch porn with their husbands and boyfriends, while men view it alone). Men masturbate more in adolescence and their later years, and men who masturbate tend to be healthier than men who do not. Is this an effect of masturbation, or is increased masturbation a result of a man being healthier and having a higher sex drive as a result of his healthiness? We do not know.

In the Victorian era, medicine declared war on masturbation. Semen was seen as vital to a man's physiological functioning, giving masculinity, the hairs on his body and beard, and altering his voice and his body. Semen was believed to be made from the same fluids that were in our brains and nerves; thus masturbation and sex could rob men of their intelligence. Doctors of the day were mistaking semen and sperm for testosterone, unknown until the early twentieth century. Both sperm and testosterone are made by the male testes. Scientists of the past knew that the loss of a man's testicles affected those things that made him appear to be a man. Unfortunately, they thought that the testicles performed a single function, that of making semen. So castration, masturbation, and sex in general were viewed as an act that jeopardized a man's masculinity. Use of the word *come* to describe male orgasm is a recent invention; for many more centuries, the word *spend* was used instead, to describe a man expending vital resources during orgasm, giving up something of value in exchange for the pleasure of orgasm.

Gender Differences

For decades, researchers and sexologists have attempted to discount, or at least minimize, the differences that exist in sexuality between men and women. But these differences are significant, substantial, and at this point undeniable. Entire texts can be written on these differences, and there are too many to enumerate fully here. The core difference lies, simply, in the greater male desire for sex, and everything, including differences in masturbation, can be seen to emerge from this core difference. But in respect to the tenets of sex addiction, some of these gender differences are particularly relevant:

- After age thirty, rising numbers of women report no significant sexual activity, including masturbation. In contrast, it is rare for men to report no sexual activity in the past year until around age seventy.[16]
- Most women would decline to have sex with someone without emotional commitment, while a majority of men report that this would rarely or never be a reason for them to decline sex.
- Half of all men report they would never decline sex, for any reason, a stance that no women share.[17]
- 46 percent of men between the ages of eighteen and forty-four describe the idea of group sex as appealing, compared to 9 percent of similarly aged women.

- 34 percent of men eighteen to forty-four are interested in having sex with a stranger, compared to only 10 percent of women.
- 40 percent of men would enjoy watching other people have sex in public; only 20 percent of women find the idea of watching public sex arousing.[18] The stigma and bias against group sex, noncommitted sex, and public sex is a bias that clearly impacts males, and male sexuality, far more than women.
- 50 percent of males think about sex more than once a day, compared to only 19 percent of females.
- Over 40 percent of males have purchased pornography or visited a strip club in the past year, compared to only 16 percent of females.[19]
- When men have casual sex, it decreases feelings of depression and increases self-esteem. In women, casual sex increases depression and decreases self-esteem.[20]
- Men see anal sex as a positive, pleasurable activity, while most women view it negatively.
- In bed, women worry about their appearance, while men worry about their performance, skills, and stamina, and their ability to bring their partner to orgasm.

Male Insecurity

I find the behavior of men when they are sexually aroused funny.

—Anka Radakovich[21]

Men brag to other men about sexual conquests and adventures. The chance to have sex with a supermodel, if you must keep it secret, is nowhere near as good as being able to tell your friends about it. Sexual adventurism is one of the ways men establish their manhood and masculinity, by having sex with women and gaining "masculinity points" from other men.

Men are more likely (three times more likely) than women to have sex when they don't actually want to, usually because the men feel like they need to in order to defend their masculinity, show off to friends, or not be seen as shy or unmanly. A man who declines sex may be challenged by a woman, "What's wrong with you? All men want sex all the time. Are you gay or something?"

The sexual self-concept, and feelings of sexual confidence, of teenage boys is far less secure than that of teenage girls.[22] Across the life span, men always feel more insecure about their sexuality, in general, compared to women. A teenage boy is worried about everything he doesn't know, and an adult man is worried about what he might not be able to do.

Men judge other men by their sexual prowess and confidence. Rapper Eminem admitted on MTV that he called other men "faggot" because it was a way to take away the manhood of other males, to assault and challenge their masculinity. Aggression and violence are two of the main ways men banish their insecurity and the shame they feel. Male sexual embarrassment and perceived failings quite often lead to violence. A huge percentage of domestic murders occur in response to a man's belief that his wife has been sexually unfaithful, cuckolding him, and leaving him feeling powerless, trod upon by another man.

The best example of what men are absolutely terrified of is exemplified in the adventures of Duke University senior Karen Owen. With a bit of time on her hands, and a wicked, satirical bent to her soul, Karen prepared a multimedia presentation, a mock senior thesis, where she evaluated the performance of thirteen different men she had hooked up with over her Duke career. She described the encounters and went so far as to describe the men's penis size and their skills (or lack thereof) in bed. The witty young woman even created bar charts and graphs, analyzing the ratings of the men.[23]

Her presentation, intended to be shared with just a few close friends, was, predictably, shared widely across the Internet, ending up on the national news and generating plenty of controversy.

Karen's evaluations are exactly what men have always feared is happening within the minds of their sexual partners. Now, sadly, we have to fear that not only are we being evaluated, but that at some point such evaluations may be developed into statistical measures and shared with the world via the wonders of self-publishing software.

Female sexual desire is different from that of males. It's not just socialization. In twenty years or a thousand, female sexual behaviors and psychology will still be different from those of men. Many of these differences underlie the concept of sex addiction, bolstering the argument that sex addiction is, in part, an effort to constrict and control male sexuality. One of the most notable differences lies in the male use of pornography, and the social fears of that form of media, exemplified by the field of sex addiction.

11

Watching It

I fucking love porn, I really do, and during my ten-year relationship
I'd come to master the clandestine rigmarole that cohabitating males
must go through to purchase, stash, and view it without getting busted.

—Alan Wieder[1]

$\mathscr{P}$ornography is a unique expression of aspects of male sexuality and male
sexual desires. Though increasing numbers of women use pornography,
through the safe anonymity of the Internet, the majority of pornography
produced around the world is made to appeal to the desires of men. American men spend more on pornography (around $12 billion annually) than the
combined ticket revenues of professional baseball, football, and basketball.
Far more Americans spend money and time on pornography than on attending the dramatic arts such as theater and dance. Each year, pornography has
around fifty million viewers in the United States. Like it or not, "pornography
is mainstream entertainment for America."[2]

Case Example

*Tom, a forty-six-year-old man in the Midwest, writes, "For what must be the 20th
time, my wife has found 'evidence' that I've been looking at porn online. We've been
together for twenty years in a relationship with little sex. This weekend I said that
this is not a secret; it's just private. I've masturbated to porn since I was a teenager,
so it is not just that she doesn't want sex that has me looking at porn all the time. I
get off on the fantasy of porn. It would improve my relationship if I dropped all porn,
since she stops all sex for a long time after she catches me again. And without porn I
would have an incentive to work on my real-life sexual relationship with her. But sex
has proven elusive (but at times pretty hot when it happens) for our entire marriage.
I'll admit my time on the Internet looking at porn is a bit much . . . an hour or more*

163

a night. I don't want to give it up or make promises I'm unlikely to keep. I would make a hell of a run at it if I had some confidence that I could get sex more often (once a week would be excellent, compared to once every six weeks now).

Unfortunately, sharing porn together is out . . . she finds it disgusting. She caught me jacking off to porn, and the accusations of "sex addict" and "porn addict" started whenever she wanted to hurt my feelings.

I've tried many, many long talks about revving up our sexuality and have had short-term efforts that fade away. I flat out enjoy looking at porn online, on amateur websites. They're the only sites I go to because it is real, and people there are welcoming. So putting it behind me is a loss of companionship in an online way. I feel so lonely. I wish divorce was an option, but I don't want to leave. I just want to improve this part of our marriage, but that's obviously an impossibility at this point, even though I always continue to try.

Gender differences and little-known facts about male pornography use:

Compared to 16 percent of women, 40 percent of men have used porn in the last year, and 85 to 90 percent of men use porn in their lives, compared to less than half of women.

When women use porn, it is almost always with a husband or boyfriend as a part of mutual sex—78 percent of men would like to share porn with their wives or girlfriends.[3]

When men use porn, it is almost always alone, as a part of masturbation.

Men who use porn actually tend to be men who desire *more* emotional intimacy with their female partners, not less. Porn use may be a way for men to fill an unmet emotional need.[4]

Men use the Internet for fantasy stimulation, to explore the ideas of naughty sex they're not having in real life, with women they don't actually know.

Women use Internet sex to explore their own sexual horizons, learn from others, process and examine their feelings, and bring sexual energy back to their personal relationships.

Men with higher levels of education are more likely to use the Internet to access pornography. This may reflect the greater access that educated men have to the Internet and computers, but similar findings have been shown in men accessing porn in movies and magazines. More-educated men are less likely to keep to rigid social boundaries and limits and are less likely to internally accept the social demonization of their sexual desires.

Neuroscience research has shown that when men watch pornography, the thing they attend to most is a woman's face, not her genitals. Watching porn, men actually look at a woman's face on screen sooner and more than women do. When we try to reduce men's sexuality to just being about a hard penis, we lose and ignore the real issues of relationships and arousal that are happening behind the scenes.[5]

Women who watch porn are more sensitive to criticism and are more concerned about their attractiveness to their partners, while men show no such changes.

When couples watch pornography together, it can be healthier for their relationship than when one partner watches it alone, and couples who watched pornography together report higher levels of sexual satisfaction.

Somewhat higher rates of infidelity are reported in those people who use pornography, either alone or together, but it is important to note that couples who have never viewed pornography still report infidelity about 10 percent of the time. So watching pornography *might* increase chances of infidelity or might simply reflect higher levels of libido and/or other personality factors that predict both pornography use and infidelity, but not using pornography does not prevent infidelity from happening.[6]

If pornography and more subtle forms of sexual exploitation objectify and subvert women as individuals, they also allow the male onlooker to identify with the "disembodied" female body.
—John Ross[7]

The biggest consumers of pornography are not in those sexual hotbed cities like San Francisco, Los Angeles, and New Orleans. In fact, per capita, the highest levels of porn purchased on the Internet are bought from people in Utah. Research shows that the great majority of porn is bought in states that actively work to restrict sexuality and sexual expression. Eight of the ten states with the highest levels of porn consumption are "red" states that voted for the Republican tickets in the last few presidential elections. People bought more pornography on the Internet if they were from states where the majority of citizens oppose gay marriage and endorse the concept that AIDS may be a punishment from God for sin.[8]

People who go to church, believe in God, and read the bible may buy less porn on Sunday. But they often then buy more porn during the rest of the week and keep their average even with those folks who don't go to church and do buy porn on Sundays. "One natural hypothesis is something like repression: if you're told you can't have this, then you want it more."[9]

One of the appeals in pornography for men may be the fact that it involves "low-emotion, high-intensity" sex, and it feeds the male desire for a satisfied, willing sexual partner. Even as women are contorted into outland-ish positions, cramped, sweating, and penetrated from every direction, the actresses appear to be having the time of their lives, and the thing they seem to want most in the world is more sex, more men, and more orgasms. Never doubt that porn actresses are indeed actresses; they must feign desire, lust, and abandon in order to allow men to surrender to sexual selfishness, assured in the satisfaction and willingness of their virtual video lover.[10] John Stol-tenberg is an antipornography activist who says that "pornography tells lies about women. But pornography tells the truth about men." He argues that pornography portrays women as though they are sex crazed and can experi-ence casual, meaningless sex in the same way that men can, and that this is one of the great lies of pornography. He suggests that the portrayal of men in pornography, as beings led by their penises, is essentially true.

But in fact research shows that men's levels of sexual satisfaction within emotional relationships is greater than what they experience with casual sex. Stoltenberg is as guilty as others of demonizing male sexuality and idealizing fe-male eroticism. There are women out there who get off on hot, dirty, no-strings-attached sex, and there are men who cannot get erections if they are not in love.

If anything, one of the greatest lies in pornography is a false assurance to men, that sexually satisfying a woman is easy. In porn, all men have to do is show up, get an erection (maybe bring a friend or two), and pump away while the woman screams in ecstasy. This is a soothing fantasy world for men, who approach physical intimacy with insecurities and fear of vulnerability. In porn, the men are invulnerable, and the women are easily orgasmic and eternally grateful.

Porn and Impotence?

Can pornography cause impotence? Some are concerned that behavioral conditioning and brain changes experienced during porn viewing can in-terfere in male sexual functioning when they are with their female partners. There's basically no empirical research that supports this, and given the high, almost universal use of pornography among some populations (young males), it seems unlikely. Anecdotal descriptions of the effects of porn use on male sexuality do include descriptions of impotence, and of porn users "requiring" porn to get erect in "normal" sexual encounters with their partners. I remem-ber a minister once describing to my university class that he had counseled a couple where the husband had to have a *Playboy* magazine on the bed open next to his wife in order to have sex with her and maintain an erection. This argument is merely an antiporn argument, based on fear and speculation, not science. No one has established, for instance, that men who use pornography and develop erectile dysfunction would not have developed this problem without the porn, or that their erectile dysfunction might not be due to some other unrelated issue, such as male sexual anxiety.

Marnia Robinson is a sexuality counselor and writer who cites many quotes from men describing how they restored their sexual response to situations that didn't involve porn, slowly, by stopping or decreasing their porn use and focusing on different aspects of sexuality in their sexual encounters. Her blog offers examples of men who asserted themselves and independently took control of their sexuality, their sexual behaviors, and the role that pornography had in their lives. They didn't require months of expensive residential treatment, the lack of a diagnosis made no difference in their lives, they weren't "lifelong addicts," and their porn use had not in fact progressed into more and more extreme areas of consumption. Instead, self-will was successful in taking control of their sexuality and their lives.

———— ∞ ————

"After a 90-day period of abstinence from porn/masturbation, I noticed that I was more sensitive than before; I didn't need any other stimulation to make me horny. Now that I have returned to some masturbation, I notice that I have been the most interested in women (and have ended up in bed with them) during my experiments with low masturbation frequency."[11]

———— ∞ ————

Hotel Porn

Senator Sam Brownback, Republican from Kansas and an opponent of pornography, offers an example which illustrates a point that was probably unintentional. During congressional hearings on pornography, Brownback explained that he had friends who had to personally and intentionally limit their time in their hotel rooms in order to avoid the temptation of porn. His point, surely, was to highlight the dangerous and seductive temptation of the porn available in hotel rooms across the country, and to support his efforts to legally restrict that availability. But his point better highlights the degree of active control asserted by these men in response to something in their life and the world. Isn't that the healthier message? If we are constantly trying to eradicate things in life that are dangerous, seductive, controlling, and tempting, we die the death of a thousand cuts. Technology and free-market economic forces are always going to have a new "drug" around the corner. We can fight these things best not by trying to erase them, but by building up in ourselves the ability to identify them, to understand the impact they have on us, and to make healthy, informed, and self-determined choices about whether we want them in our lives or not.

———— ∞ ————

Sociologist Michael Kimmel suggests that porn is a way for men to regain some of the power and control they feel they have lost to women, given the fact that women hold the power to grant sex or not. By watching women be sexually used and humiliated, men can "level the playing field just a little bit."[12] For men, the ability to explore sexuality online, through the electronic environment of the Internet, offers a way for them to pursue sexual variety, to safely pursue sexual "adventure," and to be sexually free in a way that is not open to men today. Through online pornography, men can express themselves sexually in a way they cannot in the real world. On the Internet, with no fear of rejection or judgment, men can express their deepest sexual desires, their most shameful feelings and interests, and can even find others who share their desires.

Sex addiction therapists worry a lot about the various men they see who appear to be stuck in fantasyland, choosing to masturbate to fantasy or pornography rather than engaging with other people in intimate, monogamous relationships. Regina Lynn, online sex columnist, makes a delightful and insightful point in her book *The Sexual Revolution 2.0*.[13] She points to the plethora of men ostensibly "addicted" to online porn and masturbation, and suggests the unique question, "Do we really want these guys reproducing?" Like the Darwin Awards, which celebrate the ridiculous stupidity of those who remove themselves from the gene pool, there may be an overall positive effect to removing those men (and some very few women), who can't and don't do well at "real-life" relationships, from the reproductive evolutionary cycle. And perhaps to make her point more realistic, the world of detached, impersonal online sex may offer an adaptive means of sexual satisfaction and expression for those men who struggle with interpersonal relationships.

Case Example

Hugh Hefner
At age eighty-five, Hugh Hefner lives in the Playboy Mansion with three girlfriends, all former or current Playboy models. This is a step down from the time just a few years ago when he had as many as seven different girlfriends, all living with him. Hefner first married in 1949; while he was in the army, his wife Mildred had an affair. She later allowed him to have sex with other women to make up for her own infidelity, but this was not enough to save their marriage. Throughout the creation of his media empire, Hefner has supported political, social, and legal causes that support his vision of a more egalitarian society without racism and with greater sexual freedom and equality. Hefner has been married one other time, to model Kimberly Conrad, with whom he had two children. This marriage came after Hefner

suffered a stroke and began to "rethink" his life. He has asserted that during their decadelong marriage, Hefner was monogamous. After their separation, he had seven live-in girlfriends, all Playboy *models, who would stand around his bed cheering him on as he had sex with each one in turn. Hefner distinguishes his lifestyle from that of famously unfaithful men like Tiger Woods and Jesse James: "I am very open about what I do. . . . The real immorality of infidelity is the lying."[14] The sexual icon doesn't believe in sex addiction, calling it a "cop-out," that men pursue sex because they can get away with it, not because they are addicted. Hefner lives the life of an adolescent male's dreams—dreams influenced no doubt by the pages of the fantasies in Hefner's magazine—and is described by some as having an "adolescent" form of love for women that just doesn't last. "My life is constantly filled with young women. And with young women's laughter. And that is what keeps me alive."[15]*

In watching pornography, it is only sexual imagery and material that the viewer is at least neutral to that affects the viewer's behavior. In other words, if someone who has absolutely no interest in bestiality watches a movie containing animal-human sex, it's *not* going to make that person want to have sex with an animal. But if a person who has no strong opinions against anal sex watches a movie of anal sex scenes, then yes, that person might be likely to express some increased interest in anal sex and might be more likely to engage in anal sex if it's available or offered. The same holds true for violence and aggression in pornography. If someone has some tendency toward positive attitudes about violence toward females and they watch a pornographic movie with sex and violence, then yes, they are likely to be more sexually aggressive toward women. But the reverse is not true; violence in porn does not create violence in those not already inclined toward it.[16]

There are no easy answers on pornography. It is not a black-and-white phenomenon, no matter how strongly we would like to make it one. Like human sexuality in general, it includes both good and bad, and it has the potential for both benefit and harm. It is an economic giant now, a genie that is not going to be squashed back into the bottle. First Amendment laws have been clear that rights to access and view pornography are, in most cases, protected rights. Reviewing the decades of research on pornography, one finds polemic arguments on all fronts, arguments that ignore or overlook the complexities of these issues.

Research has shown that the effects of aggressive images in pornography upon viewers can be nullified when the viewers are in an inhibiting social environment and where the viewers understand the negative and damaging effects of these aggressive images.[17] Men who gravitate toward violent images in porn are men who are already disposed toward violence and aggression. Thus, what is needed are efforts to address not the porn, but the tendencies in our society to encourage and allow violent tendencies to go unchecked, unconfronted, and unaddressed until it is too late. Finally, research on the effects of porn use suggests that there is great variability across cultures and that there are qualities of our culture and society that predispose us to be susceptible to the effects of media influence.

It's all Al Gore's fault, at least according to the many addictionologists who blame the Internet for sex addiction. Patrick Carnes has said, "There are also many individuals who never would have experienced sexual compulsive behavior had it not been for the Internet."[18] But this argument ignores the issues of personal responsibility and falls into the flaw of overstating the impact of a single factor. It also ignores the changing role of media in our lives, of which Internet pornography is only a single piece.

Because pornography in many cases reflects extreme types of sex such as promiscuity, fetishistic sex, group sex, and the like, there is confusion anymore about what is normative in sexuality. This further complicates the issues in diagnosing sex addiction, which ostensibly rely upon the ability to distinguish normal from abnormal and unhealthy levels and types of sexual practice. Men and women in our society receive much of their education about sexuality from mainstream media and pornography. But we as a society are not doing much to offer these individuals the knowledge to understand their biological functions, the ways in which evolution has shaped their desires, and how it is that pornography uses these things to make people become more aroused, more quickly, and more frequently, "clicking through" more and more. Labeling these problems as "addiction" does little to address the problem but merely gives an excuse and labels it a disease. It also ignores the powerful lessons about male sexuality that can be found in pornography.

> No man in an enjoyable, healthy sexual relationship would choose to look at pornography instead of making love with his flesh-and-blood partner, says San Francisco Bay Area sex therapist and author Dr. Marty Klein. If, however, a wife or girlfriend is uncomfortable with a man's porn use, she can claim that he has a "porn addiction." If a wife claims that porn use is infidelity, if a girlfriend claims that porn use means he isn't attracted to her, a disease is one way to handle all the complex feelings. What then typically happens is she puts her foot down—"Porn or me!"— and he promises that he'll stop watching. And some guys actually do stop.
> The rest will do what they did when they were 14—they'll do it in secret, feel bad about it and hope they won't get caught. And so a life of lying about sex continues. You can imagine what that will do to the couple's closeness.
> —Marty Klein, PhD[19]

12

The Expression of
Male Sexual Desire

Because men have enjoyed a history of sexuality that places them in
the dominant role of pursuer, sex becomes an addiction only when
heterosexual monogamy becomes blatantly (publicly) threatened,
that is, when monogamy had to be reasserted as normal, in which
case infidelity becomes psychologically excusable rather than morally inexcusable.

—Jeffrey Falla, PhD[1]

$\mathcal{T}$he theories of sex addiction set low limits on the level of sex and number of sex partners that are judged to be healthy and normal. But there are
dramatic differences between the genders in terms of sexual desire. Men
desire more sex and more sexual partners than women. Period. Even when
researchers have tried to experimentally "lift" the fears of pregnancy, disease,
and social judgment that are involved in female attitudes toward sexuality,
men still desire more sexual partners than women. In one study, researchers
found that in the "ideal" situation, with no fears or problems, men desired
almost thirteen partners a year, compared to fewer than five desired partners
for women, and the greatest number of women desire only a single sexual
partner, in their ideal.[2] Other studies have shown that men on average desire
as many as sixty-four sexual partners in a lifetime, while women on average
desire fewer than three. In one 1978 (pre-AIDS) study that compared gay
men to lesbian women, results were astounding, showing that 43 percent of
white gay men reported having over five hundred sexual partners, while none
of the lesbian women reported such high numbers.[3] The limits on "healthy"
sexual desire and frequency that are set by sex addictionologists are most
similar to the female norms and ignore these gender differences.

One study suggested that the rates of sexual experiences reported by male sex addicts are actually consistent with the number of sexual partners and sexual experiences that non–sex addicts *wish they could have*. Thus, male sex addicts may differ only in their level of sexual success, not in their level of desire or sexual interest.[4]

Novelty Chickens and Male Sexual Variety

President Calvin Coolidge and his wife once toured a chicken farm. During the tour, the First Lady took note of the fact that a single rooster had sex many times in a day and requested that this fact be conveyed to her husband the president. Hearing this, the president clarified that the rooster was having sex many times in a day, not with a single hen, but with many different females, and requested that this point be conveyed to his wife.

The "Coolidge effect" thus describes the pattern that over time men lose sexual arousal and response to "known" females, but they respond powerfully to novelty, to new, unknown females. In a study conducted at the State University of New York, Stony Brook, young men were shown images of either the same couple having sex or different couples. The men shown different images maintained high levels of sexual arousal, while the men who were shown the same image repeatedly slowly lost their erections and arousal.

Among mammals, few species live in monogamous arrangements, and fewer maintain sexual fidelity within those relationships. Man certainly does not seem to be one of them. Rates of infidelity range from 15 to 75 percent, though the most consistent findings suggest that about 25 percent of women admit infidelity across their lifetime, with 40 percent of men acknowledging violations of monogamy within their lives. When men do cheat, they cheat more than women, usually reporting as many as three times the number of extramarital encounters and partners than is reported by unfaithful women. Men frequently describe a history of multiple one-night stands, whereas women are more likely to describe longer-term love relationships that happened outside their marriage.

When we look at same-sex couples, the difference is dramatic. Among men in homosexual relationships, 82 percent admit to infidelity, compared to only 28 percent of women in lesbian relationships. Put simply, men are far more inclined to participate in infidelity than women, and these results do not appear to reflect different levels of social pressure upon women, but rather core differences in the way male and female sexual drives and attitudes affect infidelity.[5]

Embedded in the concept of sexual addiction are complex moral assumptions about sexuality, and about infidelity in particular. Carnes says it powerfully: "When your partner chooses other sexual partners, the sword cuts deeper and detachment is much more elusive."[6] He suggests that in a relationship with sexual betrayal, a betrayed partner can move into codependency, becoming sexually volatile, having affairs of their own, becoming "hypersexual" for their partner, or deadening their sexuality and becoming asexual.

I don't buy the idea that cheating, or sexual behavior of any kind, is addictive. It's too easy an answer, and it's really just a nonanswer. Labeling something as an addiction doesn't help us understand it.

There is not just one answer, but many to explain why infidelity is so compelling, so powerful, so tempting. Extramarital sex involves a complex pattern of behaviors that includes biological influences, psychological factors, social contexts, and the influence of the evolutionary history that shaped our sexual behaviors. Within each person, the reasons and factors vary.

Psychological factors can include things like how people feel about themselves and their relationship. Some people are seeking the sense of power and confidence they get from being desired by multiple people, along with the sense of control that their desire gives them. I've also seen people cheat because they want to get caught so that their marriage can end. For others, infidelity is an escape hatch, a back door, a pressure relief valve, a sense of freedom, or sometimes it's just something that "is for me, and me alone. Not for my husband, my kids, or my job. Just for me." A chronic male philanderer wrote in *Esquire* magazine that infidelity was a way for him to escape details that "fill" and "deaden" his life, allowing him to be free and to express new, different parts of himself.[7]

When a sexual relationship first starts, our brains are flooded with neurochemicals that foster feelings of excitement, obsession, and impulsivity. Oxytocin and dopamine are particularly influential at this stage. When these chemicals are raging in our brain, we can often do nothing but think about our new lover, doodling their name, daydreaming about being with them, and taking every opportunity to be near them. Sex with this new lover is exceptionally powerful, as these chemicals enhance our physical reactivity. Oxytocin alone makes our skin far more sensitive to touch, creating the sensation of trails of pleasure that linger behind our lover's touch. With our primary mate, these chemicals have faded, replaced by hormones that foster us to think about long-term plans, to nurture, and to provide for our mate and any children that might result from the frenzy of sex that is prompted by the earlier state of our brain chemicals. A new relationship with a new lover triggers these chemicals again, and in many cases we carry this same level of excitement and passion home with us. This is one reason spouses often detect infidelity by the changes in our energy, our moods, and even our increased interest in sex.

Sex with a new lover is powerful and exciting. A male with a new lover is able to have more sex, for longer, more frequently, and more vigorously, and he ejaculates harder, with more sperm in that ejaculate. His body is attempting to compete against any other men his new lover might be sleeping with. His physiology starts acting like that of an alpha male, flooded with testosterone. For a woman, leaving her husband at home as she takes a new lover can often make her intensely orgasmic, her body responding sexually and physically to this new man in a way she often has not felt in years. Her body responds to this new male and to the chance of having children with him, her children who will have the benefit of the new, diverse genes he carries. When she is at the most fertile point of her cycle, a wife often finds herself attracted to men she would normally avoid, men unlike her husband, who is a good caregiver, stable, calm, and nurturing to her and her children. When she's tempted to cheat, the wife is drawn to men who have an edge of aggression and dominance, men who will never truly commit to monogamy, to being tied down. And her body responds powerfully to these men, her sexuality becoming aroused, her heart quickening, her skin longing for his touch. She achieves orgasm with this new man within moments and often has more orgasms with him than she may have believed possible.

> The concept of sex addiction has become a convenient way of explaining why so many people break the rules of monogamy today without examining the tensions and contradictions within monogamy itself. Marital infidelity never becomes an opportunity to examine why sexual exclusivity and "love" must always occur together for all couples. Instead, our attention is directed toward understanding why the failure to buy into this definition of love is an illness. Public figures whose reputations are destroyed by infidelity can only salvage their image by submitting to public shaming and the completion of "sex addiction therapy."
> —Curtis Bergstrand, PhD[8]

Most people in America believe that sexual infidelity is morally wrong—even most of the people who cheat. Those who cheat will say, "I'm not the sort of person who cheats," even as they are having extramarital sex. This is a clear example of the distinction between our behaviors and beliefs, and strong evidence that beliefs and values do not always predict behaviors or choices.

Americans actually aren't cheating all that much, when you look at recent surveys and results. Although lifetime rates of infidelity are higher, only around 4 to 5 percent of American men and 3 percent of American women report extramarital sex in the past year, with higher rates over a lifetime. But this number changes dramatically when you look at groups within populations. For instance, in some predominantly African-American areas of Chicago, rates of infidelity among men were as high as 39 percent in the past year, in contrast to only 8 percent in women.[9] National reports show that there is more male infidelity in cities and in people with lower household incomes. As household (and national) incomes go up, female infidelity increases, but as they go down, male infidelity increases. Interestingly, when female income goes up, especially when it is higher than the husband's income, the husband is at increased risk of infidelity, perhaps because having a more successful female partner calls into question a man's masculinity.

Similar patterns are suggested by worldwide research, where poorer Third World countries report drastically higher rates of male infidelity than wealthier, developed countries. Rates of last-year male infidelity in Mexico City are around 15 percent, Haitian men at 25 percent, and Mozambique males as high as 29 percent. The African countries of the Ivory Coast, Cameroon, and Togo report rates of last-year male infidelity as high as 36 and 37 percent.

Rates and attitudes toward infidelity vary dramatically between different cultures. While France actually has less, not more, infidelity than America, they have different views of it and snicker at American turmoil and angst over the drama of infidelity. "They don't think extramarital sex points to larger moral failings."[10] Other commentators agree: "While huge portions of the French populace, of course, are faithful to their partners, my impression is that a sizable portion expects and even admires male infidelity and libidinousness."[11]

In Russia, there is an almost universal social acceptance of infidelity. Even respected psychologists view extramarital sex as a healthy, normal part of people's lives.[12] In Japan, many marriages involve very little sex between husbands and wives. Male infidelity in these marriages is extremely high, feeding a booming Japanese industry of prostitution, pornography, and sex work, and male sexual exploits are simply seen as games, as "boys out for some fun."[13] Sex with a prostitute doesn't even meet Japanese legal definitions of adultery.

In African countries where rates of HIV and AIDS are very high, so are rates of infidelity. In fact, rates of infidelity are so high, and so intrinsically linked to the spread of AIDS, that attempts at reducing extramarital sex have been a critical part of the movement to prevent HIV transmission. But despite enormous efforts and publicity, extramarital sex continues to be rampant, particularly among poor farmworkers. But no one blames this epidemic on unrestrained sexual desires, on male sexuality, or sex addiction. The continued AIDS epidemic is blamed on poverty, and on the social dynamics that prevent the use of condoms or the practice of safe sex. In South Africa, "asking someone to wear a condom implies that you don't trust him, and you need trust to feel love and passion."[14] What these people are looking for is not safety from disease, or even sex itself, but for sex to offer them feelings of love, acceptance, and a temporary escape from the crushing burdens of poverty.

> The prerequisite for a good marriage, it seems to me,
> is the license to be unfaithful.
> —Carl Jung, in a letter to Sigmund Freud[15]

In countries where male infidelity is expected, even celebrated culturally, the concept of sex addiction has not taken hold, and male sexual exploits are not seen as a sign of weakness but as a strength. Characterizing promiscuity and infidelity as a sign of weakness, a sign of physical deficit, is not supported by the evolutionary history of humanity. We all are children of promiscuous ancestors. In fact, research by Robin Baker, author of *Sperm Wars*, suggests that as many as 4 percent of all children born today are the result of extramarital sex and that almost all of us have ancestors who were not legally married to each other. In other words, infidelity and promiscuity is a fact of human existence and a long-standing component of masculine eroticism. It is only in today's Western culture that these things have been identified as an illness.

Lizard King

"I am the Lizard King, I can do anything."[16]

Neurologist Paul MacLean found that the areas of the brain that are involved with aggressive behaviors in males are extremely close to the areas of the brain that are involved with the male erection. This suggests that in the evolutionary development of the human brain, sex and aggression were linked, or at least parallel. In males, the two behaviors both emerge from similar, very primitive areas of the brain, sometimes called the "reptilian" brain.

Jim Morrison was a 1960s singer, songwriter, and poet who proclaimed himself "the Lizard King." Morrison was known for his songs involving sex and aggression. "The End" is a prime example, with its disturbing lyrics of patricide and maternal incest. Morrison never formally married but had an open relationship with his common-law wife, Pamela Courson. Throughout his short stardom, Morrison was allegedly promiscuous with countless female fans and singers from other rock groups of the day. At the time of his death in 1971, there were as many as twenty paternity suits filed against him.

Case Example

Juan is a forty-three-year-old former police officer. He lost his job for sex-related behaviors and wonders if he might have been a sex addict. Juan had always wanted to be a police officer. His dad was absent throughout his childhood, and at an early age Juan identified the power and authority inherent in the police uniform with a sense of masculinity and identity, for which he had a deep unsatisfied craving.

On his first night on the "job," Juan's supervising officer spread some cocaine out on his clipboard, took a snort, and then berated Juan for not indulging, accusing him of being a narc. On his first night as a solo officer, Juan had yet another stunning encounter. In a convenience store around midnight, a beautiful, scantily clad woman approached him and said, "You're new, aren't you? I know all the officers, and I don't know you." After a few moments, she told him to meet her later in the high school parking lot so they could get to know each other better. When he did, she had brought somebody else, her seventeen-year-old female cousin, just as scantily clad. Before he could say anything, the two women had dropped to their knees and performed oral sex on him, no questions asked.

"I was like a kid in a candy store," he told me. "Badge bunnies were every-where." Badge bunnies *is the term used to describe women who have a "thing" for men in police uniforms. They are to police and firefighters what groupies are to rock stars. Some women make it a thing, like Juan's new friends, to have sex with as many officers as they can. No-strings-attached sex was available to Juan everywhere he turned. "Women, even married women, will hop in the sack with you with no expectations just because you're a cop. They're not looking for anything from you other than the experience of screwing a police officer."*

Juan embarked on a decade more of policing, with sex on the side everywhere he turned. Even when married to female police officers, his extracurricular activities continued. "Female cops who marry male cops know what they're getting into. Police stations are just full of people cheating on each other, and I'm talking about the cops, not the people hauled in for domestic violence."

Juan's career came to an end when his current wife, a fellow police officer, pulled over one of Juan's girlfriends for a traffic violation. His girlfriend, a some-time prostitute, wasn't happy with Juan right then because he had declined to get her out of a warrant that had been issued for her arrest. "Believe it or not, I had ethics," he told me, explaining why he had refused to manipulate the law for the prostitute's protection. His girlfriend recognized the name on his wife's badge and spilled the beans. And once the beans started spilling, there were lots of beans in the jar. Juan lost his job, his marriage, and much of his identity. And without his badge and job, Juan also lost the free access to no-strings-attached sex, which had become such a part of his life.

"Like I said, I was a kid in a candy store. They put me there, put me in the candy store. And then in the end, they fired me because I ate too much."

EROTIC PRIVILEGE

> There was a period when I had fourteen women and I'd take three or four every evening, one after the other. . . . That gives you an idea of my sexuality . . . be afraid of my love. It's like a cyclone. It's tremendous. It overwhelms everything.
>
> —Benito Mussolini[17]

> He's a hard dog to keep on the porch.
>
> Hillary Clinton, describing her husband's infidelity[18]

Genetic analyses suggest that Genghis Khan may have fathered as many as a thousand different children. This estimate is based on analyses of shared genes throughout the world, which can be traced back to this mighty Asian ruler. Khan fathered so many children through his tremendous military and political power, as he and his armies swept across the continent, gathering up women as wives, concubines, and victims of rape.

Other research suggests that, in contrast to the great Khan, throughout history only about 40 percent of men have managed to reproduce, in contrast to 80 percent of women. So in order for men to reproduce and father children, they have had to be aggressive, dominant, and hypersexual. The male physiology and brain are primed to respond to sexual opportunities and to pursue dominance as a reproductive strategy.[19]

Sex on the Round Table

John F. Kennedy was no stranger to sex, even before he entered politics and brought a sexy Camelot to Washington, D.C. Prior to joining the war in the Pacific, Kennedy was embroiled in a sex scandal with a beautiful Russian spy, with FBI agents listening in on the couple's pillow talk. During his candidacy for president of the United States, Kennedy's rampant sexuality was indulged, a practice that did not abate when he entered the White House. Kennedy once told the British prime minister that he got headaches if he did not have sex with a new woman each day. His affairs with starlets like Marilyn Monroe are today notorious, though during his presidency, his indulgent infidelities were kept quiet by the press. The press at the time used an approach called "access journalism," where they maintained relationships with leaders like Kennedy, protecting stories like his infidelity in order to gain access to bigger news stories, around politics and international relations. Over time, Western journalism has moved into more of a "gotcha" style of journalism, where sensationalism has taken precedence in a style of reporting where journalists do not practice "delay of gratification" but have perhaps become "addicted" to the quick fix of a sexual scandal. Thus Bill Clinton experienced a very different relationship with the press than did his idol, JFK.[20]

⸙

In men, the more powerful and dominant they are, the more sex they have, with their wives and others. When a woman is less dominant and more submissive, she ends up having more sex, not less, as she accedes more to her male partners' requests for sex. When a male is more submissive in the relationship and less dominant, he has less sex, as he is less successful in initiating it with his female partner. When both partners in a couple are sexually dominant, they are more likely to engage in unusual sexual practices, including things like group sex, use of erotica or pornography, using sex toys, having anal sex, cross-dressing, or incorporating aspects of BDSM into their sexuality.[21]

A study conducted in the Netherlands surveyed businesspeople and found that the more power individuals held in their employment, the more likely they were to report a history of sexual infidelity. Because more men are in positions of power, it is an effect more visible in men. Personality characteristics of impulsivity and risk taking were not significant factors, compared to power. "One of the strongest effects of power is that it increases feelings of confidence. The feeling of decreased power leads to more of a focus on threat and danger. But power leads to this disinhibited sense that you can get what you want and should take risks to get it."[22]

Powerful men throughout history have enjoyed sexual privilege. In Europe, the tradition of *droigt de seigneur*, or "first night," allegedly offered noblemen the right to have sex with the new brides of men in their district. Biblically, David and Solomon both married hundreds of women, and for David, even those wives were not enough, as he coveted Bathsheba and used his power over her husband to obtain her. According to interesting results published by the Internet social site OkCupid, over 50 percent of heterosexual women prefer their mates to be dominant, and only 20 percent prefer them to be "balanced" in terms of dominance and submissive tendencies.[23]

Powerful, influential men through modern times have also enjoyed the freedom to pursue multiple women. Albert Einstein famously philandered, as revealed in his private letters. Einstein had as many as ten different lovers during his marriage, and he described them to his family, even to his wife, stating that these women would "shower him with unwanted affection."[24] Anthropologist Desmond Morris argues that geniuses like Einstein and John F. Kennedy are always unfaithful, as an expression of their creativity and their internal desire to conquer and hunt, to take risks and succeed.[25]

Victor Hugo, author of *Les Misérables,* prided himself on his sexual voracity, once boasting of having sex with four different women in a single day. On his wedding night, he bedded his young bride nine times, a pace that continued until she ceased their sexual activity after eight years and five difficult pregnancies. Hugo then embarked upon a life of sexual excess, with prostitutes, courtesans, married women, and his mistress Juliet. Though Hugo enjoyed various aspects of sexuality, such as voyeurism, using peepholes installed in the bedrooms of his home to spy on guests, Hugo's true sexual love was quantity and diversity. Juliet once estimated that in a two-year period, Hugo had sex with over two hundred different women. At the age of seventy, Hugo seduced a twenty-two-year-old woman, and at the age of eighty, his grandson found him coupling with a housemaid.[26]

Actor Richard Burton famously married Elizabeth Taylor twice. He was also a notorious philanderer, by some accounts sleeping with three different women a week for over thirty years, for an estimated total of over 2,500 different women. A close friend described Burton: "He was Don Juan, and it was a necessity in his nature to have any female who was not under age or terribly ugly."[27]

As leader of Communist China, Mao Zedong outlawed prostitution, bigamy, having concubines, and promiscuity. Infidelity wasn't outlawed but could result in severe punishments, loss of work, and banishment if an individual was reported to his or her communist work group for extramarital sex. But at the same time, Mao used his power and influence to recruit a constant stream of young women (especially virgins, which he preferred) into his bed. Mao's personal physician describes that the leader particularly liked group sex, having three, four, or even five women simultaneously.[28]

When women are elected to public office, they run different kinds of elections from men, they serve in different ways, and they may be less subject to the temptations of power as an aphrodisiac, compared to men. According to former White House Press Secretary Dee Dee Myers, "There are certain men that the more visible they get, the more bulletproof they feel. You just don't see women doing that; they don't get reckless when they're empowered."[29]

This doesn't make women better, just different. As Roy Baumeister explains in detail in his delightful book *Is There Anything Good about Men?*, men and women are different and serve different roles in our society and species. While men may be more prone to engage in sexual misbehaviors, women are more prone to engage in physical abuse of children. These differences do not indicate that men, or women, are better, just different, with different strengths *and* different weaknesses. Healthy leaders, and a healthy society, take these strengths and weaknesses into account, in themselves and in those they put in power.

Perfection in our leaders is a nice ideal, but unfortunately, in dealing with humans, and yes, particularly in dealing with human males, it can only be an ideal, never a reality. British member of parliament Paul Flynn offers advice to younger politicians, saying that it is a complete mystery to him that even ugly and foolish politicians attract members of the opposite sex, with an inescapable sexual magnetism that comes from their positions of power. He tells young politicians to take cold baths, to go to bed early, and to think about death and the negative consequences to life and career of sexual indulgence.[30]

Case Example

Eliot Spitzer, Former Governor of New York
When New York governor Eliot Spitzer faced a fall from grace, resulting from the exposure of his long-running personal relationship with prostitution, one of his advisors developed a plan whereby Spitzer would claim the effects of sex addiction and retreat to a high-priced treatment resort, an act that "symbolized his complete surrender to the reality of his sickness." In fact, the media had already labeled him a sex addict. The typical media reaction came from Dr. Tian Dayton, who wrote, "Many sex addicts feel like frauds and freaks. They lead double lives. One life they are proud to show in public, another, secret life that they feel both tantalized and deeply ashamed of. Elliot [sic] *Spitzer is probably one of them."[31]*

But Spitzer rejected the plan to pursue the label of sex addict, especially the part where he publicly blamed his behavior on an "uncontrollable compulsion."[32] Spitzer instead stood before the people of New York and stated, "I cannot allow my private failings to disrupt the people's work. Over the course of my public life I have insisted—I believe correctly—that people, regardless of their position or power, take responsibility for their conduct. I can and will ask for no less of myself."[33]

PAYING FOR IT

They [men] are starved for a moment of spontaneous, nonobligating, aggressively free sexual abandon. They go off and buy it, but the price is further damage to their already negative male self-image.

—Herb Goldberg[34]

Frequent, compulsive use of prostitutes is identified as a common component of sexual addiction. But this view of prostitution reveals the fallacy of focusing only upon the sexual behavior in prostitution and ignoring the many other psychological and emotional aspects. A manager at a Nevada brothel once told me about a man who won a million-dollar injury settlement from an insurance company. He spent over $400,000 dollars at the brothel over three months. He rarely had sex with the girls but preferred to cuddle with them, watching movies together. Former prostitutes report similar stories, with male customers paying them to go to work functions with them, make breakfast together, and simply cuddle or go to the movies with them. Like most aspects of male sexuality, visiting prostitutes involves many nonsexual aspects such as a need for connection, acceptance, and fulfilling one's internal image of identity and masculinity. Though fewer than 20 percent of men will visit a prostitute in their lives, around half of all men tend to view prostitution as somewhat acceptable.

The number of women who pay for sex with prostitutes is so small that it doesn't even register. Humorous news stories over the past few years have derided the failure of brothels with male prostitutes targeted at female customers. In both Nevada and Germany, such endeavors have failed due to lack of business; in the German effort a few years back, the male prostitutes were apprehended committing burglaries to supplement their nonexistent incomes from selling sex to women. Women don't pay for sex, because they don't have to.

The other place men pay for sex, or at least sexual contact, is in strip clubs, where female dancers disrobe for money. Sex addiction often includes visits to strip clubs, according to sex addictionologists and the DSM5 criteria for hypersexual disorder. Unfortunately, there is no research to back this up. Problems related to strip clubs are described only by anecdote, by stories told by clients and patients to therapists. Strip clubs are ubiquitous across the United States and represent a substantial part of the cash economy. As with brothels, though, there is not a significant parallel for women. Male strip shows like the Chippendales exist but make up a tiny fraction of the number of establishments and the amount of money spent on such entertainment, relative to male-oriented strip clubs.

The stimulation of seeing strange women nude triggers the male desire for variety and may even result in neurochemical and biological reactions similar to when a man first becomes physical with a new female mate. But in research with men attending strip clubs, the common reason that men give is to "relax." Men report that strip clubs are safe environments where they can be accepted for themselves and can relax their grip on trying to be sexually appropriate. In strip clubs, men can simply ogle a woman, without being afraid of judgment or reaction, or worrying that they will offend or insult the woman.

In strip clubs, men can experience a sexualized interaction, where the women praise them and work hard to make the man feel important and attractive, and where, as in porn, it seems effortless for the man to satisfy the woman—all it takes is cash. Research by Katharine Frank, PhD anthropologist and former stripper, explored the world of stripping from the experience of a woman on stage. She describes that the men she danced for were looking for acceptance and support, far more than sexual stimulation. This subtlety is lost in the views of sex addictionologists, who see only the sexuality in the acts of men who visit strip clubs and brothels, ignoring, or pathologizing, the men's loneliness and emotional needs.

Case Example

Stripped to Death
Sensational stories of obsession, death, and strippers abound. In 1997, Craig Rabinowitz allegedly strangled his young wife in order to run away with a stripper, a tale that captivated Philadelphia for months. Rabinowitz had a mountain of debt, spending $100,000 on a local stripper. Rabinowitz also had hundreds of thousands of dollars that he'd scammed from businesspeople, having developed a pyramid scheme supporting a fictional company. At last, his wife began to press him about his secret activities, and Rabinowitz killed her, attempting to make it look like an accident in order to collect on a $1.8 million life insurance policy.

In November 1997, Philadelphia psychologist Ralph Hyatt suggested that Rabinowitz's actions might reflect a sex addiction, but Rabinowitz was ultimately held responsible for his actions and sentenced to life in prison, though he tried to pawn responsibility for his actions and problems off on everyone else.[35] From prison, he told a reporter that he had grown up with a distant mother and an angry father, and that his wife's sexual distance and overmanaged life had left him feeling "emasculated," with "thirteen years of resentment." In prison, Rabinowitz was still writing to the stripper, attempting to contact her (she didn't reply and wanted nothing to do with him), and he reported that if he were released from prison, the first thing he would do was visit her.

CASUAL SEX

Sex addictionologists assert that sex without love is a path to addiction. Female sexual values prioritize intimacy, and as we've seen already, casual sex increases depression in females but decreases it in males. But the research on casual sex is complex and suggests that our problems with it have more to do with social attitudes than any true universal effects of sex without love and intimacy. Research on casual sex suggests that it is incredibly common, with between 50 and 75 percent of all college students reporting at least one incident of casual sex and hooking up in the past year.

Casual sex and college "hooking up" has been a contentious area of research, challenging many core moral concepts. Many are concerned that sex without commitment or intimacy puts people (mostly women) at risk of harm, from pregnancy, date rape, and sexually transmitted disease. Research has found that women mostly report that such experiences leave them feeling either awkward, desirable, or both. These aren't necessarily the catastrophic feelings we expect.

Casual sex does not universally result in the kind of risk and emotional harm that sex addiction theories predict. One thorough study of this phenomenon was done by Jesse Owen in 2008, where he and other researchers assessed over eight hundred college students on campuses in the western and southeastern United States. Results were fascinating. Owen's research found that there was no difference between the numbers of men and women who reported hooking up, though they reported quite different emotional experiences with casual sex. Those college students who were hooking up were not dysfunctional, disturbed, or emotionally troubled young adults. They tended to be from wealthier families, and in men at least, higher psychological "well-being" predicted more hooking up. More men reported that the experience of hooking up was positive (around 50 percent), compared to 24 percent of women, while half of all women reported that it was a negative experience.

People who view hooking up positively are more likely to have positive experiences with hooking up. If you believe it will be a good experience, or a bad experience, it seems that this becomes a self-fulfilling prophecy. So it may be the internal beliefs that casual sex is unhealthy that create the negative outcome, rather than the casual sex itself. Owen's later research shows that for individuals who are already depressed and alone, having casual sex actually helps them, improving mood and decreasing reports of loneliness. In contrast, when a person who isn't depressed has casual sex, their feelings of depression increase. But this is not a simple black-and-white effect, and the suggestion that casual, noncommitted sex is inherently destructive is not supported.

Swedish researchers Langstrom and Hanson examined sexual and mental health data from around 2,500 Swedish residents in one of the only studies that has ever examined what rates of high sexual activity actually mean in a nonclinical population. They found that, for the most part, people having lots of sex were generally healthy, with few emotional or life problems. People with higher sex drives and higher levels of sex activity were more likely to engage in fetishistic behaviors, including BDSM, voyeurism, and exhibitionism, but even these folks were still doing well in their lives. Langstrom and Hanson defined hypersexuality as representing the sexual behaviors of those who are more sexually active than 90 to 95 percent of the population. Their definition did not specify that these individuals were necessarily pathological; they merely used this statistical definition as a way to distinguish groups within their research population.

While higher rates of sex did not predict any psychosocial problems, people with high rates of "impersonal sex" and masturbation did tend to have poorer relationships, more substance abuse problems, and were generally dissatisfied with life. Their results didn't support the notion that impersonal sex itself is detrimental, just high rates of it. Langstrom and Hanson suggest that their findings indicate that any definition of "excessive" sex should focus more upon the "social and psychological meanings and not just the frequency of orgasms."[36] Again, though, we don't know which way causality goes. Are these people having more problems because they are masturbating and having more one-night stands, or are they masturbating more and having more anonymous sex because they are having more problems?

In 1994, a University of Chicago team conducted interviews using a statistically derived sampling process in one of the only large-scale studies of sexual activities in the United States on a nonclinical population.[37] They found that the more sexual intercourse a person had, the happier that person tended to be. The more masturbation a person reported, the less happy. People with only a single sex partner in the past year were happier, compared to those reporting multiple sex partners. Is it the masturbation or the multiple sex partners that is causing this unhappiness? No, certainly not. But think about the social and emotional experiences that go into those numbers. People masturbate more when they are lonely. A major reason people might report more than one sex partner in the past twelve months is not because of promiscuity, group sex, or infidelity, but simply because of divorce or other lack of a stable relationship. Divorce and loneliness create unhappiness.

Recent research in Chicago shows that casual sex can end up in emotionally committed and healthy relationships just as often as relationships that start in noncasual ways. So even though a relationship might start with "just sex," it doesn't have to stay that way, and often it does not. And casual sex doesn't hurt a person's chances of developing a real, stable, and loving relationship, despite Dear Abby's decades of advice. Even in men, other research finds that many men have more complex expectations regarding casual sex and often desire an emotional connection as a part of the casual relationship. Believe it or not, most of the men who say they are just looking for "no strings attached" are surprisingly sensitive to feelings of trust and emotions, and would prefer that there be a sense of connection with the women they're sleeping with.[38]

—∞∞∞—

Fumbling in the Dark

Gay bathhouses, where men go for anonymous sex with other men, sometimes include a special room where blackout curtains create a pitch-black environment. In the dark, visitors encounter the bodies, hands, and genitalia of unknown men. While this sounds like a hedonistic orgy, it is in fact reminiscent of a research project that revealed that this desire is normal, and that both men and women experience sexual arousal and a desire for anonymous physical contact in such settings.

In 1973, researcher Kenneth Gergen of Swarthmore College ushered five male and five female college students, one at a time, into a pitch-black room. As they entered and left the room, they did so in anonymity from the other subjects. While Gergen secretly observed using an infrared camera, the men and women interacted in the room. At first, the subjects talked, but soon, the men and women began to reach out and touch each other, seeking physical contact with the others in the darkened room. Nearly 90 percent of the subjects deliberately touched others in the room, both male and female. Half hugged other people, and a third kissed them. Eighty percent of the men and women reported that they were sexually excited by the encounters and the environment, where the imposed anonymity offered them the opportunity to express their desires for physical contact with strangers.[39]

—∞∞∞—

Male Performance on the Field of Battle

> Aggression, as a human emotion, cannot be purged from human interactions, especially not among those who love each other. Aggression is the shadow side of love. It is also an intrinsic component of sexuality, and it can never be entirely excised from sexual relationships.
>
> —Esther Perel[40]

Where past societies idolized male combat heroes, in America today, there is no higher pinnacle of modern masculine success than sports and athletics. We hold successful male athletes up as the modern role models of masculinity, celebrating their physical prowess on the court and field. These men tend to be selected for their physiques, their coordination, and their strength and speed. Society rewards men who have great sexual accomplishments, prowess, and success. Sexual conquests are seen as evidence of a man's virility, his strength, attractiveness, and level of success in the game of life. Men who have sex have "scored." In a game, who wins? The player with the highest score.

---∞---

Spur Posse

In 1993, the country was aghast at the revelations of a group of eight young men in Lakewood, California. These young men, who called themselves the "Spur Posse," devised a point system where they got points for having sex with girls. One girl, one point, went the rules, and multiple times with the same girl yielded no additional points. When the revelations broke in the media, it set off a frenzy, where the boys were sometimes defended as "red-blooded American males" who were simply acting out the testosterone-driven fantasies of every male. Only one of the eight boys was charged with a crime, for having had sex with a ten-year-old girl. The rest of the boys were lauded on daytime talk shows.

The "top scorer" of the group, young Billy Shehan, celebrated the fact of his having achieved sixty-six points with these various girls, and he boasted of the pride his father had in his conquests. None of the boys or young men appeared to show much remorse, and why would they? They were acting out the fantasies of their fathers, and when their activities were revealed, the response was a titillated fascination and instant fame.[41]

---∞---

In professional basketball, football, and baseball, casual and chronic infidelity is almost universal, and the wives of players accept, albeit reluctantly, that their husbands are often sexually unfaithful as they travel with their team. The team encourages this approach, celebrating sexual conquests and creating opportunities for teammates to stray. "A culture of adultery permeates professional sports today," says Oregon sociologist Steven Ortiz. And the wives of these athletes must simply cope and accept the sexual behaviors of their celebrity athlete husbands, who themselves are coping with "boredom, peer group pressure, team loyalty, opportunity, sense of self-importance, and the availability of women who seem to be irresistibly attracted to professional athletes."[42]

As football stars Lawrence Taylor and Keith McCants have gotten in legal problems, they have both publicly blamed their problems on sex addiction. Taylor admitted in 2004 that he was spending a thousand dollars a night on female escorts. McCants, a former Tampa Bay Buccaneers first round draft pick with a $7 million contract, is currently in prison with a history of eleven arrests for drug-related charges. Interestingly, McCants prefers to blame his problems on sex as opposed to drugs.

> I have a sex addiction, I didn't really want that to get out, but that's it. What people do for drugs, I do for sex. Drugs just happen to be in it. I've been messing with women who did drugs. Sometimes, I took the rap for them and ended up in jail. I'm not saying what I did was right, but that's what happened. For all this to go away, I know I've got to change everything about me.
> —Keith McCants[43]

We grant these top athletes extraordinary privileges and excuse horrific behaviors from them. They are frequently violent to each other, to strangers, and to their wives and girlfriends. Not only do they engage in incredibly high rates of infidelity, but the rates of rape and sexual assault are extraordinarily high in many male athletes. On many college campuses, sexual assaults by athletes make up an extraordinarily high and disproportionate percentage of the overall campus sexual assault rates. I see no evidence that society is changing its view toward the entitlements that celebrity athletes receive. What I do see is that when this approach to life and sex gets a man in trouble, it's labeled an addiction. Otherwise, it's just success.

Scoring On (and Off) the Court

Wilt Chamberlain
Wilt Chamberlain is one of the fifty greatest basketball players of all time, and he won the league's MVP award not once, but four times across his career. Wilt never married and was described by his attorney in this way: "Some people collect stamps, Wilt collected women."[44] Wilt claimed to have slept with over 20,000 different women. Though he was widely known for his prowess at "scoring" both on the court and off it, many have questioned the simple mathematics of his claim, arguing that he would have had to sleep with eight different women a week from the time of his fifteenth birthday to his death. The athlete defended his lifestyle, saying, "I was just doing what was natural—chasing good-looking ladies, whoever they were and wherever they were available." He later warned other men not to admire his lifestyle and sexual adventures, saying, "With all of you men out there who think that having a thousand different ladies is pretty cool . . . I've found out that having one woman a thousand different times is much more satisfying."

Chamberlain's sexually voracious lifestyle was not a sign of internal struggle, deficiency, and a recipe for self-destruction. Chamberlain was never alleged to have committed a crime, sexual or otherwise. Sexual adventures with women did not pall to the point of needing new, exciting thrills that he could not achieve with women, and, despite the dire predictions of sex addictionologists, Chamberlain never escalated to pursuits of pedophilia or bestiality. One of Wilt's longtime girlfriends described that he was unable to blend friendship, intimacy, and sexual relationships. But despite these emotional barriers, Chamberlain was a man who criticized the commercialism of the professional sports industry, was a strong spokesman for the Special Olympics, as well as for the plight of the poor and starving children of Africa. Sexual excess did not corrupt or subsume this man's morals, who often boasted that he never slept with a married woman, refusing to violate the bonds and oaths of another relationship.

Would Wilt's life have been different had he married? Probably. But he consciously chose never to marry, from a place of self-awareness and independent choice. "I don't have anything against marriage, but I try to be logical in my doings. A lot of people are afraid of being alone, of not being loved. But there isn't any guaranteed security that a family is going to love you. And I've never found anyone I could make a commitment to."[45] It's frankly difficult to even conceive of discussing sexual excess, particularly male sexual excess, without acknowledging the life of Wilt Chamberlain. Wilt's life stands as a credible real-world test of the claims that excessive sex causes damage to one's life and relationships.

> On the Web, men prefer images. Women prefer stories.
> Men prefer graphic sex. Women prefer relationships and romance.
> —Ogas & Gaddam[46]

Men and women differ in their approaches to relationships. Women value (and succeed at) closer, intimate relationships with a few individuals, and their communication skills and ability to express their emotions support those types of relationships. Women are interested in few sexually intimate relationships and prefer monogamy. Women enjoy the emotional and relational context of romance novels, where sexuality occurs well into the book and is driven by emotional and contextual language. But men are better at shallower relationships with larger groups of people, such as teams and armies, where the ability to withhold one's emotions and be stoic is a valuable, successful trait. Men are more attracted to sex with greater numbers of partners, and with less intimate relationships, and they are biologically and socially predisposed to respond strongly to pornography.

Men's and women's brains process pornography differently, due to instinctual, even biological processes. Visual sexual stimuli and images trigger greater neurological responses in men than they do in women. The hypothalamus and amygdala of men respond more strongly to visual erotic images than they do in women, and in men, this brain activity leads to greater sexual responsiveness, as men gain an erection in response to visual stimuli faster than women become physiologically aroused. Men's brains appear to be designed to selectively and powerfully respond to pornography and visual images of eroticism in a way that is different from that of female brains. So the strong male response to pornography is, frankly, to be expected. It is actually normal for a male to enjoy and respond to pornography, whether you look at their brains, their bodies, or the history of social and evolutionary reinforcement that males have received for millennia when they respond with quick, powerful arousal to visual images of sexuality.

It makes evolutionary sense that men would take the chance of losing their jobs and marriages in response to sexual stimuli like pornography, strippers, and infidelity. For millennia, men who took such chances increased their opportunity to reproduce, and they experienced sexual pleasure at the same time. In order to address and change the ways in which some men express sexuality in their lives, creating problems in their lives, marriages, and careers, we must change the dialogue, acknowledging that male sexuality comes from a powerful place of biology, psychology, and learning, not solely a place of low character and morals.

13

The Ignored Aspects of Masculinity

It [society] cannot afford easygoing, unproductive men. Instead, it has to get the most out of everyone—perhaps especially the elite men who need to be coming up with the advances and innovations that will push the culture ahead of its rivals.

The core achievement that defines manhood in a culture is that a man produces more than he consumes.

—Roy Baumeister, PhD[1]

In sex addiction, there is a common perception of male sexuality as intrinsically selfish, as overly focused on "scoring" and on the outward manifestations of virility. As we've seen in examples like the "Spur Posse," these aspects of male sexuality are real. But there are other, neglected sides of male sexuality. In many cases, men are far more focused upon women's needs, and upon closeness with women, than we give them credit for. "Men's love of women is often greater than their love of self," wrote Nancy Friday,[2] describing the ways in which men give up friends and male camaraderie and accept a life of economic support of women, even leading up to an earlier death, all in order to be with women. And yet, despite this simmering anger and rage against women, rage for having to give up so much of themselves in order to be with women, men more often turn that rage upon themselves sexually rather than turning it upon women. The world of BDSM is described as "bottom-heavy," where most men pursue the role of submissive or "bottom," rather than embracing a role in which they could act out as sexual aggressors, and where female dominatrixes command high prices and favored status.[3]

Case Example

Ben is thirty-four, a Jewish male from New York. Ben's father left his family when Ben was twelve, and he had to step into the "man's" role for his family. He became a father to his younger siblings, taking care of them while his mother worked two jobs to support the family. Ben worked summers and after school, giving all the money he earned to his mother. Ben graduated high school and went to night school, earning a law degree while he still lived at home supporting his mother and siblings. Ben's mother died a few years ago, just after Ben married. Ben and his wife are unable to have children after she had several miscarriages, one of which almost ended her life. Since the last miscarriage, Ben's wife has struggled with depression and anxiety, rarely leaving their home. At the same time, Ben's legal work as a public defender has become overwhelming, as budget cuts and hiring freezes have doubled and then tripled his workload. Ben found that the only place he felt he could selfishly "take" and be safely indulged was when he hired a woman to have sex. As his external life became burdened more and more with responsibility, he began to compulsively seek out escorts and sexual masseuses, as many as three or four times a week during his lunch hour and after work.

More than half of all men describe that their best sexual encounters came when they "gave a woman physical pleasure beyond her dreams."[4] Men redirect their selfishness away from their own satisfaction, and toward a sense of fulfillment and accomplishment, by giving sexual satisfaction and fulfillment. Men's health writer David Zinczenko gives numerous examples of men who responded to a magazine's survey on male sexuality and described their focus on the needs of their partners:

> The best was when I gave her seven orgasms within thirty minutes.

> My main goal in sex is to help you have a great orgasm. I know I'm going to come, so I want to make sure you do as well. In fact, I'd rather give oral than receive. It just turns me on more.

> The most beautiful thing to a man is the woman he loves having an orgasm.[5]

In fact, men's desire to sexually satisfy their partners comes at the price of their own satisfaction. When a man is unable to make his partner orgasm, many men report incredible frustration, disappointment, and self-doubt. Women even complain that men put so much pressure and intent upon helping the woman achieve orgasm that the act ceases to be pleasurable and starts to feel more like childbirth. In such cases, women fake orgasms, not for themselves, but to satisfy their partner's needs. Until a woman has an orgasm, a man doesn't think he's done his job, and his masculinity hangs in the balance.

Men are taught from a young age that they must be sexually competent and sexually powerful with exaggerated and impossible ideals. Their penis must get hard when they want it to and stay hard as long as they need it to. It should be long enough and hard enough to play baseball with, and if it isn't, they are less of a man. Men are assumed to be competent at sexually satisfying their wife, and if she cheats on him, it is evidence of the husband's inability to satisfy his wife enough so that she does not need another lover.

This is a tremendous, frightening, and pervasive burden. Nancy Friday's book on male sexual fantasies, *Men in Love*, closes with the story of Davey, a fourteen-year-old male who writes that he is good at sex, and has lots of books on sex, but is tortured by a secret failing; he does not know how to kiss, and he does not know what to do with his tongue in a girl's mouth. Writing his letter was an act of desperation, and he feared that Friday would laugh at him and ridicule his ignorance. Davey's letter mirrors the insecure desperate tragedy at the heart of every male. Am I big enough, good enough, strong enough, handsome enough, sexy enough? Do I make enough money, do I smell good enough, is my shirt white enough for me to be with a woman? Am I skilled enough in bed? Do I ejaculate too soon? A 1994 survey of sex in America found that, compared to women, men are far more insecure and anxious about their sexual performance. Nearly 30 percent of men fear that they ejaculate too soon, and one man in every six reports significant feelings of anxiety about his sexual abilities to satisfy his partner.[6]

Contrary to our belief that men are invulnerable to the same pangs that women suffer in relationships, recent research by sociologists Robin Simon and Anne Barrett found that men actually experience greater pain than women from the ups and downs of romantic relationships. In research that compared 1,000 men and women, these sociologists found that not only did the negative aspects of a romantic relationship hurt men more than women, but the positive aspects and benefits of that relationship also have greater impact upon the man than the woman. Simon and Barrett suggest that it is because women are better able to access outside support from friends and family to mediate the emotional struggles. Men are typically isolated and bear the burden alone, often with the sole "support" of substance abuse to attempt to escape the emotional pain.

As men age, their physical sexual responsiveness decreases, and their fear of failure to sexually perform increases. Young men are afraid of being unskilled. You would think, if God was in fact male, that as a man ages and gains technique, his fear of failing in sexual performance would decrease.

Alas, cruel fate and biology replace his fear of lack of technique with the fear that his body will now fail him. Urologists are now seeing more elderly men seeking penile implants as they reject the impact that aging has upon their sexual capabilities.[7]

---oœo---

Women need to understand our need for affection; it's about acceptance, reward, relief, and love as much as anything else. It's just that we need [physical affection] up front to feel loved and wanted.
—a twenty-six-year-old male radio producer
speaking to *Men's Health* writer David Zinczenko.[8]

I can handle it [sentiment], as long as it's disguised as sex.
—*Three Men and a Baby*[9]

---oœo---

For men, physical affection and sex is one of the main ways we feel loved, accepted, and regarded. For many men, it is only through physical love that we can voice tenderness and express our desire for togetherness and physical bonding. Only in sex can we let down boundaries and drop our armor enough to be emotionally vulnerable.

I was born with only one hand. For one reason or another, I was born with a shortened left arm. It is an obvious and attention-getting disability, but I'll be honest, it has truly not been that disabling. I've always been successful at finding ways to adapt and finding my own ways to do things.

People respond to disabilities with an instinctive fear and distance. Conscious or not, people fear that a disability might be contagious. Whether it's a speech impediment, mental retardation, blindness, or a missing limb, it triggers a fear of loss in people. As a therapist who works with children, I've actually found my arm to be an incredible therapeutic tool. People respond to my arm, especially children, and it opens up conversations about fear and loss. I've had clients tell me, "You're missing something on the outside, and I've always felt like I'm missing something on the inside."

But that's in my professional life, where I'm paid to be empathetic and therapeutic. In my personal life, it's painful to have people afraid to touch me, particularly to touch my arm. Granted, I think they often fear that my arm might be sensitive, and they don't want to hurt me, or embarrass me by asking, but in the end, it's left me with an occasional burning feeling of insecurity and a fear of rejection.

So, physical contact for me is a very powerful thing. And sexual physical contact is perhaps the most powerful feeling of acceptance I've experienced from another adult. To have someone tell me that they accept me, with their body, to be vulnerable to them, naked in bed, and they with me, sends a strong message that I'm not seen as deficient, or weak, or sick, or any of the other thoughts of shame that might run through your head when people don't want to touch you.

Sometimes I have had partners who like to make love even when we're arguing. But because for me sex is wrapped up intensely with feelings of acceptance, angry sex is very emotionally conflicted and confusing. So when we're fighting or angry with each other, I need time to sulk, or calm down, and for the anger to subside.

Is there anything wrong with this, with the role that sex and acceptance and my feelings about my disability play in my life? I don't think so. It works for me, and it has generally worked for my partners. And I don't think I'm all that exceptional. Sex serves as a form of acceptance for lots and lots of men, just as it serves other emotional purposes, like relief from stress, grief, and loss.

Sex plays an even greater role in the lives of men as a form of acceptance and mutual regard than it does for women. Women touch each other all the time, with hugs, holding hands, closer body contact, and smaller "personal space." Men shake hands. Really good friends might, at best, punch each other in a loving way, do a careful "man hug," or even swat each other's buttocks, if it's during an approved masculine sporting event. So the body-to-body contact that sex offers feeds an appetite, a craving, one that is often starved near to death in men.

> I took full responsibility. I cheated on my wife. Guess what. So do millions of other men. People assumed I was a dick because I didn't defend myself.
> I went into rehab thinking, all these people in this place? They are really fucked up. I figured out pretty fast I was the fucked up one. I realized I was addicted to anger. And it was going to be up to me to straighten my shit out.
> —Jesse James[10]

It seems as though everybody today accepts that men seek sexual variety, and that this is "just the way they are." This concept originates in evolutionary theory, where the argument goes that men seek to spread their sperm far and wide, with as many women as possible, in order to reproduce as much as possible. In contrast, women are generally disposed to seek out "quality" in their mates, rather than quantity, given that it is a lot more work for a woman to reproduce than for a man.

But most people don't know the rest of the story. If we accept that this evolutionary pressure to reproduce in quantity has affected men's current sexual behaviors and drives, including infidelity, the historical universality of prostitution, and their response to pornography, what else comes along with it? Some of the side effects are relatively innocuous, such as the fact that men tend, on average, to be larger than women. This is a downstream effect of evolutionary pressure, as a larger size helps the man secure more mates and fight off competitors. But another consequence of this is seen in the many men who die in their youth from doing unbelievably stupid, risky things (the show *Jackass* comes to mind), as well as the fact that men die, on average, at least ten years before most women. These risky behaviors represent high-risk, high-payout wagers, where successful men gain the opportunity for reproduction.

The fact that men develop sexual dysfunctions and fetishes at much, much higher rates than women do is also a result of this drive. The fact that men masturbate more than women and engage in things like bestiality, exhibitionism, voyeurism, and frotteurism are all ways that men express that sexual drive for variety without having to invest the time and resources needed to meet the approval qualifications of most women.

> Aggression and eroticism are deeply intertwined. Hunt, pursuit, and capture
> are biologically programmed into male sexuality. Generation after generation,
> men must be educated, refined, and ethically persuaded away
> from their tendency toward anarchy and brutishness.
> —Camille Paglia[11]

Binghamton University researcher Justin Garcia found that individuals with a certain genetically driven dopamine receptor showed higher rates of promiscuous sex, anonymous sex, and infidelity. Garcia argues that this finding supports the notion that these sexual behaviors are, and always have been, rewarded in some environments, pointing out that this dopamine receptor is more prevalent in populations where men have been encouraged and allowed to behave as "cads," rather than being rewarded for being reliable "dad" types.[12] Evolutionary biologists Randy Thornhill and Craig Palmer have challenged the notion that rape is about violence, not about sex, proposing that male rape of women is a behavior driven by the same evolutionary pressures that drive men to seek variety and quantity in their mating strategies.[13] They point to the universality of rape, occurring in every known human culture, and prevalent in animal species as well.

Thornhill and Palmer argue that to truly address the problem of rape, we must educate men about the biological and psychological pressures that might dispose them to force a woman to have sex. We must begin teaching young men to control their sexuality, from a place of self-knowledge and understanding. In this way, we can reformulate the view of male sexuality, painting it as something that can be understood and controlled, rather than teaching men that their sexual desires are the equivalent of a monster that cannot be contained if it is awoken.

Case Example

In 2011, British Columbia teen Cameron Moffat was sentenced to life imprisonment for the murder and sexual assault of an eighteen-year-old girl. At an early age, Cameron showed disturbed and violent behavior, with multiple school-related problems for aggression and violence. His disturbed behavior came after alleged sexual abuse at age three and the separation of his parents at age nine. Throughout childhood, he was assaultive and physically threatening to his family. As early as age ten, Cameron began drinking alcohol and reportedly became fascinated with sexual sadism.

In 2010, Moffat and another teenage boy planned and executed a brutal, horrific assault upon a young woman they knew from school, using text messages and online chats to lure her to her death. During police interrogations of the crime, Moffat told police that he had been a sex addict who turned his addictive behaviors toward playing online video games, and then, ultimately, toward the planning and execution of this crime. Moffat claimed that he had once had sex thirty times in a single day, until he found out his girlfriend was cheating on him, and he "built a wall" around his sexual feelings and began to focus on other activities that were more rewarding. Terribly, those activities included rape and murder. At trial, Moffat was described by mental health clinicians as a psychopath, and a severely disturbed individual, not as a sexual addict.[14]

Patrick Carnes, Robert Weiss, Douglass Weiss, and most of those treating sex addiction are doing so from a place of good intent, trying to serve people who are desperate for help. Treatment for sex addiction often includes clinically appropriate goals of building positive self-image, addressing issues of shame, and the need for support and healthy relationships. Issues of narcissism and selfishness are often addressed, along with the development of guidelines for behaviors and choices. But within the treatment there is an intent to "separate the behavior from the person," and to split men from their sexual desires.[15] This is an expression of the mind-body problem described in chapter 6.

The World Health Organization identifies "integration" as a core component of a healthy sexuality, advocating for "integration of the physical, emotional, intellectual, and social aspects of being sexual."[16] Research by Hans

Eysenck actually found that men who had been convicted of murder, sexual crimes, robbery, and other violent acts had extremely conservative, rejecting attitudes toward sex. They saw sex as dangerous and as something that should be for procreation alone rather than pleasure, they viewed pornography as corrupting, and they thought that access to sexual information and materials should be restricted. Sexual inhibition, rejection, and repression are not healthy strategies to teach men to deal with feelings of sexual arousal.[17]

An essential part of man is lost when we encourage men to split themselves from their sexuality, teaching them that their sexual desires are a ravening beast that is trying to assume control of their body, mind, and actions. Jungian analyst Robert Moore and mythologist Douglas Gillette argue that a valuable, even critical, part of masculinity is the persona of the Lover, and that as we teach men to be men, to understand, accept, and express their masculinity, we rarely attend adequately to the loving, nurturing, and amorous side of men.[18]

Men fear and struggle with the urges of the Lover within, just as they struggle with the demands of our aggressive, dominating, and violent urges. What is necessary for a healthy man, for a complete masculinity, is the integration, consolidation, and incorporation of these aspects. When we try to split off our desires for love and sex from ourselves, excising them from ourselves as something external and dangerous, we run the real risk of creating men without compassion, without tenderness, and without the ability to nurture. It is easy to suggest that what we are trying to excise are the base, primitive parts of men's eroticism, those desires to rape, dominate, and satisfy oneself selfishly, but in truth, those desires, as frightening as they can be, are integrally linked to male emotional desires for safety, acceptance, and belonging.

Over the past few decades, a significant change has occurred in the field of behavioral health. A field that was formerly dominated by male psychiatrists and psychologists has become a field now overwhelmingly populated by female therapists. For the past decade, I've kept a mental tally of this trend, and it is extremely rare that I am in a professional meeting where men are not outnumbered by women by a factor of at least two to one. My own impression is reflected in research, which has found that many colleges and graduate schools have great difficulty attracting males into the study or practice of psychology and counseling. Good therapy is provided by both males and females. But, when men have more traditional masculine values, they tend to do better working with male therapists and often have difficulty working with female therapists.[19]

Some female therapists either overidentify with the "masculine," or devalue and dissociate it in their own personalities. . . . Men will always need to be mentored and initiated into manhood mainly by men, not women. Now that there is a serious shortage of men remaining in or entering the psychotherapy profession, unlucky consumers have even fewer choices—not only regarding the type of treatment they receive, but which gender will provide it.
—Stephen Diamond, PhD[20]

Another social shift has paralleled this trend. In the past, medicine and the mental health field viewed men as "the norm." Women were viewed as less effective than men, less intelligent, less creative, and more prone to mental illness. But since around 1980, there has been a social shift in the view of males and masculinity, with the view now that women are nicer, healthier, easier to be around, and better communicators, and in general, "women are wonderful," what Baumeister calls the "WOW effect." Why should men be uncomfortable with the social view of masculinity?

Isn't this a case of "You made your bed, now lie in it?" Or, as Susan Faludi says in *Stiffed*, "How dare the kings complain about their castles?"[21] And yet, as both feminist author Faludi and psychologist Roy Baumeister argue, men are as constrained by the social expectations placed upon them, by the rigidity of the roles they are forced to assume, as women are. Men do not rule society but exist within it, just as women do. Men are exploited by the culture of our society as much as women are, just in different, and frankly more callous and often fatal, ways: far more men than women die as soldiers, as firefighters, as police officers, and even as truck drivers in the far frozen wastes of Alaska. While we may have more male leaders, we also have higher rates of poverty, death, mental retardation, and suicide in men.

As the field of mental health has become dominated by women and the social view of men has declined, it is interesting to note that there has been a parallel rise in the tendency to pathologize male sexuality. Women and men have different views of sexuality, valuing different behaviors and placing different values on sexuality in general. Men like pornography, and women like romance novels. This is not just a gross generalization but reflects tremendous statistical differences, differences that underscore the different ways in which men and women enjoy sexual and erotic ideas and entertainment. While the attention of sex addiction is focused on male sexuality, it ignores other aspects of masculinity, which, if celebrated, might restrain the often selfish and narcissistic behaviors of some men.

BEING A MAN

The concept of masculinity is one that has fluctuated over the centuries. The idea of masculinity is often tied to a society's current needs for men. For instance, in times of war, the qualities of a soldier, such as bravery, camaraderie, and aggression, are typically endorsed by a society, through media like posters, books, fiction, and drama.

A Real Man

Consistent concepts that come up over and over in the varying historical portrayals of the ideal in masculinity.

- Willpower: A "real man" is seen as a man who makes his own decisions and is not swayed by others;
- Sacrifice: The concept of sacrifice and giving of oneself for others has been critical in the militaristic and soldierly conception of men. A real man is one who stands with his comrades and saves them by jumping on a grenade or charging a hill. This same sense of sacrifice is evident in male ideals of fatherhood and even in the male sexual focus on their partner's fulfillment.
- Stoicism: This is the ability to suffer quietly and withstand pain and struggling while still doing the things a man needs to do. The British practice of "caning" young boys was even defended as training men to sustain and withstand pain without showing weakness.[22]
- Self-reliance: In one of my favorite Disney movies, *Mary Poppins*, the father is described as a man who soldiers on, who complains to no one, and who does his job in silent strength. "Who looks after your father? Tell me that. When something terrible happens, what does he do? Fends for himself, he does. Who does he tell about it? No one! Don't blab his troubles at home. He just pushes on at his job, uncomplaining and alone and silent."[23]
- Sexual strength: Real men are sexually successful, depending upon society's view of sex. In the nineteenth century, when masturbation was seen as destructive to society, healthy men were those who could resist the draw of sexual weakness. In fact, giving in to the draw of sexuality was seen as one of the ways a strong healthy man could be degenerated into a "pale-faced and effeminate" man.[24] In contrast, in cultures where polygamy is practiced, men with more wives are seen as the epitome

of masculine confidence and strength. In Latin American countries, "machismo" often involves men pursuing sex with many women, in a voracious manner.

- Adventurousness: From Indiana Jones to Marco Polo, men who strike out into the world and succeed at overcoming new, exciting challenges are celebrated as fulfilling the ideal of the masculine. And this celebration extends to men who succeed in sexual adventures as well. Research by psychologist Shirley Glass has found that most men who have extramarital affairs describe that they do so in pursuit of "sexual excitement."

The value of manhood, distinct from the idea of womanhood, is seen as something that boys and men must do, and must continue to do, in order to maintain it. Girls become women through the biological maturation process, through reaching puberty and menarche, and even women who do not or cannot have children are not widely seen as being "unwomanly." Women might be seen as unfeminine but are not seen as having lost their womanhood.

In contrast, manhood is seen as something that males must achieve, through rites of passage and challenges. Vision quests, battles, going to war, and losing one's virginity are all ways and actions associated with a boy becoming a man. In the 2006 film *Bachelor Party Vegas*, a group of young men are sent on a night of tribulations and challenges, arranged by their older family members in order to offer them a chance to become men. Men must constantly prove their masculinity or face its loss. Real men must be made, and created, by force of will, aggression, dominance, and success over others and over adversity.[25]

At an evolutionary level, it is probable that this view of masculinity affected reproduction. Men who publicly demonstrated their masculine prowess and dominance stood better chances of attracting female mates and reproducing. While women who were less feminine might be at risk of attracting lower-quality males, they were rarely at risk of not reproducing at all. But men who were at the bottom of the totem pole were likely to never have access to women, and might have never reproduced at all in polygamous societies where powerful men garnered more women. A majority of men throughout history did not father children, and remember that it was Genghis Khan who fathered over a thousand children. Men who struggle to contain their sexuality today are acting out the desires of their forefathers in a new and very different environment. Labeling them sexual addicts ignores this evolutionary history of male sexuality.

In order to help the men in our society take responsibility for their sexual behaviors, we must start early. And they cannot do it alone. It takes other men teaching them about what it means to be a man, and how responsible sexuality is a part of being a man. Healthy, useful, and values-based conversations between fathers and sons about sex just don't seem to happen.

Research shows that the majority of boys in our culture report that they never discussed nineteen out of twenty topics of sexuality with their fathers. When fathers do talk to their sons about sex, it is focused on information and education (physiology, perhaps even techniques), but it almost never involves explicit discussion of a father's values in sexuality. This is sad, because research with mothers and daughters shows that the better the mother-daughter communication about sex and relationships, the more responsible those daughters are when it comes to sexual behaviors and practicing safe sex.[26]

A father's involvement in his son's childhood has a direct correlation with the boy's sexual impulsivity and sexually risky behaviors as an adult, even when the fathers aren't talking about sex but are just being there, being a dad. When the dad isn't around, young boys grow into men who form brief, transient, and shallow relationships with women and are more likely to use force or coercion during sex with a woman.

Case Example

John Perry Barlow is a poet, political activist, retired Wyoming rancher, lyricist for the Grateful Dead, and an affirmed and ardent lover of women. He declares himself a "ladies' man," and a "libertine," and a dedicated fan of the sacred, sensual, and sexual in the opposite sex. He also declares that monogamy was something he was never meant to embrace. For Barlow, a lifetime of sexual monogamy with a single partner "made as much sense as declaring that I like mashed potatoes and gravy so much that I would eat nothing else for the rest of my life."

Barlow came to understand his conflict with monogamy through seventeen years of marriage, broken by his progressive pursuit of infidelity. But Barlow realized that his conflict was not with monogamy per se, but with his agreement to abide by it, and in the moral conflict this created within him. "Not realizing that women hate deceit even more than they hate infidelity—and they always know—I turned into a sneak and a liar. I became someone I couldn't respect, and so I left my marriage." Chastised for his openness as a man who is not monogamous and does not pretend to be, Barlow responded, "I am trying to learn how to live with myself. Accepting one's faults is not quite the same as approving of them."[27]

"The mistake that straight people made was imposing the monogamous expectation on men. Men were never expected to be monogamous. Men had concubines, mistresses and access to prostitutes, until everybody decided marriage had to be egalitarian and fairsey." In the feminist revolution, rather than extending to women "the same latitude and license and pressure-release valve that men had always enjoyed," we extended to men the confines women had always endured. "And it's been a disaster for marriage."
—Dan Savage[28]

Males and females are quite different, in many ways, including sexually. These differences are not good or bad; they just are. In the society we have built, we have seesawed back and forth between the privileges that males and females have, and the social views of the different genders. Today our society has highly valued the female views of sexuality, raising them ascendant. I agree with columnist Dan Savage, as he argues that we are applying female attitudes toward sex to all heterosexual relationships, and toward men. But I disagree that society should instead have extended the sexual freedoms and latitudes of men toward women. Most women simply don't want them. In order to reconcile the complicated view of marriage, monogamy, sexuality, and gender roles, society must adapt our views to incorporate these differences. Instead of universally applying values derived from one group to all relationships, we must find ways to integrate these differences between men and women.

Our view of masculinity as competent and resourceful can be reconciled with the increasing awareness of previously secret sexual behaviors and can banish the implicit acceptance that men are weak and cowering before internal forces of lust and desire. Those things that make men admired and respected—their strength, courage, independence, and assertiveness—are the same things that contribute to the differences in male and female sexuality. By condemning these characteristics, we run the real and frightening risk of abolishing those qualities that are essential to healthy masculinity.

I think it [society] turns a blind eye to certain kinds of "boys will be boys" behavior, even though in some cases we know the consequences are going to be adultery or the transmission of STDs. Call me a prude if you must, but that behavior includes sticking dollars into G-strings, indulging your "sex addiction," sleeping with prostitutes, and allowing athletes, actors, and politicians to get away with God-awful behavior just because they're famous. Men are not sexual sharks, as permanent BMOC Puck said on *Glee*. They won't die if they don't get laid. Allowing men to express a kind of helplessness when it comes to their desires just allows them to indulge those desires no matter the consequences.
—Raina Kelley[29]

14

Reclaiming Our Sexuality

When you accept the victim or addict label, you are saying that you are powerless over your problems, and therefore have no responsibility for them; because you are not responsible, you do not possess the power to change. . . . On the contrary, most people can achieve complete recovery only if they accept the responsibility and power of their own choices.

—Stan Katz and Aimee Liu[1]

*A*n intrinsic problem in the sex addiction philosophy is that it confounds arousal and behavior. In the sex addiction field, somebody who is a sex addict is someone who wants too much sex, and someone who has too much sex. There is an implicit assumption that one cannot want sex—that is, be sexually aroused—and control it. But every day people want things and learn that they can't have them, and they deal with it.

Just because there are times that I don't want to have to control my behaviors, just because it is a struggle to do the things I should do, and need to do, rather than the things I want to do, doesn't mean that I am out of control. When so-called sex addicts complain that they are unable to control their behaviors, and that they are powerless over their urges, there is far more to the story. For instance, the man cruising the streets at night for prostitutes is not so out of control that he cannot drive a car. He is not so out of control that he cannot plan lies and alibis to cover his behaviors if his spouse catches him. He is not so out of control that he is not watching for police and hoping to avoid arrest. A chronic male philanderer who wrote an article for *Esquire* magazine described in detail the extensive planning, preparation, and consideration he puts into his strategies for cheating, strategies all designed to protect him from getting caught or embarrassed.[2] In fact, this anonymous author suggests that chronic sexual behavior is the furthest thing from being out of control; "Cheating is a chance for the body to assert its dominion over the soul, to urge the individual towards his genetic rootspring, toward what feels good rather than what feels compulsory."[3] So, exactly where in these behaviors is the "loss of control?"

In research by Jason Winters, men were hooked up to physiological sensors that read their body's reaction to pornography. The men were told to either try to suppress their sexual arousal or increase it. In another part of the study, the same men watched a video of a standup comic and were told again to try to either suppress or increase their reaction to the humor. The men who did best at stoicism, suppressing their laughter and humor in response to the comedian, also did the best at suppressing their sexual responsiveness.

In this study, no men at all were able to fully suppress their sexual response, but *all* men showed at least some ability to self-regulate their sexual excitation. Further, a standard measure used by the sex addiction field to assess "sexual compulsivity" showed absolutely no relationship to men's performance on sexual self-regulation. All men *can* learn to regulate their own feelings of sexual arousal to at least some degree. The problem sexual behaviors identified in sexual addiction and sexual compulsion, as exemplified by the statements "I sometimes get so horny I could lose control" or "I have to struggle to control sexual thoughts and behavior," don't have anything to do with a man's actual ability to regulate his own sexual arousal.[4] Just because someone feels their control is threatened does not mean they are out of control.

There is not just one answer to the question of sex addiction. It is not just an impulse or a compulsion. It is not just the effect of testosterone or dopamine. The reason the concept of sex addiction is so challenging to pin down is the many different social and moral concepts that are embedded within it, where the only commonality is that the issue of sexual behavior is involved. The other issues that are involved, whether it be emotional functioning, brain functioning, relationship skills, or adaptability, are ignored by the extreme focus on sexual behaviors.

Although there is no overall evidence of an "addictive personality" underlying all addictions and chronic self-destructive behaviors, there are common characteristics, including impulsivity, difficulty delaying gratification, a devaluing of social conformity, and high levels of stress. Current research involving the functioning of dopamine in the brain suggests that there may be underlying genetic predispositions toward some problem behaviors such as gambling, compulsive shopping, and even sex, along with abuse of alcohol and drugs. This doesn't mean that people without these predispositions are inherently safe from such behaviors, nor that those with them are condemned to inevitable life problems. A person's life involves a complex interplay of interactions between their genes, their environment, and their personal choices. Through examination of these predisposing factors, we can better understand, and help, those who engage in damaging chronic sexual behaviors that feel "out of control." Looked at in this way, we can understand, and help, far more than simply calling something an "addiction."

In the 1960s, Stanford psychologist Walter Mischel began a series of experiments with small children, now known as the "marshmallow experiments."[5] In this study, Mischel left young children in a room with their favorite treats, a marshmallow, a cookie, or candy. The children were told that if they could wait until Mischel returned, they would get two treats, but if they ate it before he returned, they would get only the one. The children were filmed and observed as they waited, and the footage of the experiments reveals the struggles many of these children had in delaying gratification. Some of the children were tortured by the desire to gobble up the treat, covering their eyes so they couldn't see it, pulling on their hair, or kicking the desk in their efforts to resist the urge. About one-third of the kids were able to resist the impulse to eat the treat and waited the few minutes until Mischel returned, thus earning a second treat.

Through an accident of fate, Mischel was able to follow some of the children over their lives, and he noticed that what the kids did with the marshmallows was linked to their performance in school. The children who were able to wait for the second marshmallow had higher SAT scores and better school performance, whereas the 70 percent of kids who couldn't wait for the second treat struggled more. The ones who couldn't wait had more problems socially as well, with impatience and attention and with maintaining friendships, and they had similar career problems in jobs.

Those kids who gobbled up the marshmallows had more trouble with drugs and alcohol than the kids who were able to wait for the second treat, all those long years ago. Mischel never looked at the relationships with sexuality that might have been present, but the implications are clear. The ability to resist impulses, to manage one's behavior, is a critical life skill that affects one's life in countless ways.

Acting upon short-term goals and immediate gratification is a feature in almost all human activities. Dan Ariely, economist and author of *Predictably Irrational: The Hidden Forces That Shape Our Decisions*, offers numerous examples of places throughout each of our daily lives where we make decisions based on what we can get right now rather than on a long-term cost-benefit analysis. Here's one example he offers: "Suppose I offered you a choice between a free $10 Amazon gift certificate and a $20 gift certificate for seven dollars."[6] Overwhelmingly, people are lured by the word *free* and take the ten-dollar certificate, despite the fact that longer-range thinking reveals that even with the cost of seven dollars, the twenty dollar certificate leaves you with a "profit" of thirteen dollars, as opposed to only ten.

The field of behavioral economics is filled with examples like these that reveal the irrationality behind most of our daily decisions and actions, and the very low degree to which we are as "in control" of our behaviors as we would like to think. This is true in sexuality and in most things. And it is true for all of us, not just sexual addicts. Ariely's studies with Berkeley college students evaluated the effect of arousal on decision making and showed that after watching porn and masturbating, most men were willing to engage in behaviors they wouldn't normally engage in, and in more risky behaviors, such as not using a condom. These findings demonstrate the effect of arousal on judgment but do not suggest that there is a core loss of control. Sexual arousal affects our decision making. This is normal, for all people. But in Ariely's study, none of the students was unable to stop masturbating, or put down the computer and ran out and grabbed the first co-ed they found and raped her. None of them sued Ariely for exposing them to addictive materials that ruined their lives.

We all like to believe that we are good people. We believe that if someone cheats, on a test or on their spouse, it is because they are immoral. They have lost control of themselves. But we don't apply this thinking to ourselves, and when it is us that has cheated, we all have excuses and explanations and justifications. Behavioral economists such as Ariely have shown repeatedly that given the opportunity, with no chances of getting caught, and a belief that cheating will have little negative consequence, almost all people will take the opportunity to lie, cheat, or steal. "We usually think of ourselves as sitting in the driver's seat, with ultimate control over the decisions we make and the direction our life takes; but, alas, this perception has more to do with our desires—with how we want to view ourselves—than with reality."[7]

But we *can* assert control over our behaviors, through self-will, through our choices, and through our thoughts. Ariely has also done studies showing that just asking people to try to remember the Ten Commandments increases a person's honesty. Having those moral and religious prohibitions at the front of your mind makes people less likely to lie, cheat, or steal.

Walter Mischel found similar results in replications of the marshmallow study, showing that children could be taught to improve their ability to resist their impulses to gobble up the treats. By helping children learn to control their thoughts about the treat, to focus on other things and distract themselves from this burning need to eat the marshmallow, the children could delay eating it for longer and longer.

By helping the children to take control of their thoughts and desires, to treat them as understandable and manageable, the children's impulse control improved. The same is true in all things, including sex. People can be taught to resist sexual impulses, they can learn to control their sexual behaviors, and they can practice the skills necessary to delay the desire for immediate erotic gratification. Teaching people that they are powerless over a fearsome force within themselves does not improve their ability to resist impulses, for marshmallows or for sex.

To deal with life, and to resist the many irrational, unconscious, and subtle pulls on our daily choices, one must be conscious. We have to wake up and think about what we're doing. The writer William Burroughs described that he, like most drug addicts he knew, never really intended to become a drug addict. Instead, he just sort of drifted into it, without paying attention.[8] People's sexual behavior is something they need to think about, with an understanding of themselves, their own tendencies, and the influence of their environment and biology on their sexual desires. If they are on autopilot, they are abdicating responsibility for their actions.

Case Example

I Am Responsible

At the start of the "sex addiction" craze, a government official was convicted for several nonviolent, sex-related misdemeanors involving a woman with whom he was having an affair.

At sentencing, a psychiatrist argued that the man suffered from "a preoccupation with sexual desires" and was "addicted to sexual gratification." Nevertheless, the man was convicted; he described afterward that his career and reputation were destroyed.

Over time, though, his career did recover. Just seven years later, he was honored by a national association for his achievements. In the decades since, he has received numerous awards for his professional activities. He currently works with multiple universities and is very active in his church.

I was able to correspond with this gentleman and asked him to share where he was now. Thirty years have passed, and I was curious as to his perspective now, looking back. His words were powerful: "I do not believe I had an addiction though I know we all have compulsions and sometimes act on them impulsively without considering the consequences. . . . What a fool I was. . . . Ultimately, I am responsible for my own bad choices and their consequences."[9]

In the summer of 2011, the DSM5 task force made the decision to move the proposed hypersexual disorder to the appendix of the next DSM. Thus, it will be, at best, a set of criteria that are provided for research purposes, but not a formal diagnosis under the DSM's taxonomy. No formal announcement of this change was made, and no explanations were offered, but one can assume that the large number of scientific and peer-driven criticisms weighing against the concept mounted up to the point that formal inclusion of the disorder was not supported.

Dr. Rory Reid of the University of California, Los Angeles, is a psychologist and social worker, as well as a researcher and clinician. He is the principal investigator for the UCLA field trial of the ongoing validation studies of hypersexual disorder for the DSM5. Dr. Reid's research team is conducting the long-needed studies of validity, interrater reliability, and diagnostic discrimination with hypersexual patients at multiple sites throughout the United States. Dr. Reid asserts that their findings thus far suggest the diagnostic criteria for hypersexual disorder may be highly reliable, and, if included in the DSM5 as an appendix, these criteria will offer researchers like him the ability to begin to tease apart the complex web of issues, behaviors, and causes that are embedded in this concept.[10]

In order to ensure that the criteria for hypersexual disorder do not overpathologize individuals who merely have high libido or alternative sexual behaviors, the "bar" for the diagnosis was intentionally set high, requiring four of the five criteria of hypersexual disorder to warrant diagnosis. It is notable that this standard and the research going into hypersexual disorder are atheoretical, focusing upon specific behaviors, and do not include addiction concepts, nor many of the moralistic judgments so prevalent in sex addiction theorizing. Though I remain intensely skeptical of the hypersexual disorder concept, I do believe that careful scientific investigation may be worthwhile, especially when such investigation proceeds separately from the addiction concept. With regard to hypersexual disorder, I am willing to reserve judgment on this disorder, waiting to see what their data have to say.

But the inclusion of hypersexual disorder in the appendix of the DSM5 will change little anytime soon for the large and powerful sex addiction industry. Men exposed in the harsh lights of the media will still be diagnosed as sex addicts, and fallen stars will slink shamefacedly to sex addiction treatment. Proponents of hypersexual disorder will have to vigorously and carefully defend against interests that want to merely use the hypersexual disorder as a euphemism and smoke screen for sex addictionologists to use to continue business as usual, using addiction concepts and unsupported treatment approaches. The cult of sex addiction needs a medical and scientific masquerade to hide behind to defend their lack of scientific credibility.

The supporters of the hypersexual disorder concept will still be faced with the significant cultural limitations this behavior reflects and will have to consider whether this disorder reflects a culture-bound syndrome, involving a conflict between sexuality and the attitudes toward sex embedded in our culture.

However, it is hopeful that careful scientific research, using sound principles and theory to evaluate hypersexual disorder, may serve to disentangle the science from the morals that are so entwined in the morass of sex addiction theory.

The concept of sexual addiction reflects complex social, economic, and moral influences in our society, far more than it reflects the influence of science or medicine. Just as Carol Groneman argued that the concept of nymphomania was truly a metaphor for social views of female sexuality, sex addiction is a current social metaphor for our views of unfavorable aspects of masculine sexuality.[11] Allowing the social and media myth of sexual addiction to promulgate unchecked invites the corruption of medicine and mental health by the moral judgment of society at large.

Sexual addiction is the latest tool of an antisex morality embedded in our culture at its deepest levels, labeling sexuality as a dangerous evil temptation that must be constantly constrained and feared. Stanley Cohen penned the book *Folk Devils and Moral Panics*, describing that a moral panic was when a "condition, episode, person or group of persons emerges to become defined as a threat to societal values and interests."[12] Those who start these panics and promote them are "moral entrepreneurs," a role often filled by the media, which acts as agents of social indignation, creating a panic and controversy from which they feed. Sex addiction is a moral panic, and sex addictionologists are in league with the media as moral entrepreneurs.

The field of sex addiction is a belief system, not a scientific or medical school of thought. There *are* careful and thoughtful people involved, trying to carefully piece out the kernels of truth embedded in this muddy concept. But the cult of sex addiction is driven by charismatic and convincing leaders who espouse sensationalist and reactive views of sexuality that are based on their own experiences, conviction, and religious faith, *not* on science or valid research. As I have begun challenging and questioning these beliefs, the levels of defensiveness and anger have shocked me. Strong reactions have come from individuals and family members of the self-identified sex addicts. But even stronger reactions and ad hominem attacks have come from my colleagues, who make their livings treating and diagnosing sex addiction. Fellow psychologists have even accused me of being a sex addict myself, engaged in an effort to create a facade that I can hide behind. Notably, if I were a sex addict, by their definitions, I can't imagine that I would have had enough time to write this book, a point that is lost on these angry and defensive true believers in sex addiction. It concerns me that these professionals are so defensive and resistant to a public, open debate about the principles they so blithely accept. As I've said before, science progresses through open dialogue and debate. If they are unwilling to allow such a debate, then it is further evidence that sex addiction is not based upon science.

In the realm of scientific investigation, it is the responsibility of the believers to evaluate the validity of their hypothesis. If they cannot, then the null hypothesis, that the believers are wrong, is assumed to be true. Despite the challenges I have received in writing this book, it is not my burden to prove that sex addiction doesn't exist. Instead, the field of sex addiction must prove scientifically that it does exist. And to date, that proof is not forthcoming. Telling men with problems that they have sex addiction and then having them become evangelists for sex addiction does not constitute proof. It is possible that investigations of hypersexual disorder may demonstrate that there is some kernel of truth here, but even that will not prove that there is an addictive process at work. Until then, the scientific answer is that sex addiction most likely does not exist if it cannot be scientifically demonstrated.

The national dialogue about sexual addiction reflects the actions of a sensationalist media grasping at simple concepts like addiction in order to simplify complex motivations, and to seize the attention of viewers. Journalists Kovach and Rosenstiel write that "the press has moved toward sensationalism, entertainment, and opinion," and has moved away from traditional journalistic values of verification of information and attention to the relevance of the issues.[13] In today's world of the 24-7 news cycle, the economic needs of the media are overriding traditional journalistic values with a "journalism of assertion" that pays little heed to the validity of a statement and emphasizes the primary benefit of putting a claim into the arena of public discussion as quickly as possible. This style of news focuses on the value of black-and-white, moralistic, and easy-to-grasp concepts, like sex addiction. By offering viewers these simple concepts, they feed them simple sound bites that fit easily between commercials. These simplistic strategies rely on peoples' voyeuristic desires to see into the sexual lives of powerful people, and their simultaneous desire to condemn these powerful people for having what they themselves do not. When French diplomat and banker Dominique Strauss-Kahn was arrested in 2011 for allegedly raping a hotel maid (charges that were later dropped), he was "diagnosed" as a sexual addict by the national media within just a few hours, as the media sought for easy-to-digest concepts that they could feed viewers, to keep them tuned in.

The concept of sexual addiction is fueled by economic factors. The professionals who feed the media's need for psychological and biological explanations of sexual behaviors are the same professionals who make very good livings selling books and providing trainings and certifications to other therapists. These trained and certified therapists have careers providing treatment services to individuals who self-identify with sexual addiction after hearing the leaders of sex addiction on television. The proselytizing of sex addictionologists is a form of disease mongering, where they are using the media, hype, and fear to create a disorder where none truly exists. There is a circular pattern here, of media and sex addictionologists, all living off money from fear of sexuality. Thus, a complex and disturbing symbiotic relationship exists between the cult of sex addiction and the media, each feeding the other through their promulgation of the concept that sex is a dangerous disease.

The relational and procreational views of sex demonize sex that is for recreation, and it is predominantly men who view sex as recreational. The sex addiction movement clearly speaks from procreational and relational values, labeling as unhealthy any sexuality that occurs without intimacy, commitment, or love. Anything else is called dangerous, addictive, or destructive, despite the evidence that sex is emotionally and physically healthy, especially for men, even when it does not involve love, intimacy, or commitment.

The sex addiction label is, at least in part, an expression of fear and anger at the fact that males naturally have different sexual desires than women. Sex addictionologists would like to put that genie in a small bottle and stopper it up tightly. Even though women in the United States consume romance novels at rates comparable to the male consumption of pornography, there is no effort to remove these novels from the shelves of convenience stores, nor to pillory women found reading such novels in the workplace. The different sexual attitudes between genders drive the fear of pornography, as well as the general fear and stigmatization of male sexuality.

Why are men (including journalists, therapists, and John Q. Public) so quick to judge and label the sexual misbehaviors of other men as sexual addiction? Historically, many less-successful men were unable to reproduce, or even to have wives, as those women went to the homes of powerful, wealthy, and dominant men. But through society's requirement of monogamy, those powerful men are no longer easily able to "keep all the women to themselves." By pathologizing these men's sexuality, less-successful men bear less risk of losing women to them. Men are also apt to throw other men under the wheels of the bus of sexual judgment because it is easier to do that than to defend the actions of a man being pilloried in the press, and possibly face attack yourself.

The label of sex addiction undermines our efforts to enforce expectations of responsibility, holding ourselves, and especially men, responsible for their choices and actions. I reject the notion that sexuality is a disease, that sexual arousal is a thing that can overwhelm a man's mind and body, impairing his decisions, thoughts, and feelings, because in doing so, we create a weakened, powerless image of masculinity and turn men into victims. Remember that Jason Winters showed that *all* men in his study were able to control their sexual response to some degree, and *no* men were able to control their sexual response entirely. Instead of labeling men in our society as sexual addicts, we must encourage them to be manly, in all the positive aspects of that term. We can acknowledge that there are people who have great difficulty controlling their behaviors. We can sympathize with them, offer them support, and provide assistance in identifying what is at the root of their difficulties, but labeling their problem as sexual in nature ignores the true issues and allows the entire discussion to go off the rails into a moral morass. We must invite men to take responsibility for their behaviors and to exert control of their responses, but we must do so within a framework that acknowledges the differences in male and female sexuality.

Powerful men like Clinton, Spitzer, Strauss-Kahn, Schwarzenegger, and others have gotten to their positions of power through their strength of personality, their assertiveness, motivation, commitment, and effort. They have achieved success, in many cases, through force of will and resolve. Like men through history, when they reach those positions of power, many of these men expect the sexual privileges that come with their power and success. According to Baumeister, "Successful men do not necessarily want to have a hundred babies, but they often do want to have sex with a hundred women. And the culture they have created cooperates. . . . One reason they [men] buy into the system of work and achievement and playing the game is the implicit promise that if they do become successful, they will finally be able to have the women and the sex they want."[14] Leaders in sex scandals are acting as powerful men have acted for thousands of years, men who were polygamous by virtue of their success, able to have, protect, and support multiple wives because of their power and wealth. But polygamy and infidelity are now socially proscribed, and these men cannot act as their successful ancestors once did.

I'm not justifying or excusing the selfish, often narcissistic behaviors of these men and others. I do not want our leaders to feel that their success entitles them to selfish self-gratification and deception in sex, or in any other aspect of their lives. But at the same time that we condemn their behaviors and choices, we must ensure that we are condemning them for the right reasons, not just because of the sexual issues embedded within them. When we overattend to sexuality, we lose sight of the issues of ethics, responsibility, dignity, and leadership that we should address and require in our leaders and male role models. Then, when the men confess their sex addiction and enter sex addiction treatment, we pretend that the issues are resolved. We must return to a focus on the positive qualities of men, including an acknowledgment of the unique aspects of male sexuality, and encourage, even require, that men integrate their sexual desires within the framework of personal responsibility that is the hallmark of a true man.

A young girl named Rebecca recently told me, "I'm addicted to Harry Potter." I was stunned and tried not to laugh. What does a nine-year-old girl know about addiction?

She was listening to Harry Potter recorded audiobooks, and her parents had become concerned about how frequently she listened to them. Every chance she got, she was in her room listening to them. She'd listen to them past her bedtime and get in trouble for breaking curfew, and then turn it on again first thing in the morning. Her parents were starting to have to set limits, and when they did, this little girl's face would turn red with rage.

What were these recordings to her? Why were they so important to her? "They're like having a friend," she told me. Her neighbor playmate had recently moved away, and she said, "Nobody plays with me." She loved the story, of good versus evil, of a normal boy who triumphs over adversity. Rebecca said the tapes helped her manage her feelings, her mood and anxiety: "They're soothing to me. They help me calm down. I can listen to the story, and it helps me feel better."

In 2008, Pennsylvania psychologist Dr. Jeff Rudski suggested that she might not be alone. A survey of 4,000 Harry Potter fans showed that 10 percent of them were having symptoms of craving and withdrawals, interference with life activities, and emotional effects such as irritability, all around their high level of involvement in the Harry Potter series. Rudski first got interested in this fan-type addiction when he saw people "walking around in a daze" after the O. J. Simpson trial. The publication of the last book of the Harry Potter series offered him a chance to study the phenomenon. Rudski found that fans who had creative outlets for their interest, doing things like Harry Potter art, or pursuing other interests that related to or built upon Harry Potter, had no negative impacts from their "addiction." But those who were overinvolved in just the Harry Potter books experienced problems similar to those of addicts.[15]

I wrote to Dr. Rudski and chatted with him about his research and thoughts about addiction. He shared that even the most severe "Harry Potter addicts" in his study, who showed "withdrawal symptoms," had their symptoms resolve without treatment in three to five days. While things like Harry Potter or sex can "look" addictive, there are real differences between problem behaviors and addiction. Dr. Rudski related his research to the issue of sex addiction as well. "Not every case of excessive sexual behavior is sex addiction. You need to know the *why* of the behavior, not just the *what* of the behavior."[16]

I took all this information back to help Rebecca with her "problematic behavior." I worked with her parents to start getting her out of her room more. I encouraged her parents to spend more time with her, doing things like playing board games. Rebecca and I practiced self-soothing techniques, like taking walks. She returned the Harry Potter recordings to the library, and we encouraged her to check out other recordings, and other books.

"What is addiction?" I asked this precocious little girl.

"When you can't stop doing something," she replied.

"But you can stop, and you have," I pointed out to her.

"But it was hard," was her reply. And she's right. It is hard to stop some behaviors when they are pleasing you as much as they are hurting. It can be incredibly hard, particularly when the behaviors are as intrinsically rewarding as sex. But just because it's hard doesn't mean you can't stop; it doesn't mean that you cannot exert control over yourself. It doesn't mean you have a disease.

We must start asking the men in our lives and our world, in our media and in our government, to take responsibility for their sexual behaviors, their choices. But we must also offer them a context within which they *can* take that responsibility, and in which male sexuality is understood and seen for what it is, as different from female sexuality. We must offer them a context where a high libido, in men or women, is not seen as an unhealthy thing, but as an aspect of a person, of who they are, which they must integrate and incorporate within their lives and choices. As Rebecca said, even when things are hard, it doesn't mean they are impossible. Just because someone has chosen in the past not to control their sexuality, or just because someone has hurt themselves or others through their sexual behaviors, does not mean they cannot make a different choice in the future. With our support and encouragement, and most of all, with the message that they *can* choose to be in control of their sexuality, people can be in charge of their sexual desires and behaviors.

> The concept of mental illness also undermines the principle of personal responsibility, the ground on which all free political institutions rest. For the individual, the notion of mental illness precludes an inquiring attitude toward his conflicts which his "symptoms" at once conceal and reveal. For a society, it precludes regarding individuals as responsible persons and invites, instead, treating them as irresponsible patients.
> —Thomas Szasz[17]

> We would all like to point at an illness—a psychiatric label—and say of our weak or bad actions, "That thing, the illness, did it, not me. It." But at some point we must draw ourselves up to our full height, and say in a clear voice what we have done and why it was wrong. And we must use the word "I" not "it" or "illness." I did it. I. I.
> —Melvin Konner[18]

Notes

INTRODUCTION

1. *New York Times*, October 28, 1973, http://thinkexist.com/quotation/power_is_ the_ultimate_aphrodisiac/145796.html.

2. W. Kaminer, "Is Clinton a Sex Addict?" *Slate*, March 22, 1998, http://www. slate.com/id/2495.

3. T. Connor, "Newser's Book: Ford Saw Clinton as a Sex 'addict.'" *New York Daily News*, October 28, 2007,
http://www.nydailynews.com/news/national/2007/10/28/2007-10-28_newsers_ book_ford_saw_clinton_as_a_sex_a.html.

4. J. Hannah, "They Gotta Habit," *People*, May 30, 101.

5. J. Hannah, "They Gotta Habit," *People*, May 30, 101.

6. C. Shipman and J. Hopper, "Rep. Anthony Weiner in Treatment: Is Sex Addiction Real?" ABC News, http://abcnews.go.com/US/rep-anthony-weiner -treatment-photo-scandal-sex-addiction/story?id=13827354.

7. S. Bechtel, *The Practical Encyclopedia of Sex and Health* (Emmaus, PA: Rodale), 5.

8. M. Klein, *America's War on Sex: The Attack on Law, Lust and Liberty* (Westport, CT: Praeger, 2006).

CHAPTER ONE

1. http://www.goodreads.com/quotes/show/60780.

2. http://www.analitica.com/curiosidades/3668781.asp.

3. S. Peele, "Addiction in Society," *Psychology Today*, September 2010, http:// www.psychologytoday.com/print/49415.

4. M. Goodman, "Neurobiology of Addiction: An Integrative Review," *Biochemical Pharmacology* 75 (2008): 266–322.

5. ASAM, "ASAM Releases New Definition of Addiction," news release, August 2011, http://www.asam.org/pdf/Advocacy/PressReleases/20110815_DefofAddiction-PR.pdf.

6. Open Letter to the DSM-5 (2011), Society for Humanistic Psychology, Division 32 of the American Psychological Association, in alliance with Division of Developmental Psychology (Division 7 of the APA), the Society for Community Research and Action: Division of Community Psychology (Division 27 of the APA), the Society for the Psychology of Women (Division 35 of the APA), the Society for Group Psychology and Psychotherapy (Division 49 of the APA), the Association for Women in Psychology, the Society for Personality Assessment, the Society for Descriptive Psychology, the UK Council for Psychotherapy (UKCP), the Constructivist Psychology Network (CPN), and the Taos Institute, http://www.ipetitions.com/petition/dsm5/?utm_medium=email&utm_source=system&utm_campaign=.

7. APA, *Diagnostic and Statistical Manual: Mental Disorders* (Washington, DC: American Psychiatric Association, 1952), p. 39, http://www.psychiatryonline.com/DSMPDF/dsm-i.pdf.

8. http://www.dsm5.org/ProposedRevisions/Pages/proposedrevision.aspx?rid=415#.

9. R. Krafft-Ebing, *Psychopathia Sexualis: With Especial Reference to the Antipathic Sexual Instinct; A Medico-Forensic Study* (Whitefish, MT: Kessinger), 486.

10. Krafft-Ebing, *Psychopathia Sexualis*, 484.

11. G. Mosse, *Image of Man* (New York: Oxford University Press, 1996), 99.

12. Guillebaud, J. C., and K. Torjoc, *The Tyranny of Pleasure* (New York: Algora Publishing, 1999), 22.

13. J. Money, *Destroying Angel* (Buffalo, NY: Prometheus, 1985).

14. S. Freud, *Extracts from the Fliess Papers*, standard edition (1950), 1:272. Available at: http://www.pep-web.org/document.php?id=se.001.0173a.

15. Groneman, C., *Nymphomania: A History* (New York: Norton, 2001).

16. C. Turner, "Wilhelm Reich: The Man Who Invented Free Love," *Guardian*, July 8, 2011, http://www.guardian.co.uk/books/2011/jul/08/wilhelm-reich-free-love-orgasmatron.

17. Patrick Carnes, *Out of the Shadows: Understanding Sexual Addiction*, 2nd ed. (Minneapolis, MN: Hazelden, 1992).

18. Carnes, *Out of the Shadows*, 158.

19. http://www.askmen.com/specials/2010_great_male_survey/.

20. Patrick Carnes, *Don't Call It Love: Recovery from Sexual Addiction* (New York: Bantam, 1992).

21. S. N. Gold and C. L. Heffner, "Sexual Addiction: Many Conceptions, Minimal Data," *Clinical Psychology Review* 18, no. 3 (1998): 379.

22. Stephen Braveman, LMFT, personal communication, April 9, 2011.

23. Carnes, *Out of the Shadows*, 46.

24. Carnes, *Out of the Shadows*.

25. R. Earle and M. Earle, *Sex Addiction Case Studies and Management* (New York: Routledge, 1995).

26. M. Herkov, "What Is Sexual Addiction?" *Psych Central*, 2006, retrieved on July 13, 2011, from http://psychcentral.com/lib/2006/what-is-sexual-addiction.

27. O. Bamuhigire, "Sex Addiction: A Growing Problem," *New Vision*, http://www.aegis.org/news/nv/2006/NV060108.html.

28. A. Hart, *Thrilled to Death* (Nashville, TN: Thomas Nelson, 2007), 130.

29. R. Leedes, "The Three Most Important Criteria in Diagnosing Sexual Addictions: Obsession, Obsession and Obsession," *Sexual Addiction & Compulsivity* 8 (2001): 223.

30. A. Finlayson, J. Sealy, and P. Martin, "The Differential Diagnosis of Problematic Hypersexuality," *Sexual Addiction & Compulsivity* 8 (2001): 243.

31. J. Ross, *The Male Paradox* (New York: Simon & Schuster, 1992), 69.

32. S. Bechtel, *The Practical Encyclopedia of Sex and Health* (Emmaus, PA: Rodale, 1993), 310.

33. http://moliere-in-english.com/donjuan.html.

34. A. Goodman, "Sexual Addiction: Designation and Treatment," *Journal of Sex and Marital Therapy* 18 (1992): 312.

35. J. Money, *Destroying Angel* (Buffalo, NY: Prometheus, 1985), 134.

36. T. Sbraga, W. O'Donohue, and J. Bancroft, *The Sex Addiction Workbook* (Oakland, CA: New Harbinger, 2003), 13.

37. Case example provided by Steven Braveman, LMFT, personal communication, April 2011.

38. D. Weiss, "Is Sex Addiction Real? Do Golfer Tiger Woods and the Soon-to-Be-Former Husband of Academy Award-Winning Actress Sandra Bullock, among Many Others, Really Have No Control over Their Bedroom Antics?" *USA Today*. May 2010.

39. M. Kaplan and R. Krueger, "Diagnosis, Assessment and Treatment of Hypersexuality," *Journal of Sex Research*, March 1, 2010.

40. N. J. Rinehart and M. P. McCabe, "Hypersexuality: Psychopathology or Normal Variant of Sexuality?" *Sexual and Marital Therapy* 12 (1997): 45–60.

41. J. Winters, "Hypersexual Disorder: A More Cautious Approach," *Archives of Sexual Behavior* 39 (2010): 594–596.

42. Gold and Heffner, "Sexual Addiction," 367–381.

43. M. P. Kafka, "Hypersexual Disorder: A Proposed Diagnosis for DSM-V," *Archives of Sexual Behavior* 39 (2010): 377–400.

44. A. Kinsey, W. Pomeroy, and C. Martin, *Sexual Behavior in the Human Male* (Bloomington: Indiana University Press, 1998), 199.

45. J. Winters, K. Christoff, and B. Gorzalka, "Dysregulated Sexuality and High Sexual Desire: Distinct Constructs?" *Archives of Sexual Behavior* 39 (2010): 1029–1043, http://www.springerlink.com/content/3tp65768k2451663/fulltext.pdf.

46. See, for example, AskMen.com survey (http://www.askmen.com/specials/great_male_survey) and 2011 Playboy survey (http://www.playboy.com/magazine/sex-survey-results-2011).

47. Quoted in R. Baumeister, *Is There Anything Good about Men? How Cultures Flourish by Exploiting Men* (New York: Oxford University Press, 2010), 226.

48. D. Kotz, "Sex Addiction or Simple Cheating? How to Tell the Difference," *U.S. News & World Report*, January 27, 2010.

49. M. Elias, "Sex Addiction Is Real but Exaggerated, Experts Say," *USA Today*, August 10, 2003.

50. P. Carnes, "Addiction or Compulsion: Politics or Illness?" 1997, available at http://www.sexhelpworkshops.com/Documents/AddictionOrCompulsion-Politics OrIllness_PCarnes.doc.

51. APA, *Diagnostic and Statistical Manual: Mental Disorders* (Washington, DC: American Psychiatric Association, 1952), http://www.psychiatryonline.com/ DSMPDF/dsm-i.pdf.

52. APA, *Diagnostic and Statistical Manual: Mental Disorders*, 2nd ed. (Washington, DC: American Psychiatric Association, 1968), http://www.psychiatryonline .com/DSMPDF/dsm-ii.pdf.

53. Ronald Bayer, *Homosexuality and American Psychiatry: The Politics of Diagnosis* (Princeton, NJ: Princeton University Press, 1987), 3.

54. APA, *Diagnostic and Statistical Manual: Mental Disorders*, 3rd ed. (Washington, DC: American Psychiatric Association, 1980), 283.

55. APA, *Diagnostic and Statistical Manual: Mental Disorders*, 3rd ed. revised (Washington, DC: American Psychiatric Association, 1987), 296.

56. M. P. Kafka, "Hypersexual Disorder: A Proposed Diagnosis for DSM-V," *Archives of Sexual Behavior*, November 24, 2009, doi:10.1007/s10508-009-9574-7.

57. APA, *Diagnostic and Statistical Manual: Mental Disorders*, 4th ed. revised (Washington, DC: American Psychiatric Association, 2000), 582.

58. D. Thompson, "The 'Reality' of Sex Addiction Stirs Debate," *Healthday News*, May 12, 2010, http://news.healingwell.com/index.php?p=news1&id=636637.

59. S. Fox, DSM-V, "Healthcare Reform Will Fuel Major Changes in Addiction Psychiatry," *Medscape Medical News*, December 6, 2010, http://www.medscape.com/ viewarticle/733649

60. http://www.dsm5.org/ProposedRevisions/Pages/proposedrevision.aspx?rid=415#.

61. British Psychological Society, "Response to the American Psychiatric Association: DSM-5 Development," 2011, http://apps.bps.org.uk/_publicationfiles/ consultation-responses/DSM-5%202011%20-%20BPS%20response.pdf.

62. Kafka, *Hypersexual Disorder*, 377–400.

63. http://www.psychologytoday.com/blog/dsm5-in-distress/201003/dsm5-addiction -swallows-substance-abuse.

64. http://www.dsm5.org/ProposedRevisions/Pages/proposedrevision.aspx?rid=415.

65. C. Moser "Paraphilia: A Critique of a Confused Concept," in *New Directions in Sex Therapy, Innovations and Alternatives*, ed. Peggy Kleinplatz (Philadelphia, PA: Brunner-Routledge, 2001), 99.

CHAPTER TWO

1. Michael Bader, DMH, http://www.psychologytoday.com/blog/what-is-he -thinking/201001/sex-addiction-is-excuse-not-thinking-0.

2. E. Perel, *Mating in Captivity: Unlocking Erotic Intelligence* (New York: HarperCollins, 2007), 37.

3. Martin Shepard, MD, "In Defense of Nancy Friday," in *My Secret Garden* (New York: Pocket Books, 1973).

4. R. Wright, *The Moral Animal: Why We Are the Way We Are; the New Science of Evolutionary Psychology* (New York: Vintage, 1995), 298.

5. http://www.psychologytoday.com/blog/dsm5-in-distress/201003/dsm5-suggests-opening-the-door-behavioral-addictions?page=2.

6. http://thelastpsychiatrist.com/2011/02/hes_just_not_that_into_anyone.html.

7. http://www.tldm.org/news6/bundy.htm.

8. Mark Pilkington, "Sex on the Brain," *Guardian*, July 14, 2005, http://www.guardian.co.uk/science/2005/jul/14/farout.

9. M. Klein, *America's War on Sex: The Attack on Law, Lust and Liberty* (New York: Praeger, 2006).

10. http://www.texascriminallawyerblog.com/2010/03/internet_sex_addiction_can_lea.html.

11. Cited in Ogi Ogas and Sai Gaddam, *A Billion Wicked Thoughts: What the World's Largest Experiment Reveals about Human Desire* (New York: Dutton Adult, 2011).

12. F. Ilfeld Jr. and R. Lauer, *Social Nudism in America* (New Haven, CT: College and University Press Services, 1964).

13. http://www.eurekalert.org/pub_releases/2009-12/uom-ate120109.php.

14. See, for example, Christopher J. Ferguson and Richard D. Hartley, "The Pleasure Is Momentary . . . the Expense Damnable? The Influence of Pornography on Rape and Sexual Assault," *Aggression and Violent Behavior* 14, no. 5 (2009): 323–329, http://www.sciencedirect.com/science/article/pii/S1359178909000445; http://www.psychologytoday.com/blog/all-about-sex/200904/does-pornography-cause-social-harm.

15. D. Ariely, *Predictably Irrational: The Hidden Forces that Shape Our Decisions* (New York: HarperCollins, 2010).

16. R. Baumeister, *Is There Anything Good About Men? How Cultures Flourish by Exploiting Men* (New York: Oxford University Press, 2010), 228.

17. S. Okie, "The Epidemic that Wasn't," *New York Times*, January 27, 2009, http://www.nytimes.com/2009/01/27/health/27coca.html.

18. blogs.laweekly.com/informer/2011/04/porn_addict_internet_la.php.

CHAPTER THREE

1. *Valley Girl*, 1983, http://www.imdb.com/title/tt0086525/quotes.

2. Patrick Carnes, *Out of the Shadows: Understanding Sexual Addiction*, 2nd ed. (Minneapolis, MN: Hazelden, 1992), vii.

3. H. S. Kaplan, *The Sexual Desire Disorders: Dysfunctional Regulation of Sexual Motivation* (New York: Brunner/Mazel, 1995).

4. J. E. Grant, J. A. Brewer, and M. N. Potenza, "The Neurobiology of Substance and Behavioral Addictions," *CNS Spectrums* 11, no. 12 (2006): 924–930.

5. P. Carnes, "The Case for Sexual Anorexia: An Interim Report on 144 Patients with Sexual Disorders," http://www.sexhelpworkshops.com/Documents/ARTICLE_Case%20for%20Sexual%20Anorexa%20144%20patients_PCarnes.pdf.

6. Brenda Wolfe, personal communication, June 13, 2010.

7. S. Warmbir, "Despite Ban, Felon Got Political Job," *Chicago Sun-Times*, June 20, 2011, http://www.suntimes.com/news/politics/6019751-418/despite-ban-felon-got-political-job.html.

8. E. Loftus, "Dispatch from the (Un)Civil Memory Wars," in *Recollections of Trauma: Scientific Evidence and Clinical Practice*, ed. J. D. Read and D. S. Lindsay, 171–198 (New York: Plenum, 1997).

9. Albert Camus, http://thinkexist.com/quotes/with/keyword/intentions.

10. G. Stokes, "Karl Popper's Political Philosophy of Social Science," *Philosophy of the Social Sciences* 27, no. 1 (1997): 56–79.

11. http://www.brainyquote.com/quotes/keywords/agrees_2.html.

12. M. Farree, "Females and Sex Addiction: Myths and Diagnostic Implications," *Sexual Addiction & Compulsivity* 8 (2001): 293.

13. S. N. Gold and C. L. Heffner, "Sexual Addiction: Many Conceptions, Minimal Data," *Clinical Psychology Review* 18 (1998): 367–381, 369.

14. P. Briken, N. Habermann, W. Berner, and A. Hill, "Diagnosis and Treatment of Sexual Addiction: A Survey among German Sex Therapist," *Sexual Addiction & Compulsivity* 14, no. 2 (2007): 131–143.

15. For example, M. Miner, N. Raymond, B. Mueller, M. Lloyd, and K. Lim, "Preliminary Investigation of the Impulsive and Neuroanatomical Characteristics of Compulsive Sexual Behavior," *Psychiatry Research* 174, no. 2 (2009): 146–151, http://www.ncbi.nlm.nih.gov/pmc/articles/PMC2789480.

16. David Ortmann, LCSW, personal communication, May 2011.

17. B. Hagedorn, "The Call for a New Diagnostic and Statistical Manual of Mental Disorders Diagnosis: Addictive Disorders," *Journal of Addictions & Offender Counseling* 29 (April 2009), http://pegasus.cc.ucf.edu/~drbryce/The%20Call%20for%20a%20New%20Diagnosis%20-%20Addictive%20Disorders.pdf.

18. Alfred Kinsey, quoted in Wardell B. Pomeroy, *Dr. Kinsey and the Institute for Sex Research* (New York: Harper & Row, 1973), 316.

19. M. Levine and R. Troiden, "The Myth of Sexual Compulsivity," *Journal of Sex Research* 25, no. 3 (1988), http://www.jstor.org/pss/3812739.

20. R. Coombs, "Sex Education for Physicians: Is It Adequate?" *Family Coordinator* 17, no. 4 (1968), http://www.jstor.org/pss/582054.

21. S. Miller and E. Byers, "Psychologists' Sexual Education and Training in Graduate School," *Canadian Journal of Behavioural Science* 42, no. 2 (2010): 93–100, http://www.sciencedirect.com/science/article/pii/S0008400X10600103.

22. G. Weitzman, J. Davidson, R. Phillips, J. Fleckenstein, and C. Morotti-Meeker, "What Psychology Professionals Should Know about Polyamory," 2010, https://ncsfreedom.org/images/stories/pdfs/KAP/2010_poly_web.pdf.

23. Carnes, *Out of the Shadows*, 10.

24. Ogi Ogas and Sai Gaddam, *A Billion Wicked Thoughts: What the World's Largest Experiment Reveals about Human Desire* (New York: Dutton, Kindle edition, 2011).

25. Jason Winters, personal communication, June 12, 2011.

26. N. Langstrom and R. K. Hanson, "High Rates of Sexual Behavior in the General Population: Correlates and Predictors," *Archives of Sexual Behavior* 35 (2006): 37–52; N. Langstrom and R. K. Hanson, "Population Correlates Are Relevant to Understanding Hypersexuality: A Response to Giles," *Archives of Sexual Behavior* 35 (2006): 643–644.

27. P. Carnes, *Don't Call It Love: Recovery from Sexual Addiction* (New York: Bantam, 1992), 160.

28. David Ortmann, LCSW, personal communication, May 2011.

29. Gold and Heffner, "Sexual Addiction," 367–381.

CHAPTER FOUR

1. http://www.brainyquote.com/quotes/authors/e/eric_sevareid.html.

2. D. Hope, "Addiction Treatment Programs Say Sex Addiction More Common," *Online Journal*, April 19, 2011, http://onlinejournal.com/artman/publish/article_8564.shtml.

3. http://www.manta.com/c/mmgbv0j/a-new-freedom-corp.

4. http://www.iitap.com/about-us/iitap.

5. http://www.vh1.com/shows/sex_rehab_with_dr_drew/series.jhtml.

6. G. Hardesty, "Men Gather to Battle Sex Addiction," *Orange County Register*, April 25, 2011.

7. www.everymansbattle.com.

8. 990 IRS filings available at http://www2.guidestar.org.

9. J. Fedoroff, "Forensic and Diagnostic Concerns Arising from the Proposed DSM-5 Criteria for Sexual Paraphilic Disorder," *Journal of the American Academy of Psychiatry and the Law* 39, no. 2 (2011): 238–241, http://www.jaapl.org/cgi/content/full/39/2/238.

10. M. L. Wainberg, F. Muench, J. Morgenstern, et al., "A Double-Blind Study of Citalopram versus Placebo in the Treatment of Compulsive Sexual Behaviors in Gay and Bisexual Men," *Journal of Clinical Psychology*, 67 (2006): 1968–1973.

11. For example, http://abcnews.go.com/Health/Wellness/viagra-women-female-sexual-dysfunction-spotlight/story?id=10363004; http://www.health.harvard.edu/newsweek/What_is_female_sexual_dysfunction.htm.

12. S. Woloshin and L. Schwartz, "Giving Legs to Restless Legs: A Case Study of How the Media Helps Make People Sick," *PLoS Medicine* 3, no. 4 (2006): 170. http://www.ncbi.nlm.nih.gov/pmc/articles/PMC1434499/?tool=pmcentrez.

13. E. Silverman, "The Lowdown on Low T and AndroGel Promotions," *Pharmalot Pharma Blog*, June 28, 2011, http://www.pharmalot.com/2011/06/the-lowdown-on-low-t-and-androgel-promotions.

14. L. Davis, "Sex Addiction: The Truth Is Out There," *The Chicago Blog*, http://pressblog.uchicago.edu/2008/09/10/sex_addiction_the_truth_is_out.html.

CHAPTER FIVE

1. D. Kawashima, "Amazing Saga: The Detailed Story of How Author David Ritz Wrote 'Sexual Healing' with Marvin Gaye," http://www.songwriteruniverse. com/davidritz.html.

2. D. Arawaka, C. Flanders, & E. Hatfield, "Positive Psychology: What Impact Has It Had on Sex Research?" Copy obtained from author, 2011.

3. R. Leedes, "The Three Most Important Criteria in Diagnosing Sexual Addictions: Obsession, Obsession, and Obsession," *Sexual Addiction & Compulsivity: The Journal of Treatment & Prevention* 8, nos. 3–4 (2001): 223.

4. T. Sbraga, W. O'Donohue, and J. Bancroft, *The Sex Addiction Workbook* (Oakland, CA: New Harbinger, 2003), 175.

5. Sbraga, O'Donohue, and Bancroft, *The Sex Addiction Workbook*, 197.

6. http://www.famous-quotes.com/author.php?aid=6940.

7. B. Whipple, "The Health Benefits of Sexual Expression," in *Sexual Health*, vol. 1, *Psychological Foundations*, ed. M. Tepper and A. F. Owens, 19 (Westport, CT: Praeger, 2007).

8. G. Smith, S. Frankel, and J. Yarnell. "Sex and Death: Are they Related? Findings from the Caerphilly Cohort Study," *British Medical Journal* 315 (1997): 1641.

9. W. Cutler, *Love Cycles: The Science of Intimacy* (New York: Villard, 1991).

10. B. Whipple and B. Komisaruk, "Analgesia Produced in Women by Genital Self-Stimulation," *Journal of Sex Research* 24, no. 1 (1988): 130–140, http://www. jstor.org/pss/3812827.

11. Susie Bright, http://susiebright.blogs.com/susie_brights_journal_/pregnancy.

12. R. R. Baker and M. A. Bellis, "Human Sperm Competition: Ejaculate Manipulation by Females and the Function of the Female Orgasm," *Animal Behaviour* 46 (1993): 887–909.

13. "Sex and Pregnancy: It's Hard Making Babies," *Daily Star*, August 16, 2010.

14. http://www.bbc.co.uk/news/uk-england-berkshire-11284331.

15. R. Burch and G. Gallup, "The Psychobiology of Human Semen," in *Female Infidelity and Paternal Uncertainty*, ed. S. M. Platek and T. K. Shackelford, 141–172 (New York: Cambridge University Press, 2006).

16. "Headache Prevention?," *Daily News*, July 22, 1999, p. 15.

17. B. Mooney, "The Madness of Offering the Mentally Disabled Sex with Prostitutes at Taxpayers' Expense," *Mail Online*, August 18, 2010.

18. K. Oxford, "Sex Trade," *GQ Magazine*, April 2011, http://www.gq.com/ news-politics/mens-lives/201105/fellatio-sex-bartering-tips.

19. E. Perel, *Mating in Captivity: Unlocking Erotic Intelligence* (New York: HarperCollins, 2007), 16.

20. http://www.imdb.com/title/tt0089886/quotes.

21. S. Peabody, *Addicted to Love: Overcoming Obsession and Dependency in Relationships* (Berkeley, CA: Celestial Arts, 1994).

22. R. Karim, "Cutting Edge Pharmacology for Sex Addiction," California Society for Addiction Medicine, http://www.csam-asam.org/pdf/misc/Sex_Addiction.pdf.

23. P. Carnes and J. Schneider, "Recognition and Management of Addictive Sexual Disorders: Guide for the Primary Care Clinician," *Primary Care Practice* 4, no. 3 (2000).

24. N. Friday, *Men in Love* (New York: Delta, 1998), 468.

25. T. V. Hicks and H. Leitenberg, "Sexual Fantasies about One's Partner versus Someone Else: Gender Differences in Incidence and Frequency," *Journal of Sex Research* 38, no. 1 (2001): 43–50.

26. J. Bivona and J. Critelli, "The Nature of Women's Rape Fantasies: An Analysis of Prevalence, Frequency, and Contents," *Journal of Sex Research* 46 (2009): 33.

27. B. Kahr, *Who's Been Sleeping in Your Head?* (New York: Basic Books), 39.

28. W. Maltz and S. Boss, *Private Thoughts: Exploring the Power of Women's Sexual Fantasies* (Charleston, SC: Booksurge, 2008).

29. Maltz and Boss, *Private Thoughts*.

30. *Savage Love*, July 1, 2010, http://www.thestranger.com/seattle/SavageLove?oid=4362335&hpr.

31. Kahr, *Who's Been Sleeping in Your Head?*, 356–377.

32. Kahr, *Who's Been Sleeping in Your Head?*, 35.

33. Kahr, *Who's Been Sleeping in Your Head?*, 376.

34. Kahr, *Who's Been Sleeping in Your Head?*, 49.

35. Kahr, *Who's Been Sleeping in Your Head?*, 431.

36. Kahr, *Who's Been Sleeping in Your Head?*, 444.

CHAPTER SIX

1. S. Freud, *Civilization and Its Discontents* (New York: Norton, 1989).

2. http://www.dsm5.org/ProposedRevisions/Pages/proposedrevision.aspx?rid=415.

3. R. Jennings, "His Streak Is Alive at 7,788—and Counting," *USA Today*, April 28, 2011, 13.

4. S. Peabody, *Addiction to Love: Overcoming Obsession and Dependency in Relationships* (Berkeley, CA: Celestial Arts, 2005), xv.

5. M. Klein, "Why There's No Such Thing as Sexual Addiction—and Why It Really Matters," http://www.sexed.org/archive/article08.html.

6. D. Weiss, "Is Sex Addiction Real? Do Golfer Tiger Woods and the Soon-to-Be-Former Husband of Academy Award-Winning Actress Sandra Bullock, among Many Others, Really Have No Control over Their Bedroom Antics?" *USA Today*, May 2010.

7. B. Hagedorn, "The Call for a New Diagnostic and Statistical Manual of Mental Disorders Diagnosis: Addictive Disorders," *Journal of Addictions & Offender Counseling* 29 (April 2009), http://pegasus.cc.ucf.edu/~drbryce/The%20Call%20for%20a%20New%20Diagnosis%20-%20Addictive%20Disorders.pdf.

8. V. Yoder, T. Virden, and K. Amin, "Internet Pornography and Loneliness: An Association?" *Sexual Addiction & Compulsivity* 12, no. 1 (2005): 19–44.

9. R. Fullerton and G. Punge, "Kleptomania: A Brief Intellectual History," in *The Romance of Marketing History*, http://faculty.quinnipiac.edu/charm/CHARM%20

proceedings/CHARM%20article%20archive%20pdf%20format/Volume%2011%20 2003/201%20fullerton%20punj.pdf.

10. http://www.dsm5.org/ProposedRevisions/Pages/proposedrevision.aspx?rid=415.

11. C. Kasl, *Women, Sex, and Addiction: A Search for Love and Power* (New York: HarperCollins, 1990), 9.

12. P. Carnes, *Don't Call It Love: Recovery from Sexual Addiction* (New York: Bantam, 1992).

13. J. Money, *Destroying Angel* (Buffalo, NY: Prometheus Books, 1985), 81.

14. M. Raviv, "Personality Characteristics of Sexual Addicts and Pathological Gamblers," *Journal of Gambling Studies* 9, no. 1 (1993): 17–30.

15. J. Carroll, K. Volk, and J. Hyde, "Differences between Males and Females in Motives for Engaging in Sexual Intercourse," *Archives of Sexual Behavior* 14 (1985): 131–139.

16. http://www.torontosun.com/2011/06/10/sex-addict-rocker-launches-porn-dvd.

17. http://forums.studentdoctor.net/showthread.php?t=652186.

18. N. Friday, *Men in Love* (New York: Delta, 1998), 3.

19. E. Perel, *Mating in Captivity: Unlocking Erotic Intelligence* (New York: Harper, 2007), 29.

20. Personal communication, Rory Reid, PhD, November 18, 2011.

21. D. Thompson, "The 'Reality' of Sex Addiction Stirs Debate," *U.S. News and World Report*, http://www.usnews.com/mobile/articles_mobile/the-reality-of-sex -addiction-stirs-debate.

22. R. Michael, J. Gagnon, E. Lauman, and G. Kolata, *Sex in America: A Definitive Survey* (New York: Little, Brown, 1994), 126.

23. M. P. Kafka and J. Hennen, "The Paraphilia-Related Disorders: An Empirical Investigation of Nonparaphilic Hypersexuality Disorders in 206 Outpatient Males," *Journal of Sex and Marital Therapy* 25 (1999): 305–319.

24. J. Winters, K. Christoff, and B. Gorzalka, "Dysregulated Sexuality and High Sexual Desire: Distinct Constructs?" *Archives of Sexual Behavior* 39, no. 5 (2010): 1041, doi:10.1007/s10508-009-9591-6.

25. S. Kalichman and D. Cain, "The Relationship between Indicators of Sexual Compulsivity and High Risk Sexual Practices among Men and Women Receiving Services from a Sexually Transmitted Infection Clinic," *Journal of Sex Research* 41 (2004).

26. S. Buzwell and D. Rosenthal, "Constructing a Sexual Self: Adolescents' Sexual Self-Perceptions and Sexual Risk-Taking," *Journal of Research on Adolescence* 6 (1996): 489–513.

27. R. A. Lippa, "Sex Differences in Sex Drive, Sociosexuality, and Height across 53 Nations: Testing Evolutionary and Social Structural Theories," *Archives of Sexual Behavior* 38 (2009): 631–651.

28. N. Rinehart and M. McCabe, "An Empirical Investigation of Hypersexuality," *Journal of Sexual and Relationship Therapy* 13, no. 4 (1998): 369–384, http://www .informaworld.com/smpp/title%7Edb=all%7Econtent=t713446685%7Etab=issueslist %7Ebranches=13.

29. E. Blumberg, "Lives and Voices of Highly Sexual Women," *Journal of Sex Research* 40, no. 2 (2003): 150.

30. J. Bancroft and Z. Vukadinovic, "Sexual Addiction, Sexual Compulsivity, Sexual Impulsivity or What? Toward a Theoretical Model," *Journal of Sex Research* 41 (2004): 225–234.

31. J. Bancroft, C. Graham, E. Janssen, and S. Sanders, "The Dual Control Model: Current Status and Future Directions," *Journal of Sex Research* 46, no. 2–3 (2009): 121–142.

32. Jack Morin, http://www.jackmorin.com/SexTherapy.en.html.

33. C. Kasl, *Women, Sex, and Addiction: A Search for Love and Power* (New York: HarperCollins, 1990), 27.

34. W. Henkin, "The Myth of Sexual Addiction," originally published in *Spectator*, 1998, 8, copy obtained from author.

35. Personal communication; Dr. Tory Clark is a sexologist in Nevada.

36. D. Linden, *The Compass of Pleasure: How Our Brains Make Fatty Foods, Orgasm, Exercise, Marijuana, Generosity, Vodka, Learning, and Gambling Feel So Good* (New York: Viking, 2011).

37. http://benoitdenizetlewis.com/2010/02/10/nightline-sex-addiction-and-the -excuse-narrative.

38. http://www.onthemedia.org/transcripts/2008/12/26/05.

39. http://www.npr.org/2011/06/23/137348338/compass-of-pleasure-why-some -things-feel-so-good?ps=cprs.

40. G. Koob, P. Sanna, and F. Bloom, "Neuroscience of Addiction," *Neuron* 21 (September 1998): 467–476, http://dionysus.psych.wisc.edu/Lit/Articles/ KoobG1998a.pdf.

41. J. R. Garcia, J. MacKillop, E. L. Aller, A. M. Merriwether, D. S. Wilson, "Associations between Dopamine D4 Receptor Gene Variation with Both Infidelity and Sexual Promiscuity," *PLoS ONE* 5, no. 11 (2010): 6, e14162. doi:10.1371/ journal.pone.0014162; http://psychology.uga.edu/ecpl/publications/pdf/Garcia%20 et%20al.%20-%202010%20-%20PLoS%20ONE.pdf.

42. M. Richtel, "Your Brain on Computers," *New York Times*, June 6, 2010, http:// www.nytimes.com/2010/06/07/technology/07brain.html?pagewanted=3&th&emc=th.

43. M. Miner, N. Raymond, B. Mueller, M. Lloyd, and K. Lim, "Preliminary Investigation of the Impulsive and Neuroanatomical Characteristics of Compulsive Sexual Behavior," *Psychiatry Research* 174, no. 2 (2009): 146–151, http://www.ncbi .nlm.nih.gov/pmc/articles/PMC2789480.

44. R. Reid, B. Carpenter, and T. Fong, "Letter to Editor," *Surgical Neurology International* 2, no. 64, http://www.surgicalneurologyint.com/article.asp?issn=2152 -7806;year=2011;volume=2;issue=1;spage=64;epage=64;aulast=Reid.

45. D. Ley, *Insatiable Wives: Women Who Stray and the Men Who Love Them* (Lanham, MD: Rowman & Littlefield, 2009), 107–116.

46. R. Earle and M. Earle, *Sex Addiction: Case Studies and Management* (New York: Routledge, 1995), 65.

47. T. Szasz, *The Myth of Mental Illness* (New York: Harper & Row, 1974), 22.

48. C. Lane, *How Normal Behavior Became a Sickness* (New Haven, CT: Yale University Press, 2007).

49. http://thinkexist.com/quotes/benjamin_franklin.

CHAPTER SEVEN

1. Chuck Palahniuk, *Choke* (New York: Doubleday, 2001), 292.

2. J. DeLamater, "Social Control of Sexuality," *Annual Review of Sociology* 7 (1981): 266.

3. M. Levine and R. Troiden, "The Myth of Sexual Compulsivity," *Journal of Sex Research* 25, no. 3 (1988): 353.

4. R. Michael, J. Gagnon, E. Lauman, and G. Kolata, *Sex in America: A Definitive Survey* (Boston, MA: Little, Brown, 1994), 236.

5. Levine and Troiden, "The Myth of Sexual Compulsivity," 355.

6. http://www.psychologytoday.com/blog/women-who-stray/201111/the-profit -in-sex-addiction/comments.

7. http://www.unfpa.org/rights/rights.htm.

8. Y. Tan, "Law Report: Consensual Sado-masochistic Acts Unlawful: *Regina v Brown and Others*—House of Lords (Lord Templeman, Lord Jauncey of Tullichettle, Lord Lowry, Lord Mustill and Lord Slynn of Hadley)," *Independent*, March 11, 1993, http://www.independent.co.uk/news/uk/law-report-consensual -sadomasochistic-acts-unlawful-regina-v-brown-and-others—house-of-lords-lord -templeman-lord-jauncey-of-tullichettle-lord-lowry-lord-mustill-and-lord-slynn -of-hadley-11-march-1993-1497180.html.

9. APA, *Diagnostic and Statistical Manual of Mental Disorders*, DSM-IV-TR, 4th ed. (Washington, DC: American Psychiatric Association, 2000), xxxi.

10. http://www.apa.org/ethics/code/index.aspx.

11. C. Ryan and C. Jetha, *Sex at Dawn: The Prehistoric Origins of Modern Sexuality* (New York: Harper, 2010), 294.

12. D. Marshall, "Sexual Behavior on Mangaia," in *Sources: Notable Selections in Human Sexuality*, ed. Gary Kelly (Guilford, CT: Dushkin/McGraw-Hill, 1998).

13. http://en.wikiquote.org/wiki/Osho_%28Bhagwan_Shree_Rajneesh%29.

14. "India's Most Influential Gurus," *Daily News and Analysis*, June 13, 2011, http://www.dnaindia.com/india/slideshow_india-s-most-influential-gurus_1554241#top.

15. P. Druckerman, *Lust in Translation* (New York: Penguin, 2007), 125.

16. Druckerman, *Lust in Translation*, 126.

17. http://www.stanford.edu/group/womenscourage/Repro_Latin/ekobash_HIV-machismo_Latin.html.

18. Druckerman, *Lust in Translation*, 198.

19. http://news.bbc.co.uk/2/hi/8491375.stm.

20. http://www.sa.org/sexaholic.php.

21. P. R. Amato and D. D. DeBoer, "The Transmission of Marital Instability across Generations: Relationship Skills or Commitment to Marriage?" *Journal of*

Marriage and Family 63 (2001): 1038–1051; B. D'Onofrio, E. Turkheimer, R. Emery, A. Heath, P. Madden, W. Slutske, et al., "A Genetically Informed Study of the Processes Underlying the Association between Parental Marital Instability and Offspring Adjustment," *Developmental Psychology* 42, no. 3 (2006): 486–499; D. J. Weigel, K. K. Bennett, and D. S. Ballard-Reisch, "Family Influences on Commitment: Examining the Family of Origin Correlates of Relationship Commitment Attitudes," *Personal Relationships* 10 (2003): 453–474.

22. J. Owen et al., "'Hooking Up' among College Students: Demographic and Psychosocial Correlates," *Archives of Sexual Behavior*, http://www.chs.fsu.edu/~ffincham/papers/ASB%20Owen%20et%20al.pdf.

23. R. Earle and M. Earle, *Sex Addiction Case Studies and Management* (New York: Routledge, 1995), 11.

24. Female swinger quoted in C. Bergstrand and J. Sinski, *Swinging in America* (New York: Praeger, 2009), 20.

25. http://www.janetwhardy.com.

26. Janet Hardy, personal communication, June 7, 2010.

27. L. Fisher, "Sex, Romance, and Relationships: AARP Survey of Midlife and Older Adults," 2010, http://www.aarp.org/relationships/love-sex/info-05-2010/srr_09.html.

28. www.medicalnewstoday.com/articles/184329.php.

29. G. Weitzman, J. Davidson, R. Phillips, J. Fleckenstein, and C. Morotti-Meeker, "What Psychology Professionals Should Know about Polyamory," 2010, https://ncsfreedom.org/images/stories/pdfs/KAP/2010_poly_web.pdf.

30. C. Kasl, *Women, Sex, and Addiction: A Search for Love and Power* (New York: HarperCollins, 1990), 227.

31. B. Traeen and T. S. Nilson, "Use of Pornography in Traditional Media and on the Internet in Norway," *Journal of Sex Research* 43, no. 3 (2006): 245–254, http://goliath.ecnext.com/coms2/gi_0199-5754055/Use-of-pornography-in-traditional.html.

32. J. Albright, "Sex in America Online: An Exploration of Sex, Marital Status, and Sexual Identity in Internet Sex Seeking and Its Impacts," *Journal of Sex Research* 45, no. 2 (2008), 175–186.

33. V. Cass, "Homosexual Identity Formation: A Theoretical Model," *Journal of Homosexuality* 4, no. 3 (1979): 219–235.

34. J. Kort, "Has Anything Changed in What We Know about Satyriasis from Its Original Identification of the Disorder?," PhD diss., http://www.google.com/url?sa=t&source=web&cd=7&ved=0CD8QFjAG&url=http%3A%2F%2Fwww.esextherapy.com%2Fdissertations%2FJoe_Kort_Dissertation_Master_Turabian%2520January%25203%2C%25202010.doc&rct=j&q=joe%20kort%20satyriasis&ei=NqcfTvP1FjTiAK_3_GrAw&usg=AFQjCNHsF0gQgYo3z3uosx2zOyHgg4AKMQ&cad=rja.

35. S. C. Kalichman and D. Cain, "The Relationship between Indicators of Sexual Compulsivity and High Risk Sexual Practices among Men and Women Receiving Services from a Sexually Transmitted Infection Clinic," *Journal of Sex Research* 41 (2004): 235–241.

36. C. H. Hoff and S. C. Beougher, "Sexual Agreements among Gay Couples," *Archives of Sexual Behavior* 39 (November 2007): 774–787.

37. C. Panati, "Faithful in Our Fashion," *The Advocate*, June 23, 1998, 11.

38. Benzinga Staff, "Sexual Recovery Institute Amplifies Their Support of Non-Addictive, Sex-Positive, Intimate Relationships among Same-Sex Couples," June 21, 2011, http://www.benzinga.com/press-releases/11/06/b1188936/sexual-recovery-institute-amplifies-their-support-of-non-addictive-sex.

39. D. Symons, *The Evolution of Human Sexuality* (New York: Oxford University Press, 1979).

40. R. Baumeister, K. Catanese, and K. Vohs, "Is There a Gender Difference in Strength of Sex Drive? Theoretical Views, Conceptual Distinctions, and a Review of Relevant Evidence," *Personality and Social Psychology Review* 5, no 3 (2001): 242–273.

41. O. Ogas and S. Gaddam, *A Billion Wicked Thoughts: What the World's Largest Experiment Reveals about Human Desire*, Kindle ed. (New York: Dutton Adult, 2011), location 410.

42. M. S. Weinberg and C. J. Williams, "Men Sexually Interested in Transwomen (MSTW): Gendered Embodiment and the Construction of Sexual Desire," *Journal of Sex Research* 47, no. 4 (2010): 374–383.

43. S. Faludi, *Stiffed: The Betrayal of the American Man* (New York: Harper Perennial, 2000), 607.

44. American Psychological Association, "Resolution on Appropriate Affirmative Responses to Sexual Orientation Distress and Change Efforts," 2011, www.apa.org/about/governance/council/policy//sexual-orientation.aspx.

45. M. L. Hatzenbuehler, "The Social Environment and Suicide Attempts in Lesbian, Gay, and Bisexual Youth," *Pediatrics* 127 (2011): 5.

46. W. Henkin, "The Myth of Sexual Addiction," originally published in *Spectator* magazine, 1998, copy obtained from author.

47. John Leo, "Doing the Disorder Rag," *U.S. News and World Report*, October 27, 1997.

CHAPTER EIGHT

1. http://sexademic.wordpress.com/2011/05/08/explaining-porn-watching-with-science.

2. http://sexaddict.com/store/cart.php?m=product_list&c=4.

3. Douglas Weiss, *The Final Freedom: Pioneering Sexual Addiction Recovery*, 2nd ed., http://www.sexaddict.com/eBooks/FreedomeBk.pdf.

4. *Daily Telegraph*, "Ex-Sex Addict and Christian Democrat Peter Madden to Clean Up 'Dirty' Sydney," January 26, 2011, www.pedestrian.tv/arts-and-culture/news/mardi-gras-pash-protest 2/28/11.

5. http://www.freedomeveryday.org.

6. http://www.sofm.org.

7. http://www.cancerministry.com.

8. J. Leland, "Church Counsels Women Addicted to Pornography," *New York Times*, May 3, 2010, http://www.nytimes.com/2010/05/03/us/03addiction

.html?_r=1&scp=1&sq=Counseling%20for%20Women%20Addicted%20to%20 Pornography%20&st=cse.

9. Tony Keim, "Man's Child Sex Addiction Blamed on Religious Cult Upbringing," *Herald Sun*, May 6, 2011.

10. http://www.x3pure.com/samesex.

11. P. Strudwick, "Conversion Therapy: She Tried to Make Me 'Pray Away the Gay,'" *Guardian*, May 27, 2011.

12. J. Winters, K. Christoff, and B. Gorzalka, "Dysregulated Sexuality and High Sexual Desire: Distinct Constructs?" *Archives of Sexual Behavior* 39 (2010): 1029–1043.

13. K. Drury, *Money, Sex and Spiritual Power* (Indianapolis, IN: Wesley Press, 1992), http://www.drurywriting.com/keith/9male.htm.

14. D. Murrow, *Why Men Hate Going to Church* (Nashville, TN: Thomas Nelson, 2004), 207.

15. E. Bower, "Therapist Opens Clinic in Corner of Church to Treat Sexual Addictions," *Peterborough Examiner*, July 12, 2011, http://www.thepeterboroughexaminer .com/ArticleDisplay.aspx?e=3208798.

16. Staff report, "First Sex Addiction Program to Be Offered at College," *Shawnee Dispatch*, August 17, 2011.

17. P. Antze, quoted in J. Schaler, "Addiction Is a Choice," *Psychiatric Times* 19, no. 10 (October 2002).

18. Office of Juvenile Justice and Delinquency Prevention, "Using 'Sober Support' Groups in Your Juvenile Court," *Technical Assistance Bulletin*, 2010, http://www .ncjfcj.org/images/stories/dept/jfl/sobersupport.pdf.

19. Steven Braveman, LMFT, personal communication, March 2011.

20. D. Akst, "Interview with Gene M. Heyman: Is Addiction a Choice?," *Boston Globe*, August 9, 2009, http://www.boston.com/bostonglobe/ideas/articles/ 2009/08/09/qa_with_gene_m_heyman.

21. Jeffrey Schaler, "Addiction Is a Choice," *Psychiatric Times* 19, no. 10 (October 2002).

22. Associated Press, "Steger Man Claims Sex Addiction Led to Child Abuse," May 27, 2011,
http://abclocal.go.com/wls/story?section=news/local&id=8155942.

23. Staff, "Sex Addict Jailed Again for Rapes," ABC News Australia, June 2, 2011, http://www.abc.net.au/news/stories/2011/06/02/3233645.htm?section=justin.

24. C. Schmitz, "5th Circuit Nixes Claim That Drug Caused Gambling Problem," *Inside Counsel Business Magazine*, June 2010, http://www.insidecounsel.com/Issues/2010/ June-2010/Pages/5th-Circuit-Nixes-Claim-that-Drug-Caused-Gambling-Problem .aspx?page=2.

25. http://boards.medscape.com/forums?14@@.29fa173d!comment=1.

26. B. Hagedorn, "The Call for a New Diagnostic and Statistical Manual of Mental Disorders Diagnosis: Addictive Disorders," *Journal of Addictions & Offender Counseling* 29 (April 2009), http://pegasus.cc.ucf.edu/~drbryce/The%20Call%20for%20 a%20New%20Diagnosis%20-%20Addictive%20Disorders.pdf.

27. A. Jenkins, *Invitations to Responsibility* (Adelaide, South Australia: Dulwich Centre Publications, 1990), 12.

28. A. Frances, "Rape, Psychiatry, and Constitutional Rights: Hard Cases Make for Very Bad Law," *Psychiatric Times* 27, no. 9 (2010), http://www.psychiatrictimes.com/sexual-offenses/content/article/10168/1595945.

29. British Psychological Society, "Response to the American Psychiatric Association: DSM-5 Development," 2011, http://apps.bps.org.uk/_publicationfiles/consultation-responses/DSM-5%202011%20-%20BPS%20response.pdf.

30. E. Schermele, "How Effective Is Sex-Offender Rehabilitation?" KXLH News, November 2, 2011, http://www.kxlh.com/news/how-effective-is-sex-offender-rehabilitation-/.

31. J. Bancroft and Z. Vukadinovic, "Sexual Addiction, Sexual Compulsivity, Sexual Impulsivity, or What? Toward a Theoretical Model," *Journal of Sex Research* 41 (2004): 225–234.

32. M. Kafka, "Hypersexual Disorder: A Proposed Diagnosis for DSM-V," *Archives of Sexual Behavior* 39 (2010): 377–400.

33. http://getridofaddiction.info/social-worker-accused-of-having-child-porn-being-treated-for-addiction-contra-costa-times.

34. W. Miller and S. Rollnick, *Motivational Interviewing: Preparing People for Change*, 2nd ed. (New York: Guilford Press, 2002).

35. C. Courcol and M. Hood, "Fine Line between Serial Seducer and Sex Addict," *AFP News*, May 17, 2011.

36. R. Baumeister, *Evil* (New York: Freeman, 1997), 40.

37. Hart, *Thrilled to Death*, 130.

CHAPTER NINE

1. D. Prager, "Judaism's Sexual Revolution: Why Judaism Rejected Homosexuality," http://www.catholiceducation.org/articles/homosexuality/ho0003.html.

2. Betty Friedan, quoted on back cover of B. Lefkowitz, *Our Guys* (New York: Vintage, 1998).

3. http://www.crimemagazine.com/weird-news.

4. S. Arnott, *Sex: A User's Guide* (New York: Random House Digital, 2010).

5. *Telegraph*, "Man Admits Having Sex with 1,000 Cars," May 21, 2008, http://www.telegraph.co.uk/news/newstopics/howaboutthat/2000899/Man-admits-having-sex-with-1000-cars.html.

6. C. Groneman, *Nymphomania: A History* (New York: Norton, 2000), xxii.

7. E. Blumberg, "Lives and Voices of Highly Sexual Women," *Journal of Sex Research* 40, no. 2 (2003): 151.

8. M. Turner, "Female Sexual Compulsivity: A New Syndrome," *Psychiatric Clinics of North America* 31 (2008): 715.

9. M. Farree, "Females and Sex Addiction: Myths and Diagnostic Implications," *Sexual Addiction and Compulsivity* 8 (2001): 287–300.

10. C. Groneman, *Nymphomania: A History* (New York: Norton, 2000), 177.

11. M. P. Kafka, "Hypersexual Disorder: A Proposed Diagnosis for DSM-V," *Archives of Sexual Behavior* 39 (2010): 377–400.

12. J. Falla, "Disorderly Consumption and Capitalism: The Privilege of Sex Addiction," *College Literature* 28, no. 1 (Winter 2001).

13. Falla, "Disorderly Consumption and Capitalism."

14. http://www.slutwalktoronto.com.

15. D. Easton and C. Liszt, *The Ethical Slut: A Guide to Infinite Sexual Possibilities* (San Francisco, CA: Greenery Press, 1997), 4.

16. C. Millet, *Sexual Life of Catherine M.* (New York: Grove), 142.

17. J. Henley, "How Catherine Millet Discovered Jealousy," *Guardian*, October 29, 2009, http://www.guardian.co.uk/lifeandstyle/2009/oct/29/catherine-millet-jealous.

18. M. Burns, "Cases of Persecuted Sexual Activity," http://www.solresearch.org/~SOLR/rprt/bkgrd/JSOcases.asp.

19. C. Sommers, *The War against Boys: How Misguided Feminism Is Harming Our Young Men* (New York: Simon & Schuster, 2000), 212.

20. M. P. Kafka, "Hypersexual Disorder: A Proposed Diagnosis for DSM-V," *Archives of Sexual Behavior* 39 (2010): 377–400.

21. H. Zonana, "Sexual Disorders: New and Expanded Proposals for the DSM-5—Do We Need Them?" *Journal of the American Academy of Psychiatry and the Law* 39, no. 2 (2011): 245–249, http://www.jaapl.org/cgi/content/full/39/2/245.

22. S. Stark, quoted in S. Faludi, *Stiffed: The Betrayal of the American Man* (New York: Harper Perennial, 2000), 532.

23. J. Hannah, "They Gotta Habit," *People*, May 30, 1998, 109–110.

24. S. Lamb, quoted in Sommers, *War against Boys*, 55.

25. N. Kazantzakis, *Zorba the Greek* (New York: Simon & Schuster, 1996), 103.

26. D. Hill, "Differences and Similarities in Men's and Women's Sexual Self-Schemas," *Journal of Sex Research* 44, no. 2 (2007): 135–144.

27. E. Blumberg, "Lives and Voices of Highly Sexual Women," *Journal of Sex Research* 40 (2003): 2.

28. C. Ryan and C. Jetha, *Sex at Dawn: The Prehistoric Origins of Modern Sexuality* (New York: Harper, 2010), 85.

CHAPTER TEN

1. Ogi Ogas and Sai Gaddam, *A Billion Wicked Thoughts: What the World's Largest Experiment Reveals about Human Desire*, Kindle ed. (New York: Dutton Adult, 2011), location 3707.

2. Blake Edwards' film *Skin Deep*, 1989, http://www.1-famous-quotes.com/quotes/movie/Skin+Deep.

3. Sari Van Anders, "Multiple Partners Are Associated with Higher Testosterone in North American Men and Women," *Hormones and Behavior* 51 (2007): 454–459.

4. P. Sapienza, L. Zingales, and D. Maestripieri, "Gender Differences in Finan-cial Risk Aversion and Career Choices Are Affected by Testosterone," *Proceedings of the National Academy of Sciences*, August 24, 2009, doi:10.1073/pnas.0907352106, http://www.pnas.org/content/early/2009/08/20/0907352106.

5. NPR, *This American Life*, 220, http://www.thisamericanlife.org/radio-archives/episode/220/testosterone.

6. David Zincenko, *Men, Love & Sex: The Complete User's Guide for Women* (Em-maus, PA: Rodale Books, 2006).

7. S. J. Stanton, J. C. Beehner, E. K. Saini, C. N. Kuhn, and K. S. LaBar, "Dominance, Politics, and Physiology: Voters' Testosterone Changes on the Night of the 2008 United States Presidential Election," *PLoS ONE* 4, no. 10 (2009): e7543, doi:10.1371/journal.pone.0007543, http://www.plosone.org/article/info%3Adoi%2F10.1371%2Fjournal.pone.0007543.

8. P. Markey and C. Markey, "Changes in Pornography-Seeking Behaviors Fol-lowing Political Elections: An Examination of the Challenge Hypothesis," *Evolution and Human Behavior* 31 (2010): 442–446.

9. For example, M. McIntyre et al., "Romantic Involvement Often Reduces Men's Testosterone Levels—but Not Always: The Moderating Role of Extrapair Sexual Interest," *Journal of Personality and Social Psychology* 91, no. 4 (2006): 642–651; and S. van Anders and N. Watson, "Relationship Status and Testosterone in North American Heterosexual and Non-heterosexual Men and Women: Cross-sectional and Longitudinal Data," *Psychoneuroendocrinology* 31 (2006): 715–723.

10. S. van Anders and K. Goldey, "Testosterone and Partnering Are Linked via Relationship Status for Women and 'Relationship Orientation' for Men," *Hormones and Behavior* 58 (2010): 820–826.

11. http://www.thisdayinquotes.com/2010/02/real-origin-of-live-fast-die-young-and.html.

12. H. Ellis, *Studies in the Psychology of Sex*, vol. 5, *Erotic Symbolism, the Mechanism of Detumescence, the Psychic State in Pregnancy* (Originally published 1927), 185. E-text prepared by Juliet Sutherland and the Project Gutenberg Online Distributed Proof-reading Team (http://www.pgdp.net), 2004, available at http://www.gutenberg.org/files/13614/13614-h/13614-h.htm.

13. L. G. Bouchereau, "Nymphomania," in D. Hack Tuke, ed., *A Dictionary of Psychological Medicine* (London: J & A Churchill, 1892): 864.

14. M. Oliver and J. Hyde, "Gender Differences in Sexuality: A Meta-analysis," *Psychological Bulletin* 114, no. 1 (1993): 29–51.

15. Nigel Cawthorne, *Sordid Sex Lives* (London: Quercus Publishing, 2010), 156–159.

16. M. Reece et al., "National Survey of Sexual Health and Behavior (NSSHB)," 2010, http://www.nationalsexstudy.indiana.edu.

17. B. Zilbergeld, *The New Male Sexuality: The Truth about Men Sex and Pleasure* (New York: Bantam, 1993), 114.

18. R, Michael, J. Gagnon, E. Lauman, and G. Kolata, *Sex in America: A Definitive Survey* (Boston, MA: Little, Brown), 146–147.

19. Michael et al., *Sex in America*, 157.

20. D. P. Welsh, C. M. Grello, and M. S. Harper, "No Strings Attached: The Nature of Casual Sex in College Students," *Journal of Sex Research* 43, no. 3 (2006): 255–267.

21. Anka Radakovich, quoted in S. Faludi, *Stiffed: The Betrayal of the American Man* (New York: HarperPerennial, 2000), 521.

22. Rostosky et al., "Sexual Self-Concept and Sexual Self-Efficacy in Adolescents: A Possible Clue to Promoting Sexual Health?" *Journal of Sex Research* 45, no. 3 (2008): 277–286.

23. http://www.huffingtonpost.com/2010/10/07/karen-owen-duke-sex-rati_n_754186.html.

CHAPTER ELEVEN

1. A. Wieder, *Year of the Cock: The Remarkable True Account of a Married Man Who Left His Wife and Paid the Price* (New York: Grand Central Publishing, 2009), 99.

2. M. Klein, *America's War on Sex: The Attack on Law, Lust and Liberty* (New York: Praeger, 2006), 141.

3. David Zinczenko, with Ted Spiker, *Men, Love & Sex* (Emmaus, PA: Rodale, 2006).

4. M. Popovic, "Pornography Use and Closeness with Others in Men," *Archives of Sexual Behavior*, July 23, 2010.

5. Staff, "Gender and Porn: Where Men and Women Look First," *Science 2.0 Scientific Blogging*, http://www.science20.com/news_articles/gender_and_porn_where_men_and_women_look_first.

6. A. Maddox, G. Rhoades, and H. Markman, "Viewing Sexually-Explicit Materials Alone or Together: Associations with Relationship Quality," *Archives of Sexual Behavior* 40, no. 2 (2011): 441–448, doi:10.1007/s10508-009-9585-4, http://www.springerlink.com/content/444771404n122377.

7. J. Ross, *The Male Paradox* (New York: Simon & Schuster, 1992), 58.

8. B. Edelman, "Markets Red Light States: Who Buys Online Adult Entertainment?" *Journal of Economic Perspectives* 23, no. 1 (2009): 209–220.

9. E. Callaway, "Porn in the USA: Conservatives Are Biggest Consumers," *New Scientist*, February 27, 2009, http://www.newscientist.com/article/dn16680-porn-in-the-usa-conservatives-are-biggest-consumers.html.

10. A. Giddens, *The Transformation of Intimacy* (Stanford, CA: Stanford University Press), 119.

11. http://www.psychologytoday.com/blog/cupids-poisoned-arrow/201003/porn-goes-performance-goes-down.

12. M. Kimmell, *Guyland: The Perilous World Where Boys Become Men* (New York: Harper, 2008), 183.

13. R. Lynn, *The Sexual Revolution 2.0: Getting Connected, Upgrading Your Sex Life and Finding True Love—or at Least a Dinner Date—in the Internet Age* (Berkeley, CA: Amorata Press), 86.

14. *Huffington Post,* "Hugh Hefner Slams Tiger Woods, Jesse James & Sex Addiction," April 13, 2010, http://www.huffingtonpost.com/2010/04/13/hugh-hefner-slams-tiger-w_n_535635.html.

15. B. Berman, *Hugh Hefner, Playboy, Activist, and Rebel,* 2009, http://www.hugh hefnerplayboyactivistrebel.com; http://www.huffingtonpost.com/2010/07/12/hugh -hefner-i-have-sex-tw_n_643303.html.

16. C. Davis and R. Bauserman, "Exposure to Sexually Explicit Materials: An Attitude Change Perspective," in *Sources: Notable Selections in Human Sexuality,* ed. Gary Kelly (Guilford, CT: Dushkin/McGraw-Hill, 1998).

17. N. Malamuth, T. Addison, and M. Koss, "Pornography and Sexual Aggression: Are There Reliable Effects and Can We Understand Them?" *Annual Review of Sex Research* 11 (2000): 26–91.

18. P. Carnes and J. Schneider, "Recognition and Management of Addictive Sexual Disorders: Guide for the Primary Care Clinician," *Primary Care Practice* 4, no. 3 (2000).

19. M. Klein, personal communication, September 12, 2011.

CHAPTER TWELVE

1. J. Falla, "Disorderly Consumption and Capitalism: The Privilege of Sex Addiction," *College Literature* 28, no. 1 (2001).

2. A. Fenigstein and M. Preston, "The Desired Number of Sexual Partners as a Function of Gender, Sexual Risks, and the Meaning of 'Ideal,'" *Journal of Sex Research* 44, no. 1 (2007): 89–95.

3. R. Baumeister, K. Catanese, and K. Vohs, "Is There a Gender Difference in Strength of Sex Drive? Theoretical Views, Conceptual Distinctions, and a Review of Relevant Evidence," *Personality and Social Psychology Review* 5, no. 3 (2001): 242–273.

4. M. Quadland, "Compulsive Sexual Behavior: Definition of a Problem and an Approach to Treatment," *Journal of Sex and Marital Therapy* 11 (2001): 121–132.

5. Baumeister, Catanese, and Vohs, "Is There a Gender Difference in Strength of Sex Drive?"

6. P. Carnes, *Don't Call It Love: Recovery from Sexual Addiction* (New York: Bantam, 1992), 160.

7. Anonymous, "Why Men Cheat," *Esquire,* April 2010.

8. Curtis Bergstrand, PhD, personal communication, August 15, 2011.

9. P. Druckerman, *Lust in Translation: The Rules of Infidelity from Tokyo to Tennessee* (New York: Penguin, 2007), 69.

10. Druckerman, *Lust in Translation,* 126.

11. Liesl Schillinger, "Are French Women More Tolerant?" *New York Times,* May 20, 2011, http://www.nytimes.com/roomfordebate/2011/05/18/are-french-women-more-tolerant/discretion-for-the-libertine.

12. Druckerman, *Lust in Translation,* 151.

13. Druckerman, *Lust in Translation,* 179.

14. Druckerman, *Lust in Translation*, 211.

15. Carl Jung, in a letter to Sigmund Freud, January 30, 1910, http://www.pep-web.org/document.php?id=zbk.041.0288a.

16. http://www.youtube.com/watch?v=R6EnwYKNAiA.

17. Nigel Cawthorne, *Sordid Sex Lives* (London: Quercus Publishing, 2010), 147.

18. Hillary Clinton, describing her husband's infidelity, 1999, http://www.capitol hillblue.com/Aug1999/080199/hillary080199.htm.

19. R. Baumeister, *Is There Anything Good about Men? How Cultures Flourish by Exploiting Men* (New York: Oxford University Press, 2010).

20. L. Flynt and D. Eisenbach, *One Nation under Sex: How the Private Lives of Presidents, First Ladies and Their Lovers Changed the Course of American History* (New York: Palgrave Macmillan, 2011).

21. J. Browning, D. Kessler, E. Hatfield, and P. Choo, "Power, Gender and Sexual Behavior," *Journal of Sex Research* 36, no. 4 (1999): 342–347.

22. M. Szalavitz, "Sex and Politics: Are Powerful Men Really More Likely to Cheat?" *Time*, April 28, 2011.

23. http://blog.okcupid.com.

24. A. Akbar, "Einstein's Theory of Infidelity," *Independent*, July 11, 2006.

25. V. Clarke, "Forget Equations, Einstein's Genius Was to Disprove Monogamy Theory," *Independent*, http://www.independent.ie/opinion/analysis/forget-equations-einsteins-genius-was-to-disprove-monogamy-theory-132432.html.

26. Cawthorne, *Sordid Sex Lives*, 61.

27. T. Rubython, "Hollywood's First Sex Addict: Never Mind Liz Taylor—a New Book Reveals Richard Burton Slept with Three Women a Week for 30 Years," *Mail Online*, May 14, 2011, http://www.dailymail.co.uk/femail/article-1386878/Richard-Burton-slept-women-week-30-years.html.

28. Druckerman, *Lust in Translation*, 257.

29. S. Stolberg, "Naked Hubris," *New York Times*, June 12, 2011, http://www.nytimes.com/2011/06/12/weekinreview/12women.html?_r=1&hp=&pagewanted=all.

30. BBC News, "All MPs Have Sexual Magnetism, MP Paul Flynn Says," August 3, 2011, http://www.bbc.co.uk/news/uk-politics-14387836.

31. T. Dayton, "Is Eliot Spitzer a Sex Addict?" *Huffington Post*, http://www.huffingtonpost.com/dr-tian-dayton/is-eliot-spitzer-a-sex-a_b_94268.html.

32. A. Elkind, *Rough Justice: The Rise and Fall of Eliot Spitzer* (New York: Portfolio, 2010), 259.

33. Elkind, *Rough Justice*, 262.

34. H. Goldberg, *Hazards of Being Male: Surviving the Myth of Masculine Privilege* (New York: Signet, 1987), 48.

35. R. Hyatt, "Sex Addiction: Who Should Be Blamed for Lack of Self-Control?" *USA Today*, http://www.people.com/people/archive/article/0,,20122535,00.html; http://findarticles.com/p/articles/mi_m1272/is_n2630_v126/ai_20004055.

36. Letter to editor, *Archives of Sexual Behavior* 35 (2006): 643–644.

37. R. Michael, J. Gagnon, E. Lauman, and G. Kolata, *Sex in America: A Definitive Survey* (Boston, MA: Little, Brown, 1994).

38. M. Epstein, J. P. Calzo, A. P. Smiler, and L. M. Ward, "Anything from Making Out to Having Sex: Men's Negotiations of Hooking Up and Friends with Benefits Scripts," *Journal of Sex Research* 46, no. 5 (2009): 414–424.

39. K. J. Gergen, M. M. Gergen, and W. H. Barton, "Deviance in the Dark," *Psychology Today* 7 (1973): 129–130.

40. E. Perel, *Mating in Captivity: Unlocking Erotic Intelligence* (New York: Harper, 2007), 69.

41. J. Smolowe and E. Lafferty, "Sex with a Scorecard," *Time*, http://www.time.com/time/magazine/article/0,9171,978157,00.html#ixzz1SEm6BRp4.

42. http://oregonstate.edu/ua/ncs/archives/2001/aug/study-athletes-wives-must-cope-adultery-culture.

43. http://sports.yahoo.com/nfl/news?slug=nfp-20110515_keith_mccants_i_dont_want_anybody_to_feel_sorry_for_me.

44. D. Shaw, "A Gracious Man, but Driven to Win," *Los Angeles Times*, October 13, 1999, http://articles.latimes.com/1999/oct/13/news/mn-21800.

45. R. Novak, "Wilt Chamberlain," *People*, http://www.people.com/people/archive/article/0,,20088351,00.html.

46. Ogi Ogas and Sai Gaddam, *A Billion Wicked Thoughts: What the World's Largest Experiment Reveals about Human Desire*, Kindle ed. (New York: Dutton Adult, 2011), location 439.

CHAPTER THIRTEEN

1. R. Baumeister, *Is There Anything Good about Men? How Cultures Flourish by Exploiting Men* (New York: Oxford University Press, 2010), 195.

2. N. Friday, *Men in Love* (New York: Delta, 1998), 5.

3. R. Baumeister, *Escaping the Self: Alcoholism, Spirituality, Masochism, and Other Flights from the Burden of Selfhood* (New York: Basic Books, 1991).

4. David Zinczenko, with Ted Spiker, *Men, Love & Sex* (Emmaus, PA: Rodale, 2006), 48.

5. Zinczenko, *Men, Love & Sex*, 48.

6. R. Michael, J. Gagnon, E. Lauman, and G. Kolata, *Sex in America: A Definitive Survey* (Boston, MA: Little, Brown, 1994), 126.

7. Dr. Wayne Kuang, PA, Albuquerque Urology Associates, June 27, 2011.

8. David Zinczenko, *Men, Love & Sex*, 18.

9. http://www.script-o-rama.com/movie_scripts/t/three-men-and-a-baby-script.html.

10. http://gossiponthis.com/2011/05/15/jesse-james-i-cheated-on-my-wife-guess-what-so-do-millions-of-other-men.

11. C. Paglia, "It's a Jungle Out There," http://users.ipfw.edu/ruflethe/itsajungleoutthere.htm.

12. J. R. Garcia, J. MacKillop, E. L. Aller, A. M. Merriwether, D. S. Wilson, et al., "Associations between Dopamine D4 Receptor Gene Variation with Both Infidelity

and Sexual Promiscuity," *PLoS ONE* 5, no. 11 (2010): e14162, doi:10.1371/journal. pone.0014162, http://psychology.uga.edu/ecpl/publications/pdf/Garcia%20et%20 al.%20-%202010%20-%20PLoS%20ONE.pdf.

13. R. Thornhill and M. Palmer, *A Natural History of Rape* (Cambridge, MA: MIT Press, 2000).

14. http://www.ctvbc.ctv.ca/servlet/an/local/CTVNews/20110407/bc_cameron_moffat_interrogation_110406/20110407?hub=BritishColumbiaHome; http://www.timescolonist.com/Editorial+must+face+evil+deeds+Kimberly+Proctor+killers/4581248/story.html.

15. P. Carnes, *Out of the Shadows: Understanding Sexual Addiction*, 2nd ed. (Minneapolis, MN: Hazelden, 1992), 131.

16. World Health Organization, *Education and Treatment in Human Sexuality: The Training of Health Professionals*, WHO Technical Report Series no 572 (Geneva: WHO, 1975).

17. S. Modgil and H. J. Eysenck, *Hans Eysenck: Consensus and Controversy* (Philadelphia, PA: Psychology Press, 1986), 276.

18. R. Moore and D. Gillette, *The Lover Within: Accessing the Lover in the Male Psyche* (New York: Morrow, 1993).

19. B. Carey, "Female Take-over in Counseling," *New York Times*, May 29, 2011, http://www.ocala.com/article/20110529/WIRE/110529819?p=all&tc=pgall.

20. http://www.psychologytoday.com/blog/evil-deeds/201105/the-feminization -psychotherapy-does-your-therapists-sex-really-matter.

21. S. Faludi, *Stiffed: The Betrayal of the American Man* (New York: HarperPerennial, 2000), 13.

22. G. Mosse, *The Image of Man: The Creation of Modern Masculinity*, Studies in the History of Sexuality (New York: Oxford University Press, 1998), 101.

23. http://en.wikiquote.org/wiki/Mary_Poppins_%28film%29.

24. Mosse, *The Image of Man*, 83.

25. J. Vandello, J. Bosson, D. Cohen, R. Burnaford, and J. Weaver, "Precarious Manhood," *Journal of Personality and Social Psychology* 95, no. 6 (2008): 1325–1339.

26. S. T. Lehr, A. S. Demi, C. Diloro, and J. Facteau, "Predictors of Father-Son Communication about Sexuality," *Journal of Sex Research* 42, no. 2 (2005): 119–129.

27. http://www.nerve.com/personalessays/barlow/shameless?page=1.

28. M. Oppenheimer, "Married, with Infidelities," *New York Times*, http://www.nytimes.com/2011/07/03/magazine/infidelity-will-keep-us-together .html?_r=2&seid=auto&smid=tw-nytimesmagazine&pagewanted=all.

29. R. Kelley, "Don't Let Boys Be Boys," *Newsweek*, May 13, 2010, http://www.newsweek.com/2010/05/13/don-t-let-boys-be-boys.html.

CHAPTER FOURTEEN

1. S. Katz and A. Liu, *The Codependency Conspiracy* (New York: Warner Books, 1991), 124.

2. Anonymous, "Why Men Cheat," *Esquire*, April 2010.

3. Anonymous, "Why Men Cheat."

4. S. C. Kalichman, J. R. Johnson, V. Adair, D. Rompa, K. Multhauf, and J. A. Kelly, "Sexual Sensation Seeking: Scale Development and Predicting AIDS-Risk Behavior among Homosexually Active Men," *Journal of Personality Assessment* 62 (1994): 385–397.

5. J. Lehrer, "Don't: The Secret of Self-Control," *New Yorker*, May 2009, http://www.newyorker.com/reporting/2009/05/18/090518fa_fact_lehrer.

6. D. Ariely, *Predictably Irrational: The Hidden Forces That Shape Our Decisions* (New York: HarperCollins, 2010), 58.

7. D. Ariely, *Predictably Irrational: The Hidden Forces That Shape Our Decisions* (New York: HarperCollins, 2010), 243.

8. W. Burroughs, *Junky* (New York: Penguin, 1977), xv.

9. Personal communication, author's name withheld by request.

10. Personal communication, Dr. Rory Reid, November 21, 2011.

11. C. Groneman, *Nymphomania: A History* (New York: Norton, 2000), xxii.

12. S. Cohen, *Folk Devils and Moral Panics* (New York: Routledge Classics, 2011).

13. B. Kovach and T. Rosenstiel, *Warp Speed: America in the Age of Mixed Media* (New York: Twentieth Century Fund, 1999), xxx.

14. R. Baumeister, *Is There Anything Good about Men? How Cultures Flourish by Exploiting Men* (New York: Oxford University Press, 2010), 75, 210.

15. http://www.mtv.com/news/articles/1582149/20080222/story.jhtml.

16. J. Rudski, personal communication, June 3, 2010.

17. T. Szasz, *The Myth of Mental Illness: Foundations of a Theory of Personal Conduct* (New York: HarperCollins, 1974), 262.

18. M. Konner, "The I of the Storm," *LA Times Magazine*, October 8, 1989.

Selected Bibliography

Akbar, Arifa. "Einstein's Theory of Infidelity." *Independent*, July 11, 2006.

Albright, J. "Sex in America Online: An Exploration of Sex, Marital Status, and Sexual Identity in Internet Sex Seeking and Its Impacts." *Journal of Sex Research* 45, no. 2 (2008): 175–186.

American Psychiatric Association. *Diagnostic and Statistical Manual: Mental Disorders*. Washington, DC: American Psychiatric Association, 1952. http://www.psychiatryonline.com/DSMPDF/dsm-i.pdf.

———. *Diagnostic and Statistical Manual: Mental Disorders*. Washington, DC: American Psychiatric Association, 1952. http://www.psychiatryonline.com/DSMPDF/dsm-i.pdf.

———. *Diagnostic and Statistical Manual: Mental Disorders*. 2nd ed. Washington, DC: American Psychiatric Association, 1968. http://www.psychiatryonline.com/DSMPDF/dsm-ii.pdf.

———. *Diagnostic and Statistical Manual: Mental Disorders*. 3rd ed. Washington, DC: American Psychiatric Association, 1980.

———. *Diagnostic and Statistical Manual: Mental Disorders*. 3rd ed. revised. Washington, DC: American Psychiatric Association, 1987.

———. *Diagnostic and Statistical Manual of Mental Disorders*. DSM-IV-TR. 4th ed. Washington, DC: American Psychiatric Association, 2000.

———. *Diagnostic and Statistical Manual: Mental Disorders*. 4th ed. revised. Washington, DC: American Psychiatric Association, 2000.

———. Resolution on Appropriate Affirmative Responses to Sexual Orientation Distress and Change Efforts. 2011. http://www.apa.org/about/governance/council/policy//sexualorientation.aspx.

Anonymous. "Why Men Cheat." *Esquire*, April 2010.

Aragon, A. "Detection of Malingering in Chronic Frotteurists." 1999. Copy obtained from author.

Ariely, D. *Predictably Irrational: The Hidden Forces that Shape Our Decisions*. New York: HarperCollins, 2010.

241

Arnott, S. *Sex: A User's Guide*. New York: Random House Digital, 2010.

Bamuhigire, O. "Sex Addiction: A Growing Problem." *New Vision*, 2006. http://www.aegis.org/news/nv/2006/NV060108.html.

Bancroft, J., C. A. Graham, E. Janssen, and S. A. Sanders. "The Dual Control Model: Current Status and Future Directions." *Journal of Sex Research* 46, nos. 2–3 (2009): 121–142.

Bancroft, J., and Z. Vukadinovic. "Sexual Addiction, Sexual Compulsivity, Sexual Impulsivity or What? Toward a Theoretical Model." *Journal of Sex Research* 41 (2004): 225–234.

Baumeister, R. *Escaping the Self: Alcoholism, Spirituality, Masochism, and Other Flights from the Burden of Selfhood*. New York: Basic Books, 1991.

———. *Evil: Inside Human Violence and Cruelty*. New York: Freeman, 1997.

———. *Is There Anything Good About Men? How Cultures Flourish by Exploiting Men*. New York: Oxford University Press, 2010.

Baumeister, R., K. Catanese, and K. Vohs. "Is There a Gender Difference in Strength of Sex Drive? Theoretical Views, Conceptual Distinctions, and a Review of Relevant Evidence." *Personality and Social Psychology Review* 5, no. 3 (2001): 242–273.

Bayer, R. *Homosexuality and American Psychiatry: The Politics of Diagnosis*. Princeton, NJ: Princeton University Press, 1987.

Bechtel, S. *The Practical Encyclopedia of Sex and Health*. Emmaus, PA: Rodale, 1993.

Bergstrand, C., and J. Sinski. *Swinging in America: Love, Sex, and Marriage in the 21st Century*. Santa Barbara, CA: Praeger, 2010.

Bivona, J., and J. Critelli. "The Nature of Women's Rape Fantasies: An Analysis of Prevalence, Frequency, and Contents." *Journal of Sex Research* 46 (2009): 33.

Blumberg, E. "Lives and Voices of Highly Sexual Women." *Journal of Sex Research* 40, no. 2 (2003): 151.

Bright, Susie. http://susiebright.blogs.com/susie_brights_journal_/pregnancy.

Briken, P., N. Habermann, W. Berner, and A. Hill. "Diagnosis and Treatment of Sexual Addiction: A Survey among German Sex Therapists." *Sexual Addiction & Compulsivity* 14, no. 2 (2007): 131–143.

British Psychological Society. "Response to the American Psychiatric Association: DSM-5 Development." 2011. http://apps.bps.org.uk/_publicationfiles/consultation-responses/DSM-5%202011%20-%20BPS%20response.pdf.

Browning, J., D. Kessler, E. Hatfield, and P. Choo. "Power, Gender, and Sexual Behavior." *Journal of Sexual Research* 36, no. 4 (1999): 342–347.

Burch, R., and G. Gallup. "The Psychobiology of Human Semen." In *Female Infidelity and Paternal Uncertainty*, ed. S. M. Platek and T. K. Shackelford, 141–172. New York: Cambridge University Press, 2006.

Burns, M. "Cases of Persecuted Sexual Activity." http://www.solresearch.org/~SOLR/rprt/bkgrd/JSOcases.asp.

Burroughs, W. *Junky*. New York: Penguin, 1977.

Buzwell, S., and D. Rosenthal. "Constructing a Sexual Self: Adolescents' Sexual Self-Perceptions and Sexual Risk-Taking." *Journal of Research on Adolescence* 6 (1996): 489–513.

Callaway, E. "Porn in the USA: Conservatives Are Biggest Consumers." *New Scientist*, February 27, 2009. http://www.newscientist.com/article/dn16680-porn-in-the-usa-conservatives-are-biggestconsumers.

Carey, B. "Female Take-Over in Counseling." *New York Times*, May 29, 2011. http://www.ocala.com/article/20110529/WIRE/110529819?p=all&tc=pgall.

Carnes, P. "The Case for Sexual Anorexia: An Interim Report on 144 Patients with Sexual Disorders." http://www.sexhelpworkshops.com/Documents/ARTICLE_Case%20for%20Sexual%20Anorexa%20144%20patients_PCarnes.pdf.

———. *Don't Call It Love: Recovery from Sexual Addiction*. New York: Bantam, 1992.

———. *Out of the Shadows: Understanding Sexual Addiction*. 2nd ed. Minneapolis, MN: Hazelden, 1992.

Carnes, P., and J. Schneider. "Recognition and Management of Addictive Sexual Disorders: Guide for the Primary Care Clinician." *Primary Care Practice* 4, no. 3 (2000): 302–318.

Carroll, J., K. Volk, and J. Hyde. "Differences between Males and Females in Motives for Engaging in Sexual Intercourse." *Archives of Sexual Behavior* 14 (1985): 131–139.

Cass, V. "Homosexual Identity Formation: A Theoretical Model." *Journal of Homosexuality* 4, no. 3 (1979): 219–235.

Cawthorne, Nigel. *Sordid Sex Lives*. London: Quercus, 2010.

Chapman, M. *What Does Polyamory Look Like?* New York: iUniverse, 2010.

Clarke, V. "Forget Equations, Einstein's Genius Was to Disprove Monogamy Theory." *Independent*, 2006. http://www.independent.ie/opinion/analysis/forget-equations-einsteins-genius-was-to-disprovemonogamy-theory-132432.html.

Cohen, S. *Folk Devils and Moral Panics*. New York: Routledge Classics, 2011.

Connor, T. "Newser's Book: Ford Saw Clinton as a Sex 'Addict.'" *New York Daily News*, October 28, 2007. http://www.nydailynews.com/news/national/2007/10/28/2007-10-28_newsers_book_ford_saw_clinton_as_a_sex_a.html.

Coombs, R. "Sex Education for Physicians: Is It Adequate?" *Family Coordinator* 17, no. 4 (1968). http://www.jstor.org/pss/582054.

Courcol, C., and M. Hood. "Fine Line between Serial Seducer and Sex Addict." AFP News, May 17, 2011.

Cutler, W. *Love Cycles: The Science of Intimacy*. New York: Villard, 1991.

Davis, C., and R. Bauserman. "Exposure to Sexually Explicit Materials: An Attitude Change Perspective." In *Sources: Notable Selections in Human Sexuality*, ed. Gary Kelly. Guilford, CT: Dushkin/McGraw-Hill, 1998.

Davis, L. "Sex Addiction: The Truth Is Out There." *Chicago Blog*, September 10, 2008. http://pressblog.uchicago.edu/2008/09/10/sex_addiction_the_truth_is_out.html.

DeLamater, J. "Social Control of Sexuality." *Annual Review of Sociology* 7 (1981): 261–290.

D'Onofrio, B., E. Turkheimer, R. Emery, A. Heath, P. Madden, W. Slutske, et al. "A Genetically Informed Study of the Processes Underlying the Association between Parental Marital Instability and Offspring Adjustment." *Developmental Psychology* 42, no. 3 (2006): 486–499.

Druckerman, P. *Lust in Translation*. New York: Penguin, 2007.

Drury, K. *Money, Sex, and Spiritual Power*. Indianapolis, IN: Wesley Press, 1992. Available at: http://www.drurywriting.com/keith/9male.htm.

Earle, R., and M. Earle. *Sex Addiction Case Studies and Management*. New York: Routledge, 1995.

Easton, D., and C. Liszt. *The Ethical Slut: A Guide to Infinite Sexual Possibilities*. San Francisco, CA: Greenery Press, 1997.

Edelman, B. "Markets Red Light States: Who Buys Online Adult Entertainment?" *Journal of Economic Perspectives* 23, no. 1 (2009): 209–220.

Elkind, A. *Rough Justice: The Rise and Fall of Eliot Spitzer*. New York: Portfolio, 2010.

Epstein, M., J. P. Calzo, A. P. Smiler, and L. M. Ward. "Anything from Making Out to Having Sex: Men's Negotiations of Hooking Up and Friends with Benefits Scripts." *Journal of Sex Research* 46, no. 5 (2009): 414–424.

Falla, J. "Disorderly Consumption and Capitalism: The Privilege of Sex Addiction." *College Literature* 28, no. 1 (2001): 46–63.

Faludi, S. *Stiffed: The Betrayal of the American Man*. New York: Harper Perennial, 2000.

Farree, M. "Females and Sex Addiction: Myths and Diagnostic Implications." *Sexual Addiction & Compulsivity* 8 (2001): 287–300.

Fedoroff, J. "Forensic and Diagnostic Concerns Arising from the Proposed DSM-5 Criteria for Sexual Paraphilic Disorder." *Journal of the American Academy of Psychiatry and the Law* 39, no. 2 (2011): 238–241. http://www.jaapl.org/cgi/content/full/39/2/238.

Fenigstein, A., and M. Preston. "The Desired Number of Sexual Partners as a Function of Gender, Sexual Risks, and the Meaning of 'Ideal.'" *Journal of Sex Research* 44, no. 1 (2007): 89–95.

Finlayson, A., J. Sealy, and P. Martin. 2001. "The Differential Diagnosis of Problematic Hypersexuality." *Sexual Addiction & Compulsivity* 8 (2001): 243.

Fisher, L. *Sex, Romance, and Relationships: AARP Survey of Midlife and Older Adults*. Washington, DC: American Association of Retired Persons, 2010. www.aarp.org.

Flynt, L., and D. Eisenbach. *One Nation Under Sex: How the Private Lives of Presidents, First Ladies, and Their Lovers Changed the Course of American History*. New York: Palgrave Macmillan, 2011.

Fox, S. DSM-V, "Healthcare Reform Will Fuel Major Changes in Addiction Psychiatry." *Medscape Medical News*. December 6, 2010. http://www.medscape.com/viewarticle/733649

Frances, A. "Rape, Psychiatry, and Constitutional Rights: Hard Cases Make for Very Bad Law." *Psychiatric Times* 27, no. 9 (2010), http://www.psychiatrictimes.com/sexualoffenses/ content/article/10168/1595945.

Freud, S. *Civilization and Its Discontents*. New York: Norton, 1989.

Friday, N. *Men in Love*. New York: Delta, 1998.

Fullerton, R., and G. Punge. "Kleptomania: A Brief Intellectual History." In *The Romance of Marketing History*. 2003. http://faculty.quinnipiac.edu/charm/CHARM%20proceedings/CHARM%20article%20archive%20pdf%20f.

Garcia, J. R., J. MacKillop, E. L. Aller, A. M. Merriwether, D. S. Wilson, et al. "Associations between Dopamine D4 Receptor Gene Variation with Both Infidelity and Sexual Promiscuity." http://psychology.uga.edu/ecpl/publications/pdf/Garcia%20et%20al.%20-%202010%20-.

Gergen, Kenneth J., Mary M. Gergen, and William H. Barton. "Deviance in the Dark." *Psychology Today*, October 1973, 129–130.

Giddens, A. *The Transformation of Intimacy*. Stanford, CA: Stanford University Press, 1992.

Gold, S. N., and C. L. Heffner. "Sexual Addiction: Many Conceptions, Minimal Data." *Clinical Psychology Review* 18 (1998): 367–381.

Goldberg, H. *Hazards of Being Male: Surviving the Myth of Masculine Privilege*. New York: Signet, 1987.

Goodman, A. "Sexual Addiction: Designation and Treatment." *Journal of Sex and Marital Therapy* 18 (1992): 312.

Goodman, M. "Neurobiology of Addiction: An Integrative Review." *Biochemical Pharmacology* 75 (1992): 266–322.

Grant, J. E., J. A. Brewer, and M. N. Potenza. "The Neurobiology of Substance and Behavioral Addictions." *CNS Spectrums* 11, no. 12 (2006): 924–930.

Groneman, C. *Nymphomania: A History*. New York: Norton, 2000.

Hagedorn, B. "The Call for a New Diagnostic and Statistical Manual of Mental Disorders Diagnosis: Addictive Disorders." *Journal of Addictions & Offender Counseling* 29 (April 2009).

Hannah, J. "They Gotta Habit." *People*, May 30, 1998, 109–110.

Hart, A. *Thrilled to Death*. Nashville, TN: Thomas Nelson, 2007.

Hatzenbuehler, M. L. "The Social Environment and Suicide Attempts in Lesbian, Gay, and Bisexual Youth." *Pediatrics* 127, no. 5 (2011).

Henkin, W. "The Myth of Sexual Addiction." Originally published in *Spectator*, 1998. Copy obtained from author, 2007.

Herkov, M. "What Is Sexual Addiction?" *Psych Central* 3 (2006). http://psychcentral.com/lib/2006/what-is-sexual-addiction/hes=13.

Hicks, T. V., and H. Leitenberg. "Sexual Fantasies about One's Partner versus Someone Else: Gender Differences in Incidence and Frequency." *Journal of Sex Research* 38, no. 1 (2001): 43–50.

Hill, D. "Differences and Similarities in Men's and Women's Sexual Self-Schemas." *Journal of Sex Research* 44, no. 2 (2007): 135–144.

Hoff, C. H., and S. C. Beougher. "Sexual Agreements among Gay Couples." *Archives of Sexual Behavior* 39 (November 2007): 774–787.

Ilfeld, F., Jr., and R. Lauer. *Social Nudism in America*. New Haven, CT: College and University Press Services, 1964.

Jenkins, A. *Invitations to Responsibility*. Adelaide, South Australia: Dulwich Centre Publications, 1990.

Jennings, R. "His Streak Is Alive at 7,788—and Counting." *USA Today*, April 28, 2011, 13D.

Kafka, M. P. "Hypersexual Disorder: A Proposed Diagnosis for DSM-V." *Archives of Sexual Behavior* 39 (2010). doi:10.1007/s10508-009-9574-7.

Kafka, M. P., and J. Hennen. "The Paraphilia-Related Disorders: An Empirical Investigation of Nonparaphilic Hypersexuality Disorders in 206 Outpatient Males." *Journal of Sex and Marital Therapy* 25 (1999): 305–319.

Kahr, B. *Who's Been Sleeping in Your Head?* New York: Basic Books, 2008.

Kalichman, S. C., and D. Cain. "The Relationship between Indicators of Sexual Compulsivity and High Risk Sexual Practices among Men and Women Receiving Services from a Sexually Transmitted Infection Clinic." *Journal of Sex Research* 41 (2004): 235–241.

Kalichman, S. C., J. R. Johnson, V. Adair, D. Rompa, K. Multhauf, and J. A. Kelly. "Sexual Sensation Seeking: Scale Development and Predicting AIDS-Risk Behavior among Homosexually Active Men." *Journal of Personality Assessment* 62 (1994): 385–397.

Kaminer, W. "Is Clinton a Sex Addict?" *Slate*, March 22, 1998. http://www.slate.com/id/2495.

Kaplan, M., and R. Krueger. "Diagnosis, Assessment, and Treatment of Hypersexuality." *Journal of Sex Research* 47, nos. 2–3 (2010): 181–198.

Kasl, C. *Women, Sex, and Addiction: A Search for Love and Power.* New York: HarperCollins, 1990.

Katz, S., and A. Liu. *The Codependency Conspiracy.* New York: Warner Books, 1991.

Kelly, R. "Don't Let Boys Be Boys." *Newsweek*, May 13, 2010. http://www.newsweek.com/2010/05/13/don-t letboys-be-boys.html.

Kimmell, M. *Guyland: The Perilous World Where Boys Become Men.* New York: Harper, 2008.

Kinsey, A. C., W. B. Pomeroy, and C. E. Martin. *Sexual Behavior in the Human Male.* Bloomington: Indiana University Press, 1998.

Klein, M. *America's War on Sex: The Attack on Law, Lust, and Liberty.* Sex, Love, and Psychology. Westport, CT: Praeger, 2006.

———. *Why There's No Such Thing as Sexual Addiction—and Why It Really Matters.* 1998. http://www.sexed.org/archive/article08.html.

Konner, M. "The I of the Storm." *LA Times Magazine*, October 8, 1989.

Koob, G., P. Sanna, and F. Bloom. "Neuroscience of Addiction." *Neuron* 21 (1998): 467–476. http://dionysus.psych.wisc.edu/Lit/Articles/KoobG1998a.pdf.

Kort, J. "Has Anything Changed in What We Know about Satyriasis from Its Original Identification of the Disorder?" PhD diss. 2009. http://www.google.com/url?sa=t&source=web&cd=7&ved=0CD8QFjAG&url=http%3A%2F%2Fwww.esextherapy.com%2Fdissertations%2FJoe_Kort_Dissertation_Master_Turabian%2520January%25203%2C%25202010.doc&rct=j&q=joe%20kort%20satyriasis&ei=NqcfTvP1FjTiAK_3_GrAw&usg=AFQjCNHsF0gQgYo3z3uosx2zOyHgg4AKMQ&c ad=rja.

Kovach, B., and T. Rosenstiel. *Warp Speed: America in the Age of Mixed Media.* New York: Twentieth Century Fund, 1999.

Krafft-Ebing, R. *Psychopathia Sexualis: With Especial Reference to the Antipathic Sexual Instinct; A Medico-Forensic Study.* Whitefish, MT: Kessinger Publishing, 2010.

Lane, C. *How Normal Behavior Became A Sickness.* New Haven, CT: Yale University Press, 2007.

Langstrom, N., and R. K. Hanson. "High Rates of Sexual Behavior in the General Population: Correlates and Predictors." *Archives of Sexual Behavior* 35 (2006): 37–52.

———. "Population Correlates Are Relevant to Understanding Hypersexuality: A Response to Giles." *Archives of Sexual Behavior* 35 (2006): 643–644.

Larson, V. "Does Porn Watching Lead to Divorce?" *Huffington Post*, May 29, 2011. http://www.huffingtonpost.com/vicki-larson/porn-and-divorce_b_861987.html.

Leedes, R. "The Three Most Important Criteria in Diagnosing Sexual Addictions: Obsession, Obsession, and Obsession." *Sexual Addiction & Compulsivity: The Journal of Treatment & Prevention* 8, nos. 3–4 (2001): 223.

Lefkowitz, B. *Our Guys.* New York: Vintage, 1998.

Lehr, S. T., A. S. Demi, C. Diloro, and J. Facteau. "Predictors of Father-Son Communication about Sexuality." *Journal of Sex Research* 42, no. 2 (2005): 119–129.

Lehrer, J. "Don't: The Secret of Self-Control." *New Yorker*, May 2009 18: 26–32.

Leo, J. "Doing the Disorder Rag." *U.S. News and World Report*, October 27, 1997.

Levine, M., and R. Troiden. "The Myth of Sexual Compulsivity." *Journal of Sex Research* 25, no. 3. http://www.jstor.org/pss/3812739.

Ley, D. *Insatiable Wives: Women Who Stray and the Men Who Love Them.* Lanham, MD: Rowman & Littlefield, 2009.

Linden, D. *The Compass of Pleasure: How Our Brains Make Fatty Foods, Orgasm, Exercise, Marijuana, Generosity, Vodka, Learning, and Gambling Feel So Good.* New York: Viking, 2011.

Lippa, R. A. "Sex Differences in Sex Drive, Sociosexuality, and Height across 53 Nations: Testing Evolutionary and Social Structural Theories." *Archives of Sexual Behavior* 38 (2009): 631–651.

Loftus, E. "Dispatch from the (Un)Civil Memory Wars." In *Recollections of Trauma: Scientific Evidence and Clinical Practice*, ed. J. D. Read and D. S. Lindsay, 171–198. New York: Plenum, 1997.

Lynn, R. *The Sexual Revolution 2.0: Getting Connected, Upgrading Your Sex Life, and Finding True Love—or at Least a Dinner Date—in the Internet Age.* Berkeley, CA: Amorata Press, 2005.

Maddox, A., G. Rhoades, and H. Markman. "Viewing Sexually-Explicit Materials Alone or Together: Associations with Relationship Quality." *Archives of Sexual Behavior* 40, no. 2 (2011): 441–448.

Malamuth, N., T. Addison, and M. Koss. "Pornography and Sexual Aggression: Are There Reliable Effects and Can We Understand Them?" *Annual Review of Sex Research* 11 (2000): 26–91.

Maltz, W., and S. Boss. *Private Thoughts: Exploring the Power of Women's Sexual Fantasies.* Charleston, SC: Booksurge, 2008.

Markeya, P., and C. Markey. "Changes in Pornography-Seeking Behaviors Following Political Elections: An Examination of the Challenge Hypothesis." *Evolution and Human Behavior* 31 (2010): 442–446.

Marshall, D. "Sexual Behavior on Mangaia." In *Sources: Notable Selections in Human Sexuality*, ed. Gary Kelly. Guilford, CT: Dushkin/McGraw-Hill, 1998.

McIntyre, M., et al. "Romantic Involvement Often Reduces Men's Testosterone Levels—but Not Always: The Moderating Role of Extrapair Sexual Interest." *Journal of Personality and Social Psychology* 91 (2006).

McNally, R. "Cognitive Processing of Trauma-Relevant Information in PTSD." *PTSD Research Quarterly* 6, no. 2 (Spring 1995). http://www.dangerousbehaviour.com/Disturbing_News/Cognitive%20Processing%20in%20PTSD.pdf.

Michael, R., J. Gagnon, E. Lauman, and G. Kolata. *Sex in America: A Definitive Survey.* Boston, MA: Little, Brown, 1994.

Miller, S., and E. Byers. "Psychologists' Sexual Education and Training in Graduate School." *Canadian Journal of Behavioural Science* 42, no. 2 (2010): 93–100, http://www.sciencedirect.com/science/article/pii/S0008400X10600103.

Miller, W., and S. Rollnick. *Motivational Interviewing,* 2nd ed., *Preparing People for Change.* New York: Guilford Press, 2002.

Millet, C. *Sexual life of Catherine M.* New York: Grove Press, 2003.

Miner, M., N .Raymond, B. Mueller, M. Lloyd, and K. Lim, "Preliminary Investigation of the Impulsive and Neuroanatomical Characteristics of Compulsive Sexual Behavior," *Psychiatry Research* 174, no. 2 (2009): 146–151, http://www.ncbi.nlm.nih.gov/pmc/articles/PMC2789480.

Modgil, S., and H. J. Eysenck. *Hans Eysenck: Consensus and Controversy.* Philadelphia, PA: Psychology Press, 1986.

Money, J. *Destroying Angel.* Buffalo, NY: Prometheus, 1985.

Moore, R., and D. Gillette. *The Lover Within: Accessing the Lover in the Male Psyche.* New York: Morrow, 1993.

Morris, D. *The Soccer Tribe.* London: Cape, 1981.

Moser, C. "Paraphilia: A Critique of a Confused Concept." In *New Directions in Sex Therapy: Innovations and Alternatives,* ed. Peggy Kleinplatz. Philadelphia, PA: Brunner-Routledge, 2001.

Mosse, G. *The Image of Man: The Creation of Modern Masculinity.* Studies in the History of Sexuality. New York: Oxford University Press, 1998.

Murrow, D. *Why Men Hate Going to Church.* Nashville, TN: Nelson, 2004.

Novak, R. "Wilt Chamberlain." *People,* July 30, 1984. http://www.people.com/people/archive/article/0,,20088351,00.html.

Office of Juvenile Justice and Delinquency Prevention. "Using 'Sober Support' Groups in Your Juvenile Court." *Technical Assistance Bulletin,* 2010.

Ogas, Ogi, and Sai Gaddam. *A Billion Wicked Thoughts: What the World's Largest Experiment Reveals about Human Desire.* Kindle ed. New York: Dutton Adult, 2011.

Okie, S. "The Epidemic that Wasn't." *New York Times,* January 1, 2009. http://www.nytimes.com/2009/01/27/health/27coca.html.

Oliver, M., and J. Hyde, "Gender Differences in Sexuality: A Meta-analysis." *Psychological Bulletins* 114, no. 1 (1993): 29–51.

Oppenheimer, M. "Married, with Infidelities." *New York Times,* July 3, 2011. http://www.nytimes.com/2011/07/03/magazine/infidelity-will-keep-ustogether.

Owen, J., et al. "'Hooking Up' among College Students: Demographic and Psychosocial Correlates." *Archives of Sexual Behavior* (forthcoming). http://www.chs.fsu.edu/~ffincham/papers/ASB%20Owen%20et%20al.pdf.

Paglia, C. "It's a Jungle Out There." 1992. http://users.ipfw.edu/ruflethe/itsajungleoutthere.htm.

Palahniuk, C. *Choke.* New York: Doubleday, 2001.

Panati, C. "Faithful in Our Fashion." *The Advocate,* no. 762 (June 23, 1998): 11.

Peabody, S. *Addicted to Love, Overcoming Obsession and Dependency in Relationships.* Berkeley, CA: Celestial Arts, 1994.

Peele, S. "Addiction in Society." *Psychology Today*, 2010. http://www.psychologytoday.com/blog/addiction-in-society/201010/the-new-world-alcohol.

Perel, E. *Mating in Captivity: Unlocking Erotic Intelligence.* New York: HarperCollins, 2007.

Popovic, M. "Pornography Use and Closeness with Others in Men." *Archives of Sexual Behavior*, July 23, 2010.

Quadland, M. "Compulsive Sexual Behavior: Definition of a Problem and an Approach to Treatment." *Journal of Sex and Marital Therapy* 11 (1985): 121–132.

Raviv, M. 1993. "Personality Characteristics of Sexual Addicts and Pathological Gamblers." *Journal of Gambling Studies* 9, no. 1 (1993): 17–30.

Reece, M., et al. "National Survey of Sexual Health and Behavior (NSSHB)." 2010. http://www.nationalsexstudy.indiana.edu.

Reid, R., B. Carpenter, and T. Fong. "Letter to Editor: Neuroscience Research Fails to Support Claims that Excessive Pornography Consumption Causes Brain Damage." *Surgical Neurology International* 2, no. 1 (2011): 64. http://www.surgicalneurologyint.com/article.asp?issn=2152-7806;year=2011;volume=2;issue=1;spage=64;epage=64;aulast=Reid;type=0.

Richtel, M. "Your Brain on Computers." *New York Times*, June 6, 2010. http://www.nytimes.com/2010/06/07/technology/07brain.html?pagewanted=3&th&emc=th.

Rinehart, N., and M. McCabe. "An Empirical Investigation of Hypersexuality." *Sexual and Relationship Therapy* 13, no. 4 (1998): 369–384. http://www.informaworld.com/smpp/title%7Edb=all%7Econtent=t713446685%7Etab=issueslist%7Ebranc.

———. "Hypersexuality: Psychopathology or Normal Variant of Sexuality?" *Sexual and Marital Therapy* 12 (1997): 45–60.

Ross, J. *The Male Paradox.* New York: Simon & Schuster, 1992.

Rostosky, S. S., et al. "Sexual Self-Concept and Sexual Self-Efficacy in Adolescents: A Possible Clue to Promoting Sexual Health?" *Journal of Sex Research* 45, no. 3 (2008): 277–286.

Rubython, T. "Hollywood's First Sex Addict: Never Mind Liz Taylor—a New Book Reveals Richard Burton Slept with Three Women a Week for 30 Years." *Mail Online*, May 14, 2011. http://www.dailymail.co.uk/femail/article-1386878/Richard-Burton-slept-women-week-30-years.html.

Ryan, C., and C. Jetha. *Sex at Dawn: The Prehistoric Origins of Modern Sexuality.* New York: Harper, 2010.

Sapienza, P., L. Zingales, and D. Maestripieri. "Gender Differences in Financial Risk Aversion and Career Choices Are Affected by Testosterone." *Proceedings of the National Academy of Sciences*, August 24, 2009. doi:10.1073/pnas.0907352106. http://www.pnas.org/content/early/2009/08/20/0907352106.

Sbraga, T., W. O'Donohue, and J. Bancroft. *The Sex Addiction Workbook.* Oakland, CA: New Harbinger, 2003.

Schaler, Jeffrey. "Addiction Is a Choice." *Psychiatric Times* 19, no. 10 (October 2002).

Shaw, D. "A Gracious Man, but Driven to Win." *Los Angeles Times*, October 13, 1999.

Silverman, E. "The Lowdown on Low T and AndroGel Promotions." *Pharmalot Pharma Blog*, June 28, 2011. http://www.pharmalot.com/2011/06/the-lowdown -on-low-t-and-androgel-promotions.

Smith, G., S. Frankel, and J. Yarnell. "Sex and Death: Are They Related? Findings from the Caerphilly Cohort Study." *British Medical Journal* 315 (1997): 1641.

Smolowe, J., and E. Lafferty. "Sex with a Scorecard." *Time*, April 5, 1993. http:// www.time.com/time/magazine/article/0,9171,978157,00.html#ixzz1SEm6BRp4.

Sommers, C. *The War against Boys: How Misguided Feminism Is Harming Our Young Men*. New York: Simon & Schuster, 2000.

Stanton, S. J., J. C. Beehner, E. K. Saini, C. M. Kuhn, and K. S. LaBar. "Dominance, Politics, and Physiology: Voters' Testosterone Changes on the Night of the 2008 United States Presidential Election." http://www.plosone.org/article/ info%3Adoi%2F10.1371%2Fjournal.pone.0007543.

Stokes, G. "Karl Popper's Political Philosophy of Social Science." *Philosophy of the Social Sciences* 27, no. 1 (1997): 56–79.

Stolberg, S. "Naked Hubris." *New York Times*, June 12, 2011. http://www.nytimes. com/2011/06/12/weekinreview/12women.html?_r=1&hp=&pagewanted=all.

Symons, D. *The Evolution of Human Sexuality*. New York: Oxford University Press, 1979.

Szalavitz, Maia. "Sex and Politics: Are Powerful Men Really More Likely to Cheat? *Time*, April 28, 2011.

Szasz, T. *The Myth of Mental Illness: Foundations of a Theory of Personal Conduct*. New York: HarperCollins, 1974.

Taormino, T. *Opening Up: A Guide to Creating and Sustaining Open Relationships*. San Francisco, CA: Cleiss Press, 2008.

Thompson, D. "The 'Reality' of Sex Addiction Stirs Debate." *Healthday News*, May 12, 2010. http://news.healingwell.com/index.php?p=news1&id=636637.

Thornhill, R., and Palmer, M. *A Natural History of Rape*. Cambridge, MA: MIT Press, 2000.

Traeen, B., and T. S. Nilson. "Use of Pornography in Traditional Media and on the Internet in Norway." *Journal of Sex Research* 43, no. 3 (2006): 245–254. http://goliath .ecnext.com/coms2/gi_0199-5754055/Use-of-pornography-in-traditional.html.

Turner, C. "Wilhelm Reich: The Man Who Invented Free Love." *Guardian*, July 8, 2011. http://www.guardian.co.uk/books/2011/jul/08/wilhelm-reich-free-love -orgasmatron.

Turner, M. "Female Sexual Compulsivity: A New Syndrome." *Psychiatric Clinics of North America* 3, no. 4 (2008): 713–727.

Van Anders, S. "Multiple Partners Are Associated with Higher Testosterone in North American Men and Women." *Hormones and Behavior* 51 (2007): 454–459.

Van Anders, S., and K. Goldey. "Testosterone and Partnering Are Linked via Relationship Status for Women and 'Relationship Orientation' for Men." *Hormones and Behavior* 58 (2010): 820–826.

Van Anders, S., and N. Watson. "Relationship Status and Testosterone in North American Heterosexual and Non-heterosexual Men and Women: Cross-sectional and Longitudinal Data." *Psychoneuroendocrinology* 31 (2006): 715–723.

Vandello, J., J. Bosson, D. Cohen, R. Burnaford, and J. Weaver. "Precarious Manhood." *Journal of Personality and Social Psychology* 95, no. 6 (2008): 1325–1339.

Wainberg, M. L., F. Muench, J. Morgenstern, et al. "A Double-Blind Study of Citalopram versus Placebo in the Treatment of Compulsive Sexual Behaviors in Gay and Bisexual Men." *Journal of Clinical Psychiatry* 67 (2006): 1968–1973.

Weigel, D. J., K. K. Bennett, and D. S. Ballard-Reisch. "Family Influences on Commitment: Examining the Family of Origin Correlates of Relationship Commitment Attitudes." *Personal Relationships* 10 (2003): 453–474.

Weinberg, M. S., and C. J. Williams. "Men Sexually Interested in Transwomen (MSTW): Gendered Embodiment and the Construction of Sexual Desire." *Journal of Sex Research* 47, no 4 (2010): 374–383.

Weiss, D. "Is Sex Addiction Real? Do Golfer Tiger Woods and the Soon-to-Be-Former Husband of Academy Award-Winning Actress Sandra Bullock, among Many Others, Really Have No Control over Their Bedroom Antics?" *USA Today*, May 2010.

———. *The Final Freedom: Pioneering Sexual Addiction Recovery.* 2nd ed. http://www.sexaddict.com/eBooks/FreedomeBk.pdf.

Weitzman, G., J. Davidson, R. Phillips, J. Fleckenstein, C. Morotti-Meeker. "What Psychology Professionals Should Know about Polyamory." https://ncsfreedom.org/images/stories/pdfs/KAP/2010_poly_web.pdf.

Welsh, D. P., C. M. Grello, and M. S. Harper. "No Strings Attached: The Nature of Casual Sex in College Students." *Journal of Sex Research* 43, no. 3 (2006): 255–267.

Whipple, B. "The Health Benefits of Sexual Expression." In *Sexual Health*, vol. 1, *Psychological Foundations*, ed. M Tepper and A. Fuglsang Owens. Westport, CT: Praeger, 2007.

Whipple, B., and B. Komisaruk. "Analgesia Produced in Women by Genital Self-Stimulation." *Journal of Sex Research* 24, no. 1 (1988): 130–140. http://www.jstor.org/pss/3812827.

Wieder, A. *Year of the Cock: The Remarkable True Account of a Married Man Who Left His Wife and Paid the Price.* New York: Grand Central Publishing, 2009.

Winters, J. "Hypersexual Disorder: A More Cautious Approach." *Archives of Sexual Behavior* 39 (2010): 594–596.

Winters, J., K. Christoff, and B. Gorzalka. "Dysregulated Sexuality and High Sexual Desire: Distinct Constructs?" *Archives of Sexual Behavior* 39, no. 5 (2010): 1029–1043. doi:10.1007/s10508-009-9591-6.

Woloshin, S., and L. Schwartz. "Giving Legs to Restless Legs: A Case Study of How the Media Helps Make People Sick." *PLoS Medicine* 3, no. 4 (2006): e170. http://www.ncbi.nlm.nih.gov/pmc/articles/PMC1434499/?tool=pmcentrez.

World Health Organization. *Education and Treatment in Human Sexuality: The Training of Health Professionals.* WHO Technical Report Series no. 572. Geneva: WHO, 1975.

Wright, R. *The Moral Animal: Why We Are the Way We Are; the New Science of Evolutionary Psychology.* New York: Vintage, 1995.

Yoder, V., T. Virden, and K. Amin. "Internet Pornography and Loneliness: An Association?" *Sexual Addiction & Compulsivity* 12, no. 1(2005): 19–44.

Zilbergeld, B. *The New Male Sexuality: The Truth about Men, Sex, and Pleasure.* New York: Bantam, 1993.

Zinczenko, D., with Ted Spiker. *Men, Love, & Sex.* Emmaus, PA: Rodale, 2006.

Zonana, H. "Sexual Disorders: New and Expanded Proposals for the DSM-5—Do We Need Them?" *Journal of the American Academy of Psychiatry and the Law* 39, no 2. (2011): 245–249.

Index

About the Author

David Ley is a clinical psychologist in practice in Albuquerque, New Mexico, and currently serves as executive director of a large outpatient behavioral health agency. He earned his bachelor's degree in philosophy from the University of Mississippi, and his master's and doctoral degrees in clinical psychology from the University of New Mexico. Dr. Ley has been treating sexuality issues throughout his career. He first began treating perpetrators and victims of sexual abuse, but expanded his approach to include the fostering and promotion of healthy sexuality, and awareness of the wide range of normative sexual behaviors.